THE GOTHAM LIBRARY
OF THE NEW YORK UNIVERSITY PRESS

The Gotham Library is a series of original works and critical studies, published in paperback primarily for student use. The Gotham hardcover edition is primarily for use by libraries and the general reader. Devoted to significant works and major authors and to literary topics of enduring importance, Gotham Library texts offer the best in literature and criticism.

Comparative and Foreign Language Literature:
  Robert J. Clements, Editor

Comparative and English Language Literature:
  James W. Tuttleton, Editor

Alfred Jarry

Nihilism and the
Theater of the Absurd

Maurice Marc LaBelle

New York University Press · New York *and* London

Copyright © 1980 by New York University

Library of Congress Cataloging in Publication Data

LaBelle, Maurice Marc, 1939-
  Alfred Jarry, nihilism and the theater of the absurd.

  (The Gotham Library of the New York University Press)
  Bibliography: p. 173
  Includes index.
  1. Jarry, Alfred, 1873-1907—Criticism and interpre-
tation. 2. Nihilism in literature. I. Title.
PQ2615.A65Z72   842′.8   79-3009
ISBN 0-8147-4995-X
ISBN 0-8147-4996-8 pbk.

Manufactured in the United States of America

To
Professor Palmer Hilty
Professor Frank W. Jones

Acknowledgements

I appreciate the support and assistance my parents, brother, and sister-in-law have given to me throughout my work. I also wish to thank Prof. Wilton Eckley for his guidance, integrity, and help; Prof. Grace Eckley; Prof. Thomas McFarland; Prof. Haskell Block; Prof. Anna Balakian; Prof. and Mrs. T. Stroud; Prof. William Bjornstad; Prof. George Katz and Prof. Julia Katz; Prof. Francis Wilhoit; Prof. Burton Leiser; Prof. J. Tomain; and Mr. Robert Brodie. I especially am indebted to Prof. Robert D. Meade.

Contents

1.

The Red and the Black:
Iconoclasm and Pessimism

"Hornpot! We won't have destroyed a thing unless we demolish even the ruins!" [1] Such was the credo of Alfred Jarry (1873-1907). Consequently, he assaulted the most sacred altars and groves of society, government, and religion with a rarely equaled zest and zeal. His troops, superbly captained by King Ubu and Dr. Faustroll, forced the enemy to yield precious ground, and as a result he did much to revolutionize modern literature. Specifically, because of *King Ubu (Ubu Roi)* he became a progenitor of one of its richest veins, the "absurdist," or non-Aristotelian theater. Seminal though this work is, it unfortunately overshadows his other contributions, especially in prose, which remain innovative and challenging. In spite of his achievements and the publicity given him by *King Ubu,* Jarry always remained a unique conqueror because he never built a single temple, shrine, or statue to commemorate his victories. A consummate iconoclast, he not only refused to be defied, but he welcomed the day when "young people will . . . find us very old-fashioned, and they will write ballads denouncing us, and there is no reason why they shouldn't" (OCBP, p. 418).

This titan of avant-garde drama was born in Laval, a small

town in Mayenne, a province in northern France. Many generations of Jarrys had been spawned there, reproduced their kind, carried on a lackluster flirtation with life, and died without venturing very far from familiar geographical or intellectual surroundings. Because no one chanced success or risked failure, the family's genealogy is of very little interest and can be quickly recapitulated. The first recorded Jarry, André, was an eighteenth-century stonemason at Grenoux, a hamlet near Laval. His son, Jean, followed the paternal trade, and in June 1754 he married Renée Billion in his father's village. One of their seven children, Julien, took as his wife Marie-Jeanne Gendren, a girl from the nearby hamlet of Louverné. Their son, Julien-René (b. August 11, 1807) became a carpenter, and in 1829 he married Emilie Grison. Eight years later (April 30, 1837) they became the parents of Anselme, who later fathered the famous man of letters.

Anselme, in spite of his son's defamation of him as an "unimportant bastard," [2] was not without admirable qualities. For instance, he courageously broke with familial trades in order to follow a business career, at which he succeeded so admirably that he eventually became a partner in a Laval linen factory. As he gained financially, so he rose socially, and was then able to do what no other male member of his family had dared: he sought a wife outside the Laval region. In Hédé, near Rennes, Brittany, he met and courted Caroline Quernest (b. November 13, 1842), the daughter of a well-to-do justice of the peace. Anselme was eager to marry her because her family's means and social standing would augment and grace his own; yet she had a liability: her mother's family had a history of insanity. In fact, Caroline's mother was confined in an asylum. However, Anselme's ambition overrode caution; he married Caroline on July 16, 1868.

Anselme soon had reason to doubt the wisdom of his decision because shortly after the marriage she displayed eccentricities which shocked the villagers and gave them cause to speculate about her rationality. For instance, she dressed in unusual clothes, used makeup, and wore her hair in tight curls—"in the English style." The last of their doubts about her sanity was dispelled when she bought a piano! Another Emma Bovary! Despite the snickering and gossip of the citizens, Caroline was a remarkable woman

who had the fortitude to follow her own ideas and assert her individuality—no small achievement in a small French provincial
town.

On February 8, 1865, Madame Jarry gave birth to Caroline-
Marie, nicknamed "Charlotte"; the first son, born four years later,
died shortly after birth. Caroline had her last child at 5:00 A.M. on
September 8, 1873. Although he was christened Alfred-Henri, the
latter name was deleted at his baptism. Alfred enjoyed the irony of
having been born on the celebration day of the Holy Virgin's
nativity; no doubt he would have been equally happy to know that
he died on All Saints' Day.

Shortly after the birth of Alfred, Anselme's business began to
decline, and soon he was bankrupt. He turned to alcohol, a crutch
and sling supported by the villagers, who commiserated with his
conclusion that he was indeed, a pitiful victim of cruel fortune in
both business and in marriage. Caroline agreed that their marriage
was a failure, and while it is true that Anselme had lost money, it
was Caroline who was the real loser. She was a social outcast married to an alcoholic living in a small provincial French town. While
she bore the disappointments of life and marriage, the birth of
Alfred forced her to take decisive action. Unable to have another
child because of the injuries sustained during his birth, she devoted
herself to him and his future. Her ambition for him, however, was
frustrated because there were so few opportunities for advancement in Laval. Alfred, of course, could become a stonemason or a
carpenter, but she was more ambitious for him than that: he
should not follow the familial, traditional, and complacent. Another alternative was business, but in light of Anselme's failure,
that option was unacceptable. The only realistic course was to find
a career through formal education. Alfred must go to a university!
The goal was easily conceived but difficult to realize because the
school in Laval, which Alfred began to attend in May 1878, could
not offer adequate preparation for the highly competitive entrance
examinations to prestigious universities. The exigency of the situation was obvious, and Caroline therefore made the only suitable
decision. In October 1879, when Alfred was six, she rejected her
husband and the Laval gossips and took her two children to St.
Brieuc where Alfred could attend a better school than the one in

Laval. Yet her decision was not altogether altruistic, for this move benefited her: now she was free.

The transplantation to St. Brieuc had a seminal influence upon Alfred. The school provided him with educational opportunities, of which he took full advantage—under his mother's supervision. True to her expectations, he became a promising pupil, winning prizes in Latin, English, and French composition in 1886, and two years later awards in French composition and Latin as well as honors in Greek, history, physical science, geography, mathematics, German, and drawing. Alfred's justified pride in his academic success was counterpointed to his hatred of St. Brieuc, which he described in an early poem called *St. Brieuc the Cabbage Patch (St.-Brieuc des Choux;* May 1886) as a place where "everything is more or less boring. . . . Two leagues from the sea, two steps from manure piles. . . . Ah, what a miserable place" (OCBP, pp. 25-26)! In spite of his detestation of St. Brieuc, Jarry sincerely admired the traditionally proud and independent Bretons, although he was born in the neighboring province. He was so devoted to the Bretons that he mastered their language, which was no small achievement in view of the French government's vigorous efforts to suppress the Breton movement to secede from France. Much of the government's attempt to thwart this agitation focused on outlawing the Breton language. Such efforts fueled Jarry's admiration for the resistance, to which he gave his allegiance by learning the forbidden tongue. He later showed his virtuosity when a fellow student at the *lycée* Henri IV in Paris challenged him to a "dialect war." This was a mock battle in which each student would demonstrate his expertise in a regional accent. Jarry readily took up the gauntlet and immediately so overwhelmed the opposition that his friend pleaded nolo contendere.

Simultaneously with his intellectual flowering, Jarry budded artistically. There are no clues to help date his initial writings or identify their content because he later deliberately destroyed them. However, there is little question of his youthful interest in writing. His first extant work was written in 1885, and during the next four years he wrote at least nine plays and thirty-three poems. He edited them, probably during 1897-98 (OCBP, p. 1081), recopied some, and gathered them together under the title *Ontogeny (On-*

togénie), meaning works which show "the development of an orga-
nism." The subtitle is "works before *The Records* [*of the Black Crest*]
and some after *King Ubu*" (OCBP, p. 1). While Jarry rightly saw
that these works do him little honor (OCBP, p. 1) in relation to his
future masterpieces, *Ontogeny* accurately represents the nascent
stages of the development of his creative talents as well as many
attitudes he held toward man and life. For instance, Jarry's early
plays, *The Brigands of Calabria (Les Brigands de la Calabre;* December
1885) and *Kroeflich, Or The Inheritance (Kroeflich Ou L'Héritage;* July
13, 1886), reflect his preoccupation with violence and misanthropy.
While these two works together are less than 250 lines, a miser is
beaten to death with a shovel, a policeman is murdered, two ban-
dits kill each other, and two brothers are locked in fratricidal combat. The only symbol of "the good" in the two plays is a policeman
in *The Brigands of Calabria,* but Jarry depicts him as being so foolish
and feeble that he is quickly overpowered and strangled. Such
scenes serve as a backdrop to Jarry's particularly jaundiced and
pessimistic view of life.

It surprising Jarry's concept of a malevolent cosmos clearly places him at the
antipodes of Christianity, but he was extremely selective even at
this young age as to what company he wanted to keep in the non-
Christian camp. He most certainly did not wish to associate with
Voltaire, whom Jarry attacks in *The Brigands of Calabria.* Scaramouche, a celebrated bandit and murderer, disguises himself as a
gardener in order to allay any suspicion by his employer, Lantimèche, that he aims to kill him and take his money. When
Scaramouche arrives, Lantimèche orders him to spade the garden,
a strange command considering that it is well after 11:00 P.M.
Nevertheless, Jarry was more interested in rejecting Voltaire than
in carefully constructing the play. Lantimèche's order refers to
Voltaire's adage in *Candide* that "We must cultivate our own gardens," that is, be tolerant and mind one's own business. Jarry has
correctly seen that this aphorism is woefully inadequate because
one's business, like that of Scaramouche, might very well be rob-
bery and murder. In fact, Scaramouche "cultivates" his "garden"
by killing Lantimèche with the spade. So much for Voltaire!

It is surprising to find such pessimism in one so young as Jarry,
but he did not have the familial or historical backgrounds which

could generate concepts of benevolence. He was an outcast in society because the separation of his parents put him in a socially undesirable situation in rural France. Jarry's attraction to violence and pessimism is also partly due to his historical "climate of opinion." He was born two years after the Franco-Prussian War and the fall of the Paris Commune, and although he later denied any influence upon him of these two catastrophic events (OCBP, p. 1030), he could not have avoided the impact of the fall of an empire, the insult to "French glory," and the destruction of the Commune. As the Dreyfus affair (1894-1906) demonstrated, the "revenge" movement permeated French culture at this time. How, then, could a precocious and perceptive teen-ager escape its aura?

The Brigands of Calabria and *Kroeflich* are significant in Jarry's canon, not only because they show some of his embryonic philosophical concepts, but also they expose his inability to consider the intellectual needs of the spectator—a flaw in many of his works. In *Kroeflich,* for instance, the protagonist explains that he and his brother, Hanswurst, have been contesting their inheritance for the past four years, during which time the money has become "an apple of discord" between them. He concludes that he will have to kill his brother if Hanswurst inherits the estate because he "will cause my misfortune" (OCBP, p. 45). Instead of explaining Kroeflich's statement, Jarry immediately proceeds with the action. A masked figure enters with the awaited decision. It is the hated Hanswurst, who gleefully announces that he has inherited the entire estate, and at once the fratricidal duel begins. While the fight attracts the spectator's attention, the effect is diminished because Jarry has failed to provide necessary answers to some important questions: Why has the estate caused trouble between the brothers? Why has Hanswurst, rather than Kroeflich, inherited everything? Why has Kroeflich concluded that he must kill his brother? By answering such questions Jarry could have considerably developed the plot and characters, thereby increasing the effect of the play on the audience. Similarly, *The Brigands of Calabria* shows how Jarry should have elaborated the subplot of the robbers, especially their conflict which leads to the fight between Scaramouche and Pulcinella, and Jarry most certainly should have explained why Scaramouche has become a servant of Satan. It is true that

Kroeflich and *The Brigands of Calabria* are so undeveloped that they should best be considered as sketches, but the embryonic efforts nevertheless show that Jarry was fascinated by the tone or mood, the climactic moment, the time of supreme effect, rather than with establishing necessary rapport with the spectator and thereby effectively introducing the proper atmosphere.

The Brigands of Calabria and *Kroeflich* are, admittedly, riddled with mistakes, but rather than overcome them Jarry suddenly turned his attention to other types of drama. The reason for this abrupt shift was that he had become a member of the students at the *lycée* and contributed to their antics. He consequently wrote several poems and plays depicting them and their capers real and imagined: *Roupias the Sepia Head (Roupias Tête-de-Seiche;* 1886), *Anecdote (Anécdote;* May 1886), *The Rat (Le Rat;* June 17, 1886), *The Adventures of a Pygmy (Les Aventures d'un Pygmée;* June 18, 1886), *Professor Sicca (Sicca Professeur;* June 22, 1886), *Pigeaux Who (Pigeaux Qui;* June 26, 1886), *The Choir and the Taurobole (Le Choeur et le Taurobole;* July 24, 1886), and *The Great Procession of the Choir of Esteem (Grande Procession du Choeur d'Estime;* August 1886). Most of these works are unimportant; the two "Antliaclastes" plays (July 13, 1886, and January 9, 10, 11, 1888) represent most of the material in the other works, show the continuity of some of Jarry's attitudes, and expose his developing dramaturgy.

Both "Antliaclastes" plays are based on schoolboy fantasies involving a group of nicknamed cohorts (Rouget, Sicca, Roupias, Pas-Fort, Ratpias, and Toga) who are the central figures in a mock-epic struggle between "The Antliatores," a Latinized expression for "the pumpers," and "The Antliaclastes," which is Greek for "the pump-breakers." The two groups war over a pump which can expel a brown igneous substance through various pipes. The principal theme of these two plays is violence and death, as the treatment of the traitor Toga demonstrates. In the first version, Toga is easily discovered, quickly sentenced to death, and hanged—the body dropping with such force that "the rope separates the head from the body" (OCBP, p. 42). In *The Antliaclastes,* the scene is extended: as Toga is hanged, his body falls to the ground, the blood about to spurt from his eyes (OCBP, p. 93). As the executioners start to drink some wine, Toga suddenly opens his eyes, curses Sicca, predicts his death, and then—finally—dies. Jarry's infatuation with violence is also shown in the last scenes of both plays. In the first version, the Chorus sings "Torch, burn, fire/ Everything we don't desire,/Fire, burn, and break/Everything we can't take" (OCBP, p. 42). As the victors prepare to set fire to the Antliator Club, the stage lighting suddenly shows that there are some barrels of gunpowder with a lighted fuse. The Antliaclastes, seeing the danger, become panic-stricken, but when they attempt to flee, some pumpers appear at a pump and spray them. As the two sides struggle, the barrels explode, and such is "The End of the Antliaclastes" (OCBP, p. 44). Jarry drastically revised the ending of the second version, and in it Sicca, who is thought by his enemies to have been dead for ten years, suddenly appears before them. While a cracking noise is heard, he informs them that the area has been undermined and that everything is going to collapse. in a lecture he gave to a meeting organized by the editors of *La Libre Esthétique* in Belgium on March 22, 1902: "passive and rudimentary, [puppets] convey concisely and accurately the outline of our thoughts" (OCBP, pp. 422-23). His conclusion was now inevitable: Puppets as symbols could express the universal and eternal which lies deep within man. With this theory, Jarry showed not only his affinity to Symbolism but his ability to direct and adapt it opening scene by delaying the depiction of the victory celebration of the Antlium forces until the second act. He substituted a scene showing a secret meeting of the Antliaclastes complete with password and torch-lit cave. This motif of the clandestine, grotesque, and macabre surfaces in the third act when the soldiers of Antlium celebrate their victory over the Antliaclastes. Suddenly, the head and arms of a masked figure appear on the parapet, and the audience quickly sees that he is carry a long package, which he throws to the ground. As some pumpers begin to open the box, the stranger, his face covered by his cloak, enters and flips his disguise aside. It is Sicca! After the men of Antlium recover from their shock at seeing their archenemy, Pigeaux opens the box and Sicca pulls out a human skeleton, which he identifies as the bones of the traitor Roupias. Immediately a cracking noise is heard. Sicca, "in a thunderous voice," informs the assembly that they are doomed because the area has been undermined (OCBP, p. 106).

Jarry continued to be fascinated with death, and in his first two extant plays there are several hangings, a fatal explosion, and a fantastic catastrophe which decimates an army. However, there is a significant change in the second version: Sicca's humorous comment as the Antliaclastes are destroyed shows that Jarry was experimenting with integrating comedy and pessimism. He forces the spectator to question whether he is to be horrified or laugh when both "good" and "evil" characters, such as Sicca and the Antliaclastes, are slaughtered as the protagonist makes a witty comment, presumably just before his own death. Jarry was so intrigued by this quandary that he continued to develop the integration of humor and tragedy until its fruition eight years later in that fiend of "black humor," Father Ubu.

The "Antliaclastes" plays also reflect Jarry's inability to develop his characters. He certainly felt no need to do so because they were his friends in school, but he failed to see that he needed to explain them to the audience. Similarly, some of the incidents are so bizarre that they strain the credulity of the spectator. For instance, at the end of the second version, Sicca states that "The ground is undermined, and everything is caving in" (OCBP, p. 106). It would have taken a herd of titanic moles to accomplish this miraculous feat! Satanic vows and midnight garden work might be accepted, but not this wonder of tunnelling.

In spite of the marked flaws in the two works, there are also admirable aspects in construction. In the second play Jarry adroitly manipulates the plot by compounding the spy motif. The spectator unexpectedly learns that Sicca's trusted lieutenant, Roupias, who was present at Toga's death in the original, is in the 1888 play another spy for Rouget. Seeking vengeance for the death of Toga, he devises a scheme by which Sicca is to be ambushed by his own men. However, as Roupias's plan is about to succeed, Sicca has a premonition of danger and escapes the trap in such a way that Roupias himself falls into it and is killed (OCBP, p. 100).

In the eighteen months between the two "Antliaclastes" plays, Jarry toyed with traditional techniques of wit and buffoonery. Once again his schoolboy friends became test tubes and beakers for his experiments called the "Bidasse" series: *Bidasse's Class (Un Cours de Bidasse;* 1886) and *Bidasse and Company (Bidasse et Compagnie;* August 1886), which focus on student-teacher and teacher-administrator relations. In *Bidasse's Class* Jarry lashes out at one of his favorite subjects, authority figures, specifically a teacher who shows his tyrannical nature by admonishing the students to be "very serious" and quiet (OCBP, p. 51). His sole disciplinary method is to order the students to copy slavishly "A hundred lines. . . . A hundred lines at once" (OCBP, p. 53). While he is a bully in front of the students, he is a milksop before two inspectors, Mr. Savant and Father Esteem. In order to test Bidasse's teaching proficiency, the latter requests a student to recite his lesson, but he is not prepared; nor is another student when Mr. Savant asks him a question. Faced with such a display of ignorance, Bidasse immediately grovels before the inspectors and explains that he only touched upon the subject. "But Everything is essential," the pedantic inspector replies, thereby showing that he cannot judiciously evaluate what students should learn. A student properly concludes that Mr. Savant is "a real fool" (OCBP, pp. 55-56).

Although brief, *Bidasse's Class* remains one of the best works in Jarry's juvenilia, and certainly the only comedy of this period worthy of attention. The play is well constructed, and the wit flows freely, effortlessly, and spontaneously. It is equally important to note that for the first time Jarry rises above his personal experiences and explains his characters and actions of the play to the spectator. Consequently, the spectator understands the tyrannical-subservient personality of Bidasse and can thereby appreciate Jarry's ridicule of him as well as the pedantic stupidity of his superiors. As a result of Jarry's care and consideration, the play emerges as a delightful cameo of students, teacher, and classroom inspectors.

The promise of *Bidasse's Class* proved ephemeral, and this precocious work was quickly swallowed up in the sophomoric and lackluster *Bidasse and Company*. It takes place in the apartment of "ex-professor" Bidasse where some students have hidden themselves. As he enters, they mischievously play "a piercing and frightening note" on a "taurobole," which, Jarry explains, is an ancient instrument found in the ruins of Jerusalem (OCBP, p. 61). Terrified, Bidasse pulls out a rusty sword, and as he brandishes it the sequestered Sicca comments that Bidasse "is really cracked"

(OCBP, p. 63). Jarry's attempt to make Bidasse a buffoon backfires because the spectator sympathizes with Bidasse's attempts to defend himself; it is the student's evaluation which is "cracked." After this dismal buffoonery, the tone and direction of the play change as Sicca tries to steal a fish from Bidasse, but the teacher discovers him, grabs a chamber pot, and threatens to dump it over Sicca's head. Confronted by such a prospect, Sicca yields, and after an act of contrition, which offers an opportunity to once again trick Bidasse, the play mercifully ends.

After completing *Bidasse and Company*, Jarry wrote some poems, and he did not return to comedy until early 1888, when he finished *The Opening Day of Fishing (L'Ouverture de la Pêche;* March 4 and 5, 1888). This is another mediocre play whose only importance is that it shows Jarry's continuing interest in buffoonery. This short piece focuses on another of Jarry's passions, fishing. The protagonist, Mr. Ripaton, is so devoted to it that his room is filled with fishing gear, and as the curtain rises he is asleep—fishing lines in each hand—dreaming of catching fish (OCBP, p. 107-9). After waking, he goes fishing and takes a place alongside the Galimard family, which includes "five or six brats" (OCBP, p. 107). Ripaton has wandered into chaos: the boisterous Galimards shout at each other to "be quiet" and "don't make noise" (OCBP, pp. 111-12). The cacophony is too much for Ripaton, and he pulls in his lines and leaves. Unfortunately, the subject matter is sophomoric, and the only interesting aspect is the buffoonery of the Galimard family. However, instead of exploiting it by linking buffoonery and social commentary, such as showing how ridiculous family recreation can be or attacking the usual drivel about how wonderful children are, Jarry immediately changes scenes. Ripaton meets Mr. Belleplume, who, in a fit of anger at not having caught a fish, grabs Ripaton by the nose, and this tiresome slapstick episode ends the play.

Jarry's early dramas give scant reason to suspect that he would create that theatrical masterpiece, *King Ubu.* These works are superficial and undeveloped, and the humor is insipid. However, *Bidasse's Class* shows that he had promise, although the basic reason why Jarry did not quickly develop his dramatic and comedic interests is that they were not his primary foci. It would be many years before he considered himself anything other than a poet.

Concomitant with the "Antliaclastes" and "Bidasse" series, Jarry wrote poetry, and it is in this genre that his artistic and philosophical capabilities are most marked. His interest in this medium was initially reflected in many of his plays, which he wrote in verse, but his attraction to poetry was accelerated by his reading of Homer, Byron, Longfellow, Coleridge, Virgil, and above all Goethe. It would be facile to conclude that he was significantly influenced by these writers. Jarry was always very selective in what he borrowed, and his literary relations with Goethe demonstrate the point.

There are more references to Goethe in Jarry's juvenilia than to any other literary or philosophical figure, yet such works as *The Sorcerer of the Harz* (*La Sorcière du Hartz;* January 23, 1887), *The Deluge* (*Le Déluge;* February 29, 1887), *The Four Horsemen of the Apocalypse* (*Les Quatre Fléaux de l'Apocalypse;* March 26, 1888), and *The Hexentanzplatz* (*Le Hexentanzplatz;* March 26, 1888) show that he completely rejected Goethe's optimism, faith in human capabilities, and idealism. Jarry did his utmost to show that walking free ground with free men [3] is impossible: man is condemned to quite a different promenade.

Rather than being intrigued by the evolution of Faust's education, Jarry was singularly drawn to the Walpurgis Night episode of *Faust.* He returned to it frequently, and his reading rekindled his interest in the fantastic and Gothic, especially Satanism, which had intrigued him as early as *The Brigands of Calabria.* This theme appears in *The Hexentanzplatz,* which begins with a description of "Sylphs, gnomes, / Hideous ghosts . . . / Demons and Sorcerers, / The dead in their shrouds / [Leaving] their biers / Dedicated to combat." Soon Beelzebub himself arrives, "because he likes to celebrate this day . . ." in which "The dead, frenzied and hideous, [have a] / Crazy and horrible dance" (OCBP, pp. 121-22). As he had done in *The Brigands of Calabria,* Jarry couples Satanism with pessimism, an integration readily seen in *The Sorcerer of the Harz.* A sorcerer is about to die and he needs a particular coffin for his funeral rites, but it is hidden in a church and secured to it by "a hundred enormous bronze chains." His demons attack the church for three days, and the hundred monks inside increasingly chant with less assurance and greater haste because of their fear. At midnight Satan triumphs, enters the church, and buries the sorcerer. The monks fall on their knees, and when one of them tries to get up, Satan "paralyzes" him. Everything, even the forces of the Lord, is powerless before "the black group" (OCBP, pp. 74-76).

Jarry's reading of Goethe's Walpurgis Night also served to guide and extend his imagination and creativity to include an apocalyptic vision of man as a helpless creature continually confronting forces which are immeasurably more powerful than himself. This theme appears in *The Sorcerer of the Harz,* but the point is more forcefully made in *The Misery of Man (Misère de l'Homme;* May 3, 1888) in which Jarry states that "Man is alone, man is weak." For example, his food supply is very fragile, in spite of his most ardent efforts at cultivation (OCBP, p. 126). "Death is everywhere! If man escapes the wild beasts, / He finds death in the broiling deserts, / In the terrible Ocean where tempests blow, / When the waves engulf his vessel." For man, Jarry continues, "there is no hope. / He weeps and that is justice" (OCBP, pp. 126-27).

Jarry completes his concept of malevolence by showing that man destroys himself because he refuses to learn. The point is most clearly made in his transformation of Coleridge's *The Rime of the Ancient Mariner,* called *The Albatross (L'Albatros;* March 1887). Jarry begins with the Ancient Mariner's tale in which he relates how "Our vessel swirled around in the middle of this gulf, / From which came vapors of tar and sulfur." Suddenly an albatross appeared, and "The sea around us grew calm . . . / But a crossbow's arrow, / Shot by this hand, pierced the albatross." Almost at once a "skeleton ship without sails" passes by, and the Mariner thinks it resembles "an enormous crossbow" (OCBP, p. 82). He sees two figures on it—Death and Life The former throws some dice and then exclaims "I've won!" At once the bow of the Mariner's vessel is struck by the skeleton ship, and fifty men fall dead. "I heard a voice murmuring: 'This man killed the albatross, the friend of the sailor; / His crime has angered the giant, the ghost, / Whose powerful hands control the winds and waves' " (OCBP, p. 83). The mariner wakes up on a beach, "And, reassured, recognizing that he has been dreaming, / He sings . . . 'Ghosts and gnomes, / Spirits and phantoms, / I laugh at you; / And, in the foam, / Birds of the mist, / Stop your cries' " (OCBP, p. 83). He has learned nothing and unknowingly awaits his fate, which is in the hands of Death.

As if man's hostile environment and ignorance were not sufficiently homicidal, man's fate is sealed by God Himself. In *The Deluge,* Jarry describes the "father of the gods" who "wants to crush Mortal men / Who have for a very long time forsaken His altars" (OCBP, p. 80). He decides to inundate the earth, and in a fine *staccato* style Jarry describes the sea rising and men being inevitably trapped. Only when "Everything is swallowed up" do the rains stop, and the poem closes with a depiction of the floating bodies serving as "pasture for filthy ravens" (OCBP, p. 81).

Jarry's misanthropy, pessimism, and cosmology are succinctly recapitulated in *The Second Life, Or Macaber (La Seconde Vie, Ou Macaber;* June 30, July 29, 1888), in which he seeks to correct what he considers to be the errors of *Faust.* In the first part, "The Sabbath," the poet depicts a "night of horror and shadow, / Night when the ghosts without number / Leave their somber cavern" to dance and sing (OCBP, p. 130). The celebration is interrupted when Death—Macaber—appears and sighs "Alas! O God! When will my indefatigable scythe cease harvesting? / I constantly hear a voice ordering me to perform / My pitiless task" (OCBP, p. 131). Immediately "The thunder / Crashes . . . / And from the fathomless depths . . . / An enormous shadow / Climbs into the air . . . / And in a halo of gold the Eternal appears." Macaber confronts "the mystery" and hears a voice which tells him that he can save a soul of his choosing—but only for one year. The rooster soon crows and dawn comes, which causes the spirits to disappear and Death to return to the abyss (OCBP, p. 132), but he has chosen "Aldern," a Breton word for "Alfred." The next part of *The Second Life* focuses on Aldern, who like Faust, wishes to examine "The unfathomable mystery" of death. But where Faust went toward the abyss and stayed on the edge, "Aldern does not hesitate: Aldern grasps the vial . . . drains it to the last drop" (OCBP, p. 133), and he dies. The third section, called "The Resurrection," begins with Aldern returning to life: "Everything is uncovered / To your enraptured eyes, to you . . . Cosmic knowledge which you have brought back from death" (OCBP, p. 135). Aldern sees the constellations "sowing in the night their radiant glimmerings," the revolving and luminescent planets, and then he sees "the black ether instead of the blue sky." He no longer thinks of hell which awaits him because the light of the sun is so striking and resplendent (OCBP, p. 134). Soon he sees the scythe and arms of Death, "And Death approaches Aldern and seizes him, / And holds him in the diaphanous ether" (OCBP, p. 134). Such is man's fate: beyond the sun is death!

The Second Life is the finest achievement of Jarry's juvenilia. Gone are the tales of schoolboy antics, the mock-epic struggles, the *études*. Here is a budding artist who has answered some of the great philosophical questions of life such as the direction of human existence and the nature of the cosmos. Moreover, *The Second Life* shows that he was able to express his views with so much verve and confidence that it is difficult indeed to realize that this is the work of a fifteen-year-old!

The nine years Jarry spent at the *lycée* in St. Brieuc were rich and seminal ones for him in which he developed his philosophical attitudes and creative abilities, especially in poetry. It is ironic that dramaturgy, for which he would be celebrated, was his weakest medium at St. Brieuc, and his comedy, which would later revolutionize modern theater, was more ludicrous than humorous, although there were moments of promise. The primary reason for these problems is that he had yet to develop the capacity to evaluate his art in view of the need to communicate rather than just to express his ideas and attitudes. Underlying his artistic inadequacies, however, was a strong mind, which was reflected in his academic record. In July 1886 he won first prize in Latin, English, reading and recitation, and honors in French composition; and in August of the following year he won first place in French composition, Latin, Greek, physical sciences, recitation, honors in English, imitative drawing, and third prize in mathematics. The significance of these academic achievements was not lost on Madame Jarry. Success breeds ambition; therefore, she began to contemplate how to advance her son. After all, if he could be successful in St. Brieuc, why not elsewhere? The next logical step was to send him to school in Rennes, the capital of Brittany. Thus, in October 1888 Madame Jarry took her two children to Rennes and enrolled Alfred in the *lycée*. Thus begins one of the most important periods of his life.

The *lycée* was a seventeenth-century convent which had been remodeled into a school, and the transformation left much to be desired. "The physics classes were taught in the old buildings. The plaster was falling off the walls and ceilings, the tables for the experiments were warped, and the corners were dirty." [4] A friend of Jarry recalls him "with his forehead like a rock . . . his voice which 'cut' in all senses of the word [, and his] walk which, with his bowlegs, looked like a fat bird walking. We called him 'Quasimodo' " (Herz, p. 75).

Jarry continued to develop artistically and intellectually, the latter being demonstrated by his winning awards on July 29, 1889, in Greek, French composition, chemistry, German, and Latin. He then passed the first part of his baccalaureate, scored in the first rank in the national examination for students in all comparable *lycées* and *collèges,* and completed his Bachelor's Degree in Letters in 1890. He continued to write, and *The Prospective Husband in Spite of Himself (Le Futur Malgré Lui;* 1889) reveals advances in drama and comedy as well as in delineating his enemies. In *Bidasse and Company* he had attacked authority figures, but in *The Prospective Husband* he began to probe more deeply into the socioeconomic foundations of his society; it was inevitable that he would discover that one of his principal antagonists was the bourgeoisie. This play was the first time Jarry threw down the gauntlet to the despised middle class, and thus began a joust which would attract him throughout his life.

One of the social institutions dear to the bourgeois is marriage, and Jarry takes delight in ridiculing it, specifically the prelude of plotting the marriage by the girl's mother. In the opening scene of *The Prospective Husband,* Madame du Toqué, whose name means "cracked" or "crazy," tries to arrange a marriage between her daughter, Gertrude, and Mr. de l'Etang, a French expression for a pool of stagnant water. She recognizes that he has all the requisites for a good husband: his family has social standing by virtue of his father being a nobleman, and the family is wealthy. Unfortunately, he has a flaw. He is in the army, which is very detrimental in Jarry's eyes because, as he would later show in *Days and Nights,* he considered the military and its uniformed bodies and minds to be despicable. But, as Jarry demonstrates in *The Prospective Hus-*

band, the bourgeoisie are incapable of understanding the true nature of the military because they, too, are automatons; the only difference is that the bourgeois is controlled by society rather than by a segment of it, as is the soldier. Madame Toqué, therefore, quickly overlooks this grievous failing of the intended (OCBP, p. 138).

Because of the superficiality of the bourgeois personality, its flaccid interpersonal and social concerns serve as a fine scenario for comedy, which Jarry exploits in this play. After some banal but extremely formal and elegant conversation, the intended husband is introduced to Gertrude, but the dialogue immediately turns from the embarrassed girl to Mr. de l'Etang, who is applauded as being a fine fisherman, musician, poet, and dancer. His protestations result in adding modesty to his list of merits, and consequently there is yet another round of formalities (OCBP, pp. 141-42). While tea is prepared, the guest is invited to show his "fine talent" at the piano, but he insists that he will perform only after Madame du Bocage (Mrs. Scrapmetal), Gertrude's aunt, who has been imported because of her knowledge of social grace, sets the example (OCBP, pp. 142-43). She immediately grasps the situation and asks Gertrude to present her pianistic ability, but the shy girl does not know which piece to perform. Madame du Bocage suggests that she play "Give Me My Fatherland," which represents the intelligence and sophistication of both aunt and niece. When the girl cannot find the music, the suitor recommends that she play "Moonlight" or "I Have Some Good Tobacco," which shows the moronic level of his taste. Gertrude finally returns with a copy of "Waltz of the Roses," a wise choice because such romantic slop benefits the bourgeoisie.

The Prospective Husband also shows that Jarry continued to strengthen and refine his interests in buffoonery, which is represented by the servant, François. He and Madame du Toqué enter, each pushing a cart with six bottles of wine. The foolish servant has unduly sampled the twelve bottles in order to select the proper ones; in fact, he has drunk up all of them. He maintains that the bottles are not empty because there are spiders in them, and at that moment "an enormous spider emerges from a bottle." Chaos erupts as the guest and hostesses flee, but the confusion is not so great that Madame du Toqué, ever attuned to the bourgeois goal of marrying off her daughter, asks the prospective husband not to leave before dinner (OCBP, p. 144).

The Prospective Husband shows that Jarry had refined his ability to construct effective dialogue. The characters in *The Prospective Husband* speak smoothly, rather than in stychomythia. Moreover, Jarry sets a comfortable tempo, rather than bombarding the spectator *alla turca*. The preparations and excitement of the dominant mother are effectively described and nicely counterpointed to the fear and trepidation of the daughter, and the bumbling servant speaks a delightfully nonaristocratic French. However, the spider episode is clumsily contrived and mars the ending.

The Prospective Husband sporadically shows the development of Jarry's comedic talents, but *The Pickled, A Chemical Opera (Les Alcoolisés, Opéra-Chimique;* June 1890) is a reminder that he had much to learn before he was ready to write his masterpiece. As he had done in St. Brieuc, so in Rennes. Jarry wrote comedies focusing on his friends and fellow students at the *lycée,* and *The Pickled* is one of them. The play mocks a classmate, Octave Priou, who was a fitting subject for ridicule, being academically so inept that the other students scoffed at him for taking so long to graduate. Jarry also jabs at his confrères when he calls them "fetuses" because they like to get "pickled" in alcohol. But Priou is acknowledged to be a "superfetus." The teacher, Professor Crocknuff, tells the assembled bottled fetuses that Priou "makes you look like pikers. . . . You're going to find this one far better than you. This sublime fetus. . . . The Holy Ghost inspires you. Assholes—I'm talking about Priou!!!" (OCBP, p. 148).

The ridicule of Priou and the teasing of the other students for their drinking habits is interspersed with abuse heaped upon the professor. In *Bidasse's Class* Jarry had attacked teachers for being tyrants before the students and cringing fops when confronting authority, and in *The Pickled* he lacerates some of their classroom techniques. Mr. Crocknuff enters the classroom, calls the roll, and then begins his lecture on the esoteric subject of "subculary villosities," but he is immediately in trouble because he cannot find his visual aids. Crocknuff quickly attempts to improvise a model by tearing up his suspenders, all the while pedantically admonishing the students to "Write everything down in your notebooks" (OCBP, p. 145). But the fetuses ignore his order; they are scandalized at his disrobing and cry, "Scandal! Horrors! The asshole. . . . He's dirty" (OCBP, pp. 145-46). The ensuing uproar is so great that Crocknuff is forced to refasten his suspenders and, turning to the spectators, informs them that the fetuses have smashed his lecture "like a turd" (OCBP, pp. 146-47).

The basic reason for this clumsy, gauche, and ineffective ridicule and iconoclasm is that Jarry had once again fallen back into his old habit of writing for a select group of students, who brought a background knowledge of the individuals being ridiculed. For instance, Jarry does not paint Priou's personality because the other students knew it, but the spectator has been slighted. Consequently, the real humor of most of the comments about Priou's stupidity and drinking is lost. Also, depicting the students as fetuses and talking from wide-mouthed bottles or singing together as a chorus is ridiculous. This miserable play would not attract the slightest interest if it were not the first time that Jarry used scientific references, which would become significant in his later works, especially *Faustroll*. Because of Jarry's fine academic background in science, it was to be expected that such vocabulary would seep into his art. An example of his utilization of scientific terms in *The Pickled* occurs when Crocknuff lures Priou to the wide-mouthed bottle in which he is to be "pickled" by explaining that "Priou, it's the new style. Instead of taking cold baths, / A platinum electrode is put in the bottles" (OCBP, p. 153). Jarry continued to refine his utilization of science and scientific expressions. He eventually used them masterfully in his analyses for constructing a time machine, calculating the dimensions of God, and his superb analysis of a floating sieve in *Faustroll*.

A second reason *The Pickled* is noteworthy is that Jarry utilized scatological expressions, such as Crocknuff's reference to his lecture being smashed "like a turd" or his calling the students/fetuses "assholes." There is also a ribald scene in which Jarry ridicules Priou for his lack of personal hygiene. Crocknuff discreetly asks Priou to show him his "inexpressible," which Priou calls his "backside," but Crocknuff corrects him by calling it his "frontside." Obviously, Priou is so much of an "inexpressible" that it really makes no difference which side he shows! Priou complies, and Crocknuff is immediately overwhelmed: "Oh, but it's dirty. This is really indecent! Don't you ever take a bath?" "Rarely," Priou answers. Crocknuff orders him to wash, but Priou dumbfoundedly asks, "Why?" (OCBP, p. 151). Such scatological expressions were preparatory to the opening word of *King Ubu*, which would do much to redirect modern drama and permit an expanded vocabulary for the dramatist.

There are two extant examples of Jarry's academic work at the school in Rennes, and they help to reveal an interesting and fundamental facet of his mind. The first, a composition for the General Examination of 1889, is a 165-word description of the style of Emperor Augustus. The points are clearly presented and organized, and the essay reflects research, attention to detail, careful selection of materials, and confidence in exposition. This academic essay expresses Jarry's foundation in the classics, interest in style, and analytical capacity. This facet of his mind is frequently beclouded by the buffoonery which would later characterize him. The essay shows that beneath that façade lurked a strong, confident, educated, and probing mind.

The second essay is *A Letter from a Parisian Humanist to an Italian Aristotelian (Lettre d'un Humaniste Parisien à un Aristotélicien d'Italie;* 1887, 1892) (OCBP, p. 1906). The format of the essay is that a Parisian replies to a letter which an Italian has sent to him in which he deifies Aristotle. The Parisian, speaking for Jarry, agrees that Aristotle was a genius who discovered many new sciences but he was only human and therefore could not know everything (OCBP, pp. 165-66); other thinkers are necessary "in order to complete what [Aristotle] had only been able to sketch in the short span of one man's life" (OCBP, p. 167). While the essay's thesis can be succinctly summarized, it is important and timely in the evolution of Jarry's thought because it marks the first time that Jarry offered a critique of Aristotle. In the past, he carefully followed many of Aristotle's suggestions about art. Specifically, he was keenly aware of Aristotle's observation that a work of art has a beginning, a middle, and an end. Consequently, Scaramouche and Kroeflich die as the curtain falls, Bidasse salutes the inspectors as they leave his classroom, and Priou enters the bottle as the Chorus of Unseen Fetuses sings a dirge. But with *A Letter from a Parisian Humanist to an Italian Aristotelian* Jarry flew his iconoclastic colors: he recognized that Aristotle's concepts were by no means sacrosanct and were subject to modification. Thus freed from a linchpin of Western aesthetics, his feet were firmly placed on the road to freedom and greatness, and soon he would create that Declaration of Rights for the Absurdists, *King Ubu.*

Jarry's academic success in Rennes fueled his mother's ambitions for him. As he had progressed from St. Brieuc to Rennes, now it was time for him to advance again—to the prestigious Ecole Normale Supérieure in Paris, the Mecca of French education. Jarry left the Lycée during the academic year of 1890-91 (October-July) in order to prepare for the very difficult entrance examinations, which he took and failed in July 1891. On a scale of 1 to 10 points, he received 3 in philosophy, 1.5 in history, 3.75 in Latin, 4 in Greek, and a similar score in French discourse.

Where must the blame be put for Alfred's failure? Mostly on his mother, whose ambitions for him overrode her rational analysis of his abilities. She did not see that while her son was a brilliant student in school, it was quite another question whether he was capable of preparing for the difficult tests without adequate supervision. Recognizing his inadequate preparation, Madame Jarry decided to send him to Paris where he could attend a school which would give him the necessary training for the examinations. Consequently, he went to Paris and enrolled as a student of advanced rhetoric at the Lycée Henri IV. He took the tests for the Ecole Normale Supérieure for the second time (1892), and although his score improved, it was still insufficient (2.75, 3, 7, 5, 3.5, and 6.5, respectively). Jarry then became quite ill from January to March 1893, and his mother came to Paris to care for him. She had no sooner seen her son recover than she died (May 10, 1893). Undaunted, he took the examinations a third time in July 1893, and while his grades were stronger than ever (5.5, 1.5, 7.75, 3.75, 6, and 9, respectively), his total of 33.5 points fell short of the required 35.25. Still confident, he registered for the examinations in July 1894, but he did not take them because he spent so much time in Laval owing to the prolonged illness of his uncle, Julien-René, who died on July 21, 1894.

Jarry's failure to enter the Ecole Normale Supérieure should not be allowed to becloud the fact that he was indeed a superior student with a diverse background. He had a fine grasp of Latin, Greek, English, German, and philosophy, geometry, zoology, botany, natural science, mysticism, Rabelais, Hellenism, macabre literatures, Symbolism, Lautréamont, Bergson, Shakespeare, and Coleridge. But the school was not the sole source of Jarry's education; Paris itself must accept both guilt and glory. Paris at the turn of the century! Stung by the defeat of Emperor Napoleon III and French glory by Prussia in 1870, and shocked by the "Red Specter" raising its head proudly and scornfully during the Paris Commune, much of the intellectual milieu of France was thoroughly shaken. Its historical convulsions gave birth to a phalanx of brilliant and ambitious "Young Turks," who were more than ready to formulate new concepts of art, society, man, and god. Jarry happily became one of them.

In *A Reply to an Inquiry: Alsace-Lorraine and the Real "Climate of Opinion" (Réponse à l'Enquête: L'Alsace-Lorraine et l'Etat Actuel des Esprits;* pub., December 1897), Jarry denies any direct influence of the Franco-Prussian War on him: "Since I was born in 1873, the war of 1870 is in my mind three years beyond the completely forgotten. It really seemed to me that this event had never occurred, and was simply a pedagogic invention feeding scholarly battalions" (OCBP, p. 1030). Such was Jarry's claim, but he was wrong. In spite of his fine academic performance in many disciplines, he was a poor student of politics and history. The truth is that he was in the midst of an intellectual tempest caused by these historical events when he frequented Mallarmé's "at homes" on Thursday afternoons and also the Tuesday afternoon receptions of the *Mercure de France.* Alfred Vallette, its editor, and his wife, whose *nom de plume* was "Rachilde," opened the *salon* in 1889 and promptly attracted "all of the luminaries of the literature of our epoch." So said Rachilde, and to a great extent she was right (Rachilde, p. 11). She welcomed the "dirty, shabby" Jarry dressed in slippers with his toes sticking out.[5] Here Jarry met Louis Libaude (pseud., "Louis Lormel"), who published some of Jarry's early works before he and Jarry became bitter enemies; Marcel Schwob, who helped edit *King Ubu* and to whom the play is dedicated; Octave Mirbeau, Catulle Mendès, Félix Fénéon, Henri de Régnier, Pierre Louÿs, A.F. Hérold, Gustave Kahn, Franc-Nohain, Maurice Ravel, Claude Terrasse (who composed and played the music for *King Ubu*), Remy de Gourmont, almost all of the Symbolist circle, and many artists, including Paul Sérusier, Toulouse-Lautrec (both of whom helped paint the backdrop for *King Ubu*), Vuillard, Gauguin (who was a roommate of Jarry),[6] and Henri Rousseau, who painted Jarry's portrait. Jarry also entered the circle of *La Revue Blanche*—that "rallying centre for the most divergent tendencies," according to Gide.[7] Founded in 1891, "it was for eleven years the best periodical of its kind that has ever been published . . . the magazine had the mark of the Lycée Condorcet, where the pupils were expected to know about everything without appearing to do any work" (Russell, p. 53). So charged and supported by his fellow combatants, Jarry became an unequaled individualist, a supreme iconoclast, the acknowledged High Priest of the Eccentric!

Jarry plunged into the *Kultur* of the Left Bank fully and joyfully. His dress at the Lycée Henri IV attests to that. He was a striking and startling figure with his hat, which was extremely tall—"a veritable observatory dome"—and his cape which reached to the floor.[8] He was short, stockily built, rather seedy-looking, and he wore a thick mustache. When not dressed in his "dome," he was usually attired in short trousers, sweater, and tennis shoes with the toes worn out. André Gide, who met Jarry but never became fond of him, describes him as "having a plaster-colored complexion, outfitted like a circus clown, playing the role of a fantastically constructed character, resolutely artificial."[9] Gide also noted Jarry's elocution—"strange, implacable, without inflection, without nuance, with a style of equally accenting each syllable, including the mute ones. A nutcracker would speak like Jarry" (Gide, p. 168). Rachilde describes his voice as something akin to "the meshing of rusted gears" (Rachilde, p. 14). Jarry's comportment and voice mesmerized the people at the *Mercure de France,* and they competed with each other "to imitate him, adopt his style, his clownery, and above all his speech" (Gide, p. 168).[10]

Beneath that abrasive and sophomoric exterior Jarry was quite a different person, a point which is too frequently forgotten in the vapid attempts to show that Jarry became the incarnate Ubu. True, Jarry told stories about Ubu, and by doing so became a clown, an entertainer, but he was Ubu in speech only. Gide was correct: Jarry was, in public, "resolutely artificial." His close friends knew him to be affectionate and very sentimental,[11] capable of close and intimate personal relationships. For instance, his friendship with the Vallettes survived even Vallette's decision in 1897 not to publish any more of Jarry's work because he thought it was becoming increasingly incomprehensible and pornographic. Jarry also became close friends with some of the most individualistic people of modern literature and art, and in his catalogue of creators in *Faustroll* Jarry lists only three people (Christian Beck, Louis Lormel, and Pierre Loti) whom he detested. His closest friend was Léon-Paul Fargue, whom Jarry met shortly after coming to Paris. The two lived in a very sleazy hotel, typified by broken stairs and pools of urine on the pavement outside. Here the two raised rats, monkeys, and parrots.[12] The youths frequently battled the philistines with shock tactics, for which Jarry was well fitted. One example occurred when Jarry and Fargue went to a café where Jarry began a discourse for the benefit of the patrons on masturbation "from personal recollections," and then Fargue asked: "what is Art but intellectual masturbation?" (Lormel, p. 606).

Jarry's friends advanced his career by seeing to it that he was awarded first prize in a prose competition offered by the *Echo de Paris Mensuel Illustré*. The magazine was edited by Marcel Schwob and Catulle Mendès. Jarry's entry was *Guignol,* which appeared in that magazine on April 23, 1893. He also published in a small review called *L'Art Littéraire,* which Lormel edited. Jarry began to collaborate with him in December 1893, but in March of the following year Lormel complained in the magazine that he was paying three quarters of the money for publication, instead of his other partners, Jarry and François Coulon, assuming their financial responsibilities. This obvious notice to them was ignored, and Lormel stopped publication in November 1894.[13]

Many of Jarry's works of this period were collected in his first major publication, *The Records of the Black Crest (Les Minutes de Sable Mémorial;* September 1894). The title is based on two symbols of heraldry: sable is one of the five enamels on a coat of arms, and black is emblematic of evil. The title, then, shows that the collection is the herald of malevolence's victory: the prose, poems, and plays prove that man is so weak that his vaunted reason and egoism can be easily overthrown and that the cosmic powers are unable to help him.

The Records of the Black Crest is a two-pronged philosophical and artistic attack, which begins by revealing that man's rationality can be wrested from an individual's control and subsequently directed and manipulated by the artist. Jarry became interested in this problem shortly after coming to Paris, and it dominates this collection. *The Report Explaining the Terrible Accident of February 30, 1891 (Mémoire Explicatif du Terrible Accident du 30 Février, 1891* (1891) [14] is a study in counterpointing reason and irrationality, logic and absurdity, in order to engender a sense of reality's illogicality. Jarry sets the tone of the work in the title in which the reader is given a "report," that is, a factual description of something which never happened on a nonexistent day. The second paragraph typifies his technique: "After listening attentively to the reports of the jurists, practical jokers, and savants, after rejecting the advice of those who, showing some propensity for insanity, dropsy, or drugs," the undisclosed author tells the strange events of this unique day. "All the inhabitants of Paris remember this terrible adventure: the heat was torrid, the Seine carried pieces of ice as big as pumpkins, and on the third platform of the Eiffel Tower the fish fainted on the surface of the waves, crying horribly because of the aridity" (OCBP, p. 161).

The work's theme is obviously fanciful; but Jarry has very skillfully interjected words and phrases, such as Paris, the Seine, the Eiffel Tower, and Notre Dame, which continuously orient the reader toward reality. Jarry also liberally intersperses the "report" with references to "fact" and "reasons," including that infallible source, the architectonic of French scholasticism, the Larousse dictionary. Counterpointed to these well-known references is the irrational: heat yet chunks of ice floating in the river, fish not getting enough water but the Seine flooding; and elsewhere in the work he mentions an actor at the Théâtre Français singing "While blowing into his ocarina without being able to open his mouth," an unidentified "accused" throwing himself "from the top of the towers of Notre Dame into Lake Geneva," and a telegraph pole having "bushlike foliage" (OCBP, p. 162).

Opium (L'Opium), which is included in *The Records of the Black Crest*, is an experiment in the same mold as *The Report of the Terrible Accident*. This work focuses on a feverish man who takes some opium and describes his hallucinations.[15] This brief introduction is much more effective than dropping the reader in the middle of a strange and bewildering situation, as Jarry did in *The Report of the Terrible Accident*. Moreover, because the reader is told that he is about to read a description of an opium experience, he understands the abrupt transition of scenes and images and he thereby willingly suspends his disbelief. The fundamental technique of *Opium* is to present the reader with a phantasmagoria of graphic but loosely connected images. A brief section exemplifies the method. After the man's "corpse" has become "astral," he enters "an immense morgue," sees dead bodies, and shortly meets a man washing them who tells him to continue down the corridor and count the years, and "At thirty years you will find a morgue where the poets snore." He follows the instructions, enters the morgue, and tells the guard that he "has come for body number four." The guard asks him for "The proof that you killed him," but in spite of his inability to produce the proof, the guard trusts his honesty and allows him to pass. In an abrupt change, the man boards a bus, sees an eagle in a cage, and then finds in his hands a book which he has written but does not know when or how. Immediately the scene shifts to a cathedral where "bacchic incantations" are sung along with a "hellish hymn." Suddenly, "The walls collapse and the arches rise like a balloon." Finally, he finds his corporeal body "in my primordial armchair, all things in place, except my opium hookah, which I am going to replenish" (OCBP, pp. 195-98).

Jarry frequently experimented with images during the 1893-94 period, and one of the most important result is *Phonograph (Phonographe)*, the second part of *Guignol*, which was published separately in *Essais d'Art Libre* (June-July 1894). Rather than using geographic references to guide the reader's rationality as Jarry had done in *The Report of the Terrible Accident*, *Phonograph* is based on the technique of a recurring motif, like a record with a scratch on it, such as "the mineral siren" and her paramour. Part of the first paragraph demonstrates the theory. The reader is informed that "The mineral siren holds her beloved by his head, like steel tweezers pinching a dress." This is followed by three clauses, each containing an image: "The book closes itself in order to crush flies, and eight halos of gas, shading the carbon lamps." Then the "scratch" occurs: "She puts her crippled hands down with a brusque gesture to the right and left of the head of her lover-of-the-day, and she, the old lover, does not wound him, nor do her claws scratch him." Carrying out the reference to the "lover-of-the-day," Jarry says that the paramour's "fingers have rolled a game of nine-pins on the ground; paralyzed, the rudimentary organs have disappeared; and like the horses after the deluge, a single bone covered with a single claw." Then the "scratch" recurs: "She the old lover, does not wound him nor do her claws scratch him" (OCBP, p. 185). The pattern repeats until the work ends on a verbatim restatement of the first sentence.

Phonograph is more sophisticated than *The Report of the Terrible Accident* because the use of cyclical motifs is more universal than geographic locations, which he employed in the former work. *Phonograph* remains an experiment because Jarry has once again failed to judge the reader's ability to relinquish his logic. Conditioned to value reason, he surrenders it only after careful seduction. Unfortunately, Jarry was too hasty, and as a result the images are either undeveloped, as in the first series, or too esoteric (such as the references to the evolution of the horse's hoof) to be readily accepted. Moreover, the images are too compact, and they follow each other so quickly that the reader's mind either balks or begins to investigate and question rather than hallucinate.

The Report of the Terrible Accident, Opium, and *Phonograph* are nondidactic *études,* but Jarry was never far away from lecturing about his views of man and cosmos. At times he coupled artistic experiments with philosophic attitudes, an integration which appears in *Being and Living (Etre et Vivre).* He published it in the March-April 1894 issue of *L'Art Littéraire,* but he did not include it in *The Records of the Black Crest,* although it belongs in the group with the other four experiments. In *Being and Living* Jarry changes the technique and format from his use of geographic references, cyclical motifs, or flight of hallucinogenic images to manipulating logic, and he does so with such mastery that *Being and Living* is a bombing range where Jarry, at ease and at home, strafes at will. The result is a *tour de force* in which Jarry immerses the reader in a quagmire of logical statements and then contradicts them with equal logic. Because everything appears reasonable, the confused reader does not know how to find the truth.

Jarry begins by asking the reader which comes first, thought or action, and then provides an answer replete with logical substantiation. Jarry concludes that "Thought is the fetus of Action," but "Thought is fixed in one of its moments [and therefore] has an almost perceptible form" (OCBP, p. 341). He immediately reverses the conclusion and argues that "Action must necessarily be at the beginning for the unfolding of present and past acts" (OCBP, p. 342). Then suddenly he gives "Thought" unusual and unexpected qualities when he states that it "is not at the beginning because It is beyond time" (OCBP, p. 342). This conclusion might very well be true if one considers time within a psychological framework; but the statement nevertheless contradicts Jarry's premise that "Thought" has "a form" and is "fixed." Now that the reader is sufficiently confused by this brief squall of logic, Jarry attacks: "You, skeleton . . . habit-ridden, snobbish, and spherically bourgeois. You're not living . . . you simply Exist" (OCBP, p. 342). Cleverly done: thrust home when the opponent is unsuspecting! His point made, Jarry immediately changes the argument and continues the essay by using "to exist" as a transition. He states that the verb can be defined in terms of "its proven antipodes, Living" (OCBP, p. 342). Instead of explaining this logical discourse, he indulges in a flight of fancy intermingled with logic when he says that the letters of the word "Living" have "only the sense of the delirium of an inside-out hook. Life equals the action of sucking from the future itself by the umbilical siphon: to perceive is to be modified . . . likewise, to be perceived is to modify, to spread out tentacularly its amoebic horn." Suddenly the reader is jerked from the imagery into a completely unexpected conclusion, replete with proper vocabulary: "Thus and therefore, one knows that *opposites are equal*" (OCBP, p. 342). The work continues with a cascade of logical verbiage: "Consequently: when being becomes

Living the Continued becomes the Discontinued, Being syllogistically Non-Being. To Live = to cease Existing" (OCBP, p. 342), which is a return to his initial assertion that "Living" and "Existing" are diametrically opposed. After a few more short examples of twisted logic, he once again contradicts his position by concluding that "Life is the carnival of Being" (OCBP, p. 343).

The next section of *Being and Living* builds upon the paralysis in the reader's mind caused by the juxtaposition of reason and imagination. Now Jarry moves into fantasy: "Symbols of Being: two Day-Blind Eyes, in effect matched cymbals, circular chrome, thereby identical with itself, A Circle without circumference, thereby undimensioned" (OCBP, pp. 343-44). Mesmerized by this mixture of logic and phantasmagoria, the reader is jerked into reality at the end of the section by a misanthropic statement: "The Powerlessness of the heart's tears, forever eternal" (OCBP, p. 344).

The final part of *Being and Living,* which is its weakest section, begins with the bizarre assertion, based on the assumption that by now the reader is sufficiently stupefied to accept it, that "All murder is beautiful." The statement is so blatantly false that it is ineffective. Unwilling to grant the rectitude of the premise, how can the reader be expected to accede to its corollary: "let us, therefore, destroy Being" (OCBP, p. 344)? Nevertheless, Jarry proceeds to delineate two methods of doing so. First, *"by sterility"* because "All organs in repose atrophy." This correct analysis is counterpointed to the irrationality of the second: *"by stupor* unconsciously with ambivalence and the frequentation of Men reading Words, and the circular vision of the Heads" (OCBP, p. 344).

Except for the last section, *Being and Living* is a fresh, clever, subtle work because Jarry deftly manipulates logic and mixes it with imagination. The newly found strength lies in his focus on logic and giving a subsidiary role to images, an equation which permitted Jarry to keep proper perspective on his imagery. Moreover, his pleasure and familiarity with logic allowed him to work with joy and deliberation; consequently, *Being and Living* is more disciplined and refined with a more measured pace than the *tempo agitato* of most of his previous experiments. However, brilliant though *Being and Living* is, it demonstrates a rather consistent flaw in Jarry's work: unable to sustain his imagery or develop his philosophy over an extended period, he wrote episodes. Sometimes they are effective, but frequently they are too succinct and are often poorly integrated. This awkward handling sometimes causes a lack of focus and direction and a consequent loss of effect or message.

The four experiments *(The Report of the Terrible Accident, Opium, Phonograph,* and *Being and Living)*, although riddled with errors and flaws, remain extraordinary achievements, the more so since Jarry wrote them between the ages of eighteen and twenty. They show that he had scant respect for vaunted reason because it can be overpowered, turned upon itself, and made to self-destruct. He tried other techniques of gaining that goal, and the result is three *Funeral Songs (Lieds Funèbres;* pub., June 18, 1893), which are also a part of *The Records of the Black Crest.* "The Miracle of St. Accroupi" ("Le Miracle de Saint-Accroupi") focuses on a famine which has struck a city, but because of the prayers of the citizens for the intercession of St. Accroupi, God terminates the famine and sends down manna from heaven. However, unknown to the citizens, Famine still lurks beneath them (OCBP, p. 175). In the second story, Jarry tells "The Plaint of the Mandrake" ("La Plainte de la Mandragore") in which a man hears a mandrake regret that it is fixed to the ground. As the person touches the plant in order to console it, he is fixed to the ground (OCBP, p. 176). In "The Incubus" ("L'Incube"), the last of the trilogy, an incubus attacks a sleeping child; confronting this victory, the angels "turn the other cheek" (OCBP, p. 177).

In each story Jarry leads the reader into optimism, such as a miracle from God, an altruistic gesture, or the expectation that somehow the slowly crawling incubus will be crushed. But Jarry's misanthropy appears at the end of each story as the reader's hopes for the intercession of a benevolent deity are convincingly shattered, and he is consequently forced to acknowledge the supremacy of evil. Prayers and miracles are of no lasting succor or avail; to be compassionate is foolhardy; and not even the angels in heaven can stop evil attacking and conquering the innocent. In each of these three prose works Jarry utilizes an embellished style to create a mood in order to seduce the reader into accepting the irrational: an incubus, a talking plant, and manna from heaven. A valid goal, but the primary reason for his failure is the brevity of the stories. Jarry does not give the reader sufficient time to become engrossed in them so that he can accept the "fact" of a miracle, that is, the unreal. These are truly marvelous events, and it takes a degree of patience to prepare the reader to accept them, especially in the age of science, materialism, and rationalism.

The Records of the Black Crest contains only one play, Haldernablou (Haldernablou; 1894), a narrative drama which is a pivotal work because many of the conclusions expressed in it remained with Jarry throughout his life. The foremost stimulus for this play was The Songs of Maldoror by Isidore Ducasse, a young Uruguayan who came to France and took the pseudonym of "the Count of Lautréamont." The circumstances and chronology of the composition of this masterpiece are unknown, although it is confirmed that he finished it in 1868. This work received scant attention for decades, and then only from the avant-garde French literati. Jarry, attuned to subterranean literary works and currents, became enthralled by it, and eventually The Songs of Maldoror proved to be one of the most influential works he read. No wonder he referred to Lautréamont as "my friend the Montevidean" (OCBP, p. 227). Jarry was immediately struck by Lautréamont's strident statement of a malevolent cosmos. Lautréamont frequently castigates God, whom he calls "the horrible Eternal One," [16] the "Great Exterior Object," "the Celestial Bandit" (OCLP, p. 279). Extending the anthropomorphic concept of God to the extreme, Lautréamont depicts Him as sitting on a throne made of "Human excrement and gold . . . robed in a shroud of unwashed hospital sheets" (OCLP, p. 121). Lautréamont aggressively attacks the concept that God is all-merciful and all-loving by arguing that if He were, He would not set fires in which children and old people perish (OCLP, p. 41) allow oceans to "engulf ships," create hurricanes and earthquakes, nor permit plagues and diseases (OCLP, p. 41).

As Lautréamont depicts God sitting on His throne raining His wrath upon mankind, so does Jarry. In Haldernablou, Jarry shows Him to be an egoist who notices men only when they disobey His commandments. God prophesies that "All those will perish who have not respected my laws . . . and those who do not want, such as I created them, to reproduce their kind: for my Rule abominates them" (OCBP, p. 212). Like Lautréamont, Jarry depicts God as being dictatorial and tyrannical, the sworn enemy of those, such as Jarry, who violate "the Norm" by formulating and following their own moral codes (OCBP, p. 212).

With the backdrop that God is uncaring, tyrannical, and homicidal, Jarry turns to investigate the world of man. He borrows another precept from Lautréamont, who concludes that man is trapped in a paradox: he is an animal as savage as any in the wilderness but he also aspires to absolutes, which fuel his barbarism. Torn between the two poles, man will kill for what he considers right and virtuous, although those judgments are all too frequently founded on ignorance, blatant stupidity, and unrelieved egotism. Moreover, man will kill without let or mercy, with a relish and lust which defies belief. Lautréamont demonstrates his point by telling the story of a mother teaching her son about some wild dogs which are tearing each other to pieces, the story being an allegory for mankind: "don't make light of what they are doing: they have an insatiable thirst for the infinite, like you, like me, like the rest of us human beings. . . . I will even permit you to stand at the window and see this spectacle, which is rather magnificent" (OCLP, p. 15). Yes, there is something "magnificent" in, for instance, the effort to bring Christianity to the West at the cost of an estimated 20 million lives.[17] And for what?

Like Lautréamont's dogs, Jarry shows that man has a lust for the infinite, abstract, and eternal, although, like Lautréamont, Jarry does not account for this impulse. Haldern sees "the only reality—Surreality"—of "sublime" and "Pure Thought" (OCBP, p. 216-17). It is impossible, however, to remain very long in empyreal realms, and Jarry's examination of why man cannot stay in the eternal regions is more profound than Lautréamont's discussion. Jarry concludes that the "harmony" of "sublime thoughts" must be inevitably broken because no one can escape the gravitation of the earth, that is, sex. Haldern exemplifies the point when he becomes sexually excited, and, turning to his servant, Ablou, confesses that "I love you and want you at my feet." Jarry depicts Haldern's descent from the realm of "Pure Thought" by his reference in a train station to a locomotive as the "metallic god," a deity of the modern world emblematic of iron, power, and movement. Concomitantly, Ablou, after his contact with Haldern, moves toward the ethereal realms while keeping various facets of his mundane nature, and soon he too comes to admire the locomotive (OCBP, p. 217).

Lautréamont saw that man is not a free agent because, like Maldoror, he is "born evil" (OCLP, p. 38). Jarry formulated a similar concept in his early works, and in them he often shows people who have inherited avaricious and homicidal tendencies, such as Scaramouche and Kroeflich. Haldern, for instance, correctly notes that he and Ablou are not longer free because "The Subterranean Fate is on us" (OCBP, p. 218). Consequently, with his feet firmly set on land, Haldern asks Ablou to kiss him "fraternally" (OCBP, pp. 219-20). The youth recognizes the sexual implications of the request, and he replies that "I've got to do it or say no" (OCBP, p. 220). But there really is no choice: the "Subterranean Fate" is indeed upon him, and in a cascade of phallic images, he yields to Haldern.

Haldern and Ablou were destined to have sexual relations (OCBP, p. 216), but this fated love is also inevitably homicidal, a theme which became one of Jarry's principal concepts and first appears in *Haldernablou*. Jarry demonstrates his conclusion when he describes Haldern's room, where the coupling occurs, as being decorated with a Madonna as well as with "a . . . sculptured head of Death" (OCBP, p. 222). The cosmic backdrop thus painted, Jarry proceeds to the earthly forefront. Instead of returning Ablou's love, Haldern is seized with religious fervor when he sees the Madonna's statue. Beginning his journey back to "Pure Thought," he insists that the lamp be turned up and asks that Ablou join him in a reading of the Bible. The book is accidentally opened to Nehemiah 2:3: "The doors of the house will be consumed by fire" (OCBP, p. 223). The phrase is prophetic: Haldern swears that he will kill his former servant "because I despise him as impure and venal" (OCBP, p. 227). This statement parallels Lautréamont's observations about the dogs and man as well as Jarry's statement about God's commandment that He will murder those "who do not want, such as I created them, to reproduce their kind" (OCBP, p. 212). "It is necessary," Haldern concludes, "to kill the beast with which one has fornicated" (OCBP, p. 227). Thus filled with religious purity, Haldern brutally kills Ablou (OCBP, p. 229).

While Lautréamont's masterpiece provides much of the philosophical underpinning of *Haldernablou,* Jarry also utilizes facets of his personal life for the presentation of the sexual motif, as shown in a letter he wrote to Vallette on May 27, 1894. Jarry was in the army at this time, and he asked Vallette to prepare the *Haldernablou* manuscript for publication. Initially Jarry called the work *Cameleo,* but he instructed Vallette to change the title to *Haldernablou,* which is a unification of the renamed principal figures. "Haldern" is a Breton form of "Alfred," which underscores that this play is partly autobiographical. The first time Haldern appears is in the poem *The Second Life, Or Macaber* in which Aldern-Alfred, more zealous than Faust in the search for total knowledge, commits suicide in order to plumb the mysteries of the universe. This view of Haldern-Alfred as seer-savant reappears in *Haldernablou* when the principal figure's mind revels in "Pure Thought." In a less overt fashion, this sagelike quality also surfaces in the Prologue, with which Jarry frequently began his major efforts. For instance, in *The Second Life* and especially in *Haldernablou* he delights in providing a backdrop, usually cosmic in nature, in which the author states his comprehension of the nature of the universe. Similarly, he frequently exposes his apocalyptic vision of man's fate as well as man's demise. Jarry continued underpinning his works with his egotism until it was checked by the failure of *King Ubu.*

The title of *Haldernablou* was a deliberate unification of the two names in order to show, Jarry wrote, "in one word of horror . . . the beast doubly coupled" (OCBP, p. 1037). The play, then, is about a homosexual affair between Haldern-Alfred and Ablou, originally named "Cameleo," a nickname for Jarry's roommate, Léon-Paul Fargue. Libaude intimates in an essay that the two were indeed homosexuals, but he made this accusation after Libaude and Jarry had become bitter enemies.[18] However, his statement is made credible by the recurring homosexual references in Jarry's work, especially in *Days and Nights,* and his nine-month association with Lord Douglas, the confrère of Oscar Wilde. Despite such indications, it is noteworthy that not one of Jarry's numerous friends and acquaintances, except Libaude, have made even the slightest allegation that he was a homosexual and that, except for *Haldernablou* and several sections of *Days and Nights,* he makes no sustained presentation of homosexuality; in fact, his last two major works, *Messalina* and *The Supermale,* deal with heterosexuality. Moreover, the picture Jarry presents of the Haldern-Cameleo homosexuality is certainly limited. For instance, was Jarry stating that he was the abstract thinker while Cameleo-Fargue was mundane? Yet in the café it was Jarry who discussed masturbation while Fargue spoke about art.

The most notable flaw in *Haldernablou* is the inordinate compression of episodes, a problem which had long plagued Jarry. Because of the dense imagery and concise dialogue, the work frequently fails to communicate effectively. For instance, Jarry does not give the reader sufficient opportunity to comprehend Haldern's descent from the empyreal realms, and the acquiescence of Ablou's mother in the homosexual coupling certainly deserves more extensive treatment than three lines. One of the most irritating facets of the play is Jarry's awkward use of the Chorus, whose lines are frequently clumsy and overextended with sometimes sophomoric if not unintelligible images, and whose entrances are usually disruptive. To compound the problem of understanding the play, the Pastor of the Owls has no valid function, and his long speech, replete with strophes, antistrophes, and epodes, is so fanciful that it damages rather than embellishes the play.

While *Haldernablou* has numerous artistic shortcomings, it is revolutionary in one significant aspect. Until 1893-94, Jarry had consciously adhered to many of Aristotle's observations about drama, most specifically that a work of art has a beginning, a middle, and an end. Although *Haldernablou* satisfies the first two requirements, it does not meet the third. The play terminates with the death of Ablou, and the invisible Chorus twisting slightly its opening ode: "The white worm of the grave leaves its abode" (OCBP, p. 229). However, Haldern lives in the rarefied atmosphere of Christian purity, and the play has convincingly shown that he cannot remain in his "sublime" realm. He will once again be inevitably seized by sexual desire, travel earthward, and kill. Thus there is no ending to the play in the Aristotelian sense. Jarry had signaled his revolt against Aristotle in *A Letter from a Parisian Humanist to an Italian Aristotelian,* and *Haldernablou* was the first manifestation of the rebellion. Fortunately, his first attempt was so successful that he continued his disregard of Aristotelian strictures, formulated his own theories, and by doing so eventually revolutionized much of modern theater.

The Records of the Black Crest emerges as an intriguing collection. Artistically, it is a fine amalgam of experiments, ranging from the mimetic *(Phonograph* and *Opium)* to the didactic, such as the *Funeral Songs* and *Haldernablou.* While all these experiments have shortcomings, they nevertheless represent a considerable spectrum of inventiveness, an unmistakable willingness to reject the customary, and marked courage to investigate the new. Philosophically, *The Records of the Black Crest* demonstrates a striking advance over his earlier works, especially in the artist's confident assumption that man's vaunted reason is a thin veneer of egoism. To Jarry, the mind is indeed malleable, and the subsequent problem for the creator is to find the proper technique to bend and twist it. *The Records of the Black Crest* also shows that Jarry was a militant misanthrope with a view of man that led inevitably to an attack on Christian cosmology, which Jarry now condemned for its homicidal nature. Thus, with *The Records of the Black Crest* Jarry had shown his crest, the banner of his knighthood: black—emblematic of iconoclasm and malevolence, and sable—rebellion.

Jarry's literary activity was temporarily restricted by his being drafted into the French army. He tried several times to avoid military service, but on November 13, 1894, he was called up. Here was the classic clash between the immovable object and the unstoppable force, and in this case Jarry won—with the help of a little subterfuge. After he entered service, his commanding officer, a captain, asked Jarry his name, and the youth replied that "my na-meh is Al-fred Jar-ry I am-meh or-ig-in-al-ly a na-tive of La-val and man-neh of let-ters from-meh Par-is." Jarry gave each syllable the same weight; there was no punctuation; and one sound was low, another high, like a "primitive chant." [19] The captain told him not to call a superior officer "Monsieur," and Jarry replied "Ver-ry well Mon-sieur. Here-after I shall call you my cap-tain" (Géroy, pp. 4-5). Always attentive and respectful, he seemingly wanted to cooperate with the officers, but he managed to disrupt and demoralize the organization so much that he was excused from parades and most of the drills. What can the forces of discipline, order, and obedience do with such a free-spirited man? He was too intelligent to be disrespectful and thereby subject to discipline, and yet he was too free to be tolerated. Therefore, he was shortly released from the army for "chronic lithiasis" (gallstones), although Jarry claimed his discharge was due to his "precocious imbecility." There was another reason for his release: unknown to the authorities, Jarry had injected himself with picric acid, which gave his skin a yellow cast. The ruse was successful: he was first hospitalized and then released, although his discharge was not formalized until December 14, 1895.

Although Jarry wrote nothing during his military service, he proceeded with his publications, including *Haldernablou* and *Emperor Antichrist (César-Antichrist)*, the latter appearing in the *Mercure de France* (October 1, 1895). The first three acts were originally separate pieces: the Prologue appeared as a one-act play in *L'Art Littéraire* (July, August 1894); and the "Heraldic" and "Terrestrial" acts were published in the *Mercure de France* in March and September, respectively. This publication history explains the disjunct organization of the work and its sometimes contradictory materials.

Jarry expressed the principal themes of *Emperor Antichrist* in *Haldernablou*, although there are nuances which differentiate the two. Similar to *Haldernablou*, he portrays man as being inescapably trapped between opposites. To Jarry in *Emperor Antichrist*, "Man is the mean between Infinity and Nothing" (OCBP, p. 280). This statement of his position is much more pessimistic than in *Haldernablou* because there is no person like Haldern, who strives for that which is greater than himself, that is, the ethereal region of "Pure Thought." A second difference between *Haldernablou* and *Emperor Antichrist* is that in the latter work Jarry deletes any mention of love. There is no moment of richness, such as Ablou experiencing beauty and perfection. *Emperor Antichrist* portrays a wasteland ruled by the Antichrist, Ubu.

Emperor Antichrist is a forceful attack on Christianity. In the Prologue, the Gold Christ, emblematic of charity and Jesus' commandment to "turn the other cheek," announces that "Those [of us] who are about to die salute you," Emperor Antichrist (OCBP,

p. 276). Shortly afterward a Herald enters and announces that "life has conceived . . . the one who will destroy it" (OCBP, p. 277). This statement is the front-line of the assault: logically, Jarry argues, the reign of Jesus must end because, according to Plato, opposites engender opposites. Plato uses this rational in *The Phaedo* to defend the position that there is life after death; Jarry, however, cleverly ridicules this defense of Christian theology. Using Christian terms, Jarry shows that the "Lamb of Love" must generate his opposite, the Lion of Hate, and Jarry concludes that God had two sons, which He acknowledges when He recognizes Emperor Antichrist as "my beloved son in whom I place all of my love" (OCBP, p. 330). A vulture then alights on Jesus, plucks out one of his eyes, and announces "Let there be light—One" (OCBP, p. 331). So Jesus, the "Prince of Peace" and the "King of Kings" is dethroned.

The Prologue is a very clever and sophisticated work, but to argue that God actually begat two sons so countermands the traditional belief that Jesus was God's only issue that the average reader will find the new revelation unacceptable. A solution would have been to be more patient with the reader by slowly and carefully presenting the argument and rationale, but Jarry still had not developed this expertise. He continued to write in a highly compressed style with little care given to explaining to others what he himself so clearly saw.

The second act of *Emperor Antichrist* focuses on the nobility, which represents the mean between the cosmic, symbolized by the demise of Lord Jesus, and the "Terrestrial," epitomized by Ubu, ex-King of Poland and Aragon. The transition to the "Heraldic" act is awkward, a problem caused by the inadequate stitching together of the separately published works. For instance, at the end of the Prologue, the Antichrist is awake and speaking (OCBP, pp. 281-82), but in the "Heraldic" he sleeps for the first seven scenes. Unfortunately, Jarry was in the army when *Emperor Antichrist* was published *in toto;* and Vallette, who had been trusted with preparing the manuscript, did not do so carefully. A second mistake is that scenes viii and ix, which are devoted to equating the Antichrist with Ubu, need much more development than fifteen lines of speech. But the conclusion is unmistakable: Ubu acknowledges that "Like an egg, a pumpkin, or a flashing meteor, I roll on this earth where I will do what I please" (OCBP, p. 293). Requisite proof is given in the third part, the "Terrestrial act," which is devoted to the exploits of Ubu; this chapter later became *King Ubu.*

Artistically, *Emperor Antichrist* shows that Jarry was learning how to employ symbols. Influenced by Mallarmé and the Symbolists at this time, he might have been expected to experiment with symbols, as *Haldernablou* demonstrates; but he had trouble using them. In *Emperor Antichrist* he exploited Christian symbols and used them with a finesse not seen in his previous works. For instance, by splitting Jesus' character into three parts (the Green Christ of Life, the Gold Christ of Charity, and the White Christ of Love of Mankind), he is able to highlight the destruction of each quality. But only the most zealous student of the Bible would recognize bronze, silver, and gold as emblematic of the idols mentioned in Revelation. Jarry makes a similar error in much of the second act when he extensively uses symbols of medieval heraldry, many of which are so obscure that only a specialist would know them.

Emperor Antichrist is a massive, esoteric frontal assault on Christianity, and while Jarry's arguments are innovative, they are of little value in refuting Christianity. After all, who accepts Plato's doctrine of opposites as proof for the existence of an afterlife? Moreover, Jarry ultimately defeats his own goal because if the good (Jesus) must inevitably spawn evil (Ubu), must not the doctrine of opposites be extended to include Ubu inevitably giving birth to Jesus? Thus, to end the play with the triumph of Ubu—as Jarry does—is illogical. Philosophically as well as artistically, the play is interesting but a failure.

Jarry continued to attack Christianity in a superb piece he wrote for *La Revue Blanche* entitled *Toward Paradise, Or The Old Man of the Mountain (Au Paradis, Ou Le Vieux de la Montagne;* May 1, 1896). He submitted the work to the editor, his friend Félix Fénéon, with considerable trepidation because of what Jarry considered to be the "length, obscenity, or vagueness" (OCBP, p. 1046). His fears were completely unfounded. It was a mark of his thoughtfulness that he gave his friend an excuse to reject the manuscript; it proved to be one of his finest achievements.

In *Emperor Antichrist* Jarry had argued that Jesus, "Lamb of Love," must generate His opposite; in *The Old Man of the Mountain*

Jarry deletes any pyrotechnical display of logic and presents Jesus as a tyrant, enslaver, and murderer. Rather than a frontal assault, which would shock the timorous and alienate them at once, Jarry tempts the reader with a fictional story of Marco Polo and Genghis Khan standing before a castle, the palace of Alaodine, a Jesus figure (OCBP, p. 897).[20] He controls the gates to paradise, which Jarry ridicules as being a land "of milk and water . . . honey and wine," which, the author underscores, is illusory. Paradise can be seen only after drinking an elixir, which has the smell of garlic and "of a hanged man's semen" (OCBP, p. 895). However disagreeable it may be, men will drink this elixir to see the mirage of heaven. Because Alaodine-Jesus controls the potion, he automatically has enormous control over the lives and thoughts of men, represented by Marco Polo and Genghis Khan. The true satanic nature of Alaodine soon appears. As the administrator of the hallucinatory drug, he is the serpent in the Garden because once man has seen heaven, he becomes addicted to it and begs for more elixir. Thus enslaved, Genghis Khan and Marco Polo are subject to Alaodine's desire to enhance his own power and position. His first order is for them to kill Father John because he has refused to surrender his daughter, Princess Belor, to Alaodine. The sycophants heartily obey. Such, then, is Jarry's attack on Christianity: its path to paradise is littered with slaves and corpses.

In spite of the traditional view of Jesus as the Prince of Peace, Jarry sees that this portrayal masks a religion of rarely equaled violence and savagery. For instance, the Christian Astrologer cannot help admiring the beauty of the Princess Belor, thus trespassing Alaodine's admonition that "If thine eye offend thee, pluck it out!" The Christian Astrologer, faithful to this stricture, plucks out his eyes, which are promptly devoured by Alaodine's mascot, a savage manticore. Moreover, the Alaodine-Jesus sycophant exonerates, justifies, and even rationalizes murder, which is exemplified by Marco Polo when he enters with Father John's head on his sword. Not only has he been a faithful servant, but at once the Princess Belor falls in love with him because, she explains, "you have killed my father, and while doing that, you, dearest, have become completely like Alaodine . . . our sheik and great prophet" (OCBP, p. 900). Although she means well, her sentiment is hardly complimentary. Thus, Alaodine-Jesus manages to turn child against father and even induces the Princess Belor to remain a virgin, although her natural impulses urge another course of action. The work ends with a bizarre and effective twist which is reminiscent of the *Funeral Songs* of *The Records of the Black Crest.* The blind Christian Astrologer has the last line: "There never was a paradise, nor a castle" (OCBP, p. 903). The sightless, like Oedipus, see: Christianity is an illusion, but the deaths are very real.

Philosophically, *The Old Man of the Mountain* augments the attack Jarry made on Christianity in *Haldernablou* and *Emperor Antichrist:* this religion is tyrannical, homicidal, illogical, suppressive, and enslaving. The view of Christianity as well as his pessimism, atheism, and misanthropy placed Jarry squarely outside the mainstream of Western culture; these works also show that he was an innovative warrior and a rigorous soldier.

Artistically, *The Old Man of the Mountain* is quite different from the two complementary works, *Haldernablou* and *Emperor Antichrist.* For instance, *The Old Man of the Mountain* is light in tone, almost comic. Alaodine-Jesus is a buffoon, and so are Genghis Khan and Marco Polo in their zest to surrender their wills. The Princess Belor is the "dumb blonde" character when she adores Marco Polo for murdering her father. Never before had Jarry been so subtle, clever, and deadly with his wit; and he was in such complete control of his humor that he could tellingly underscore his points yet stop short of making his audience laugh. While Jarry had taken admirable strides forward as a craftsman, his decision to write this work as well as *Haldernablou* and *Emperor Antichrist* as narrative dramas shows that he had yet to commit himself fully to drama.

Although *The Records of the Black Crest* is a surprisingly excellent collection, its quality is uneven. Remy de Gourmont, Jarry's close friend, noted that there were facets of the collection which did not please him but concluded that *The Records of the Black Crest* "is a delightful début, a stalk whose first blossoms promise a future of beautiful hollyhocks and passionflowers." [21]

Jarry's career took an unexpected turn when in October 1894 he founded, along with Remy de Gourmont, *L'Ymagier,* subtitled a *Magazine of Engravings.* Jarry had been interested in the editorial facets of publication as early as 1893-94 when he, Coulon, and

Lormel collaborated on *L'Art Littéraire*. Now he had his own journal which would express his interests. Its format was sumptuous, and the engravings and woodcuts are still striking. Jarry did the commentary as well as some of his own woodcuts under the pseudonym of "Alain Jans." The first issue (October 1894) was devoted to scenes of "The Passion," many of which are so elaborate that they recall biblical illumination. However, the second (January 1895), called "Monsters," was most unusual and graphic. The April 1895 issue was devoted to "The Virgin and Christ Child," and the fourth (July 1895) returned to "The Passion." The fifth (October 1895) contained five representations of "Gingerbread Figures." One of the pictures was without a signature; the other four were by Alain Jans. After that edition, Jarry and Gourmont separated and *L'Ymagier* inconspicuously expired.

On August 19, 1895, Jarry's father died—"right on schedule," according to Jarry—of the influenza epidemic. Since Alfred had little affection for him, his death was unmourned; the inheritance was gladly accepted. Using the money, Jarry rented a lavish apartment, to which he invited his friends when the Czar of Russia passed by in order to honor the recent Franco-Russian alliance. Jarry also used his inheritance to found *Perhinderion*, a Breton word for "pilgrimage," in which his goal was to present the complete works of Dürer. Jarry commissioned special plates and handset type, and the format was even more luxurious than that of *L'Ymagier*. According to the announcement, "The reproductions of the old woodcuts will be photoengraved . . . without reducing their size, and struck . . . on laid paper, which is the most similar to the original paper" (OCBP, p. 995). The cost was so great that Jarry could afford only two issues (March and June 1896). Because of *Perhinderion* and the rent on his apartment, his inheritance was quickly exhausted. By December 8, 1896, he had about thirty francs left.

Perhinderion, unfortunately short-lived, became the means for Jarry to advance himself. He sent a copy of the first number to Lugné-Poe, the director and producer of the Théâtre de l'Oeuvre, who was impressed by its sumptuousness. Thus, the requisite doors opened for the two men to meet and become friends. At the same time, Jarry exploded artistically. With an unfaltering hand, he rewrote a childhood play, which Lugné-Poe soon produced. This play became the most seminal, revolutionary and iconoclastic play of the modern theater—*King Ubu.*

Notes

1. Alfred Jarry, *Oeuvres Complètes,* Michel Arrivé (Paris: Gallimard [Bibliothèque de la Pléiade], 1972), p. 427. Hereafter cited in the text and abbreviated as "OCBP."
2. Cited in Margarite Eymery (pseud., "Rachilde"), *Alfred Jarry ou Le Surmâle des Lettres* (Paris: Bernard Grasset, 1928), p. 31. Hereafter cited in the text as "Rachilde."
3. Johann Wolfgang von Goethe, *Faust,* trans. Charles E. Passage (New York: Bobbs-Merrill, 1965), pp. 392-93, ll. 11,559-11,586.
4. Henri Hertz, "Jarry, Collégien et la Naissance d'*Ubu Roi,*" *Ecrits Nouveaux* (November 1921), vols. 8-9, p. 73. Hereafter cited in the text as "Hertz."
5. André Bellerie, "Jarry le Mystificateur," *Caliban,* no. 39 (May 1950), p. 79.
6. Jarry wrote three poems in honor of Gauguin. See OCBP, pp. 252-54; OCBP, p. 1116, n. 2.
7. Cited in John Russell, *Edouard Vuillard, 1868-1940* (Norwich, Great Britain: Jarrold and Sons, 1971), p. 120. Hereafter cited in the text as "Russell."
8. Fernard Lot, *Alfred Jarry, Son Oeuvre* (Paris: Editions de la Nouvelle Revue Critique, 1934), p. 8. Hereafter cited in the text as "Lot."
9. André Gide, "Le Groupement Littéraire qu'abritait le *Mercure de France,*" *Mercure de France* 218, nos. 999-1000 (December 1946), p. 168. Hereafter cited in the text as "Gide."
10. Gide tells a lengthy story about Jarry in the chapter entitled "The Argonaut's Dinner" in *The Counterfeiters.*
11. G. E. Clancier, *Panorama Critique de Rimbaud au Surréalisme.* (Paris: Pierre Seghers, 1953), p. 154.
12. Louis Lormel, "Entre Soi," *La Plume,* October 1, 1897, p. 605. Hereafter cited in the text as "Lormel."
13. J.-H. Sainmont, "Lormel et Jarry," *Cahiers du Collège de 'Pataphysique,* nos. 22-23, p. 59.
14. Jarry did not include *The Report of the Terrible Accident* in *The Records of the Black Crest* because it is clearly a sophomoric work. However, the style and content show its close relation to *The Records of the Black Crest.*
15. There is little doubt that Jarry was well acquainted with hallucina-

tory drugs, and a reference to laudanum in "The Antliaclastes" (OCBP, p. 38) suggests that the acquaintance occurred at an early age. Laudanum was an opiate widely used medicinally.

16. Isidore Ducasse (pseud., "le Comte de Lautréamont"), *Oeuvres Complètes* (Paris: Librairie Générale Française [Livre de Poche], 1969), p. 96. Hereafter cited in the text and abbreviated as "OCLP."

17. Homer W. Smith, *Man and His Gods* (New York: Grosset, 1957), p. 251.

18. J.-H. Sainmont speculates, with considerable justification, that the rupture in the friendship between Jarry and Lormel was Lormel's fault. Sainmont thinks that Lormel became increasingly jealous of Jarry's success as well as the loss of some of his friends to Jarry's circle. It was under these circumstanes that Lormel wrote the article for *La Plume*. See Sainmont, "Lormel et Jarry." However, the two men were reconciled shortly before Jarry's death, according to Lormel. See Lormel, *La Phalange* (December 1907), pp. 555 and 559.

19. Géroy, "Mon Ami Alfred Jarry," *Le Courrier d'Epidaure* (March-April 1949), p. 5. Hereafter cited in the text as "Géroy."

20. Jarry might well have learned of "the old man of the mountain" from reading Baudelaire's "Le Peintre de La Vie Moderne." See Baudelaire, *Oeuvres Complètes* (Paris: Gallimard, 1961), p. 1179. The expression originated in an eleventh-to-thirteenth-century Islamic sect. One of his grand masters was nicknamed "shaykh al-jabal," which is Arabic for "mountain chief"; the Crusaders mistranslated the expression as "Old Man of the Mountain." The sect considered it a religious duty to murder its enemies.

21. Remy de Gourmont, "Les Livres: *Les Minutes de Sable Mémorial* par Alfred Jarry," *Mercure de France* 12 (October 1894), p. 178.

2.

Aesthetics and Dramaturgy

Death is plagiarism, the dying poet tells the Muse in a section of *The Visits of Love* (OCBP, p. 893). Jarry epitomizes this attitude because he resolutely refused to follow the dicta of others. While stimulated by such luminaries as Goethe, Coleridge, and Lautréamont, he did not hesitate to modify their works and ideas. This pattern of borrowing and transforming, modifying and augmenting, is also seen in Jarry's aesthetic theories, most of which he developed after he came to Paris in 1891. In this artistically fecund city he benefited from his contacts with writers, musicians, and painters who also sought new goals for their art. Their trials and errors, successes and failures, made *fin de siècle* Paris one of the most exciting places and periods in Western thought, and it was fortunate that Jarry's heritage and inclination permitted him to be nurtured by this "climate of opinion."

The aura of Paris proved so electrifying that he was sometimes unable to sift adequately the various views he confronted; reflect and analyze; and then properly select, modify, and correlate them. Consequently, his aesthetic concepts are often inadequately examined, superficially conceived, and poorly presented. His drama-

turgy demonstrates the point. In June 1896 Jarry accepted the
position of Lugné-Poe's secretary. In the ensuing seven months he
became very active in the organization, wrote several essays about
the theater, revised and produced *King Ubu,* reacted to the defeat
of his play, and then left the company. He was too busy to evaluate his ideas properly; as a result, he never became a systematic
aesthetician. Nevertheless, Jarry's observations, although sometimes limited and disjointed, remain a significant contribution to
modern drama because he posed questions and suggested provocative solutions at a significant moment. His hypotheses helped
liberate dramatists from old attitudes and concepts so that they
could walk in new territory. His most significant experiment, *King
Ubu,* was a test tube in which others saw the viability of his views
and theories.

In the light of literary history, Jarry was an illuminary, but the
honors for causing the major reassessment of drama belong to his
mentor, Victor Hugo. While the "battle of *Hernani*" (1830) helped
shake French theater from its classical foundations, the revolutionary promise of *Hernani* was cut short by the political events of 1848.
The dramatic vacuum was being filled in 1887 by André Antoine,
who was using the Théâtre Libre to blaze new trails in the theater,
Paul Fort helped introduce Symbolist drama; and Aurélien Lugné-
Poe continued this development at his Théâtre de l'Oeuvre, where
he experimented with avant-garde plays, including works by Ibsen
and Maeterlinck. He allowed Jarry to present *King Ubu* at the
Théâtre de l'Oeuvre, and it was through Jarry's subsequent writings and *King Ubu* that the clearest and most demanding call was
sounded for a critical reappraisal of the theater and the formulation of new dramaturgical concepts.

Jarry wrote most of his theories of art between 1894 and 1896.
The first group of ideas focuses on the "Lintel" to *The Records of the
Black Crest* (1894). Then Jarry became involved in the theater, and
at this time he formed most of his ideas about drama. Third, he
wrote an essay, "Theater Questions" ("Questions de Théâtre";
January 1, 1897) after the production of *King Ubu* in which he tried
to answer his critics, but this essay is more of an apologia than an
extension of his previous concepts.

The first foundation stone of Jarry's aesthetics is Symbolism, with which Jarry became intimately acquainted shortly after coming to Paris in 1891. Not only were the Symbolists attractive to Jarry because of their experiments in literature, but he was drawn to the mild and gentle Mallarmé, who always gave encouragement. Although the two men had divergent personalities, they became such friends that Mallarmé was present at the première of *King Ubu* and congratulated him on his achievement. When Mallarmé died, Jarry attended the funeral—an unusual action for him. He then composed "Necrology" ("Nécrologie"; 1899) [1] in which the presence of his valued friend and mentor is depicted as being like "impetuous surface heat from timpani . . . like fire which enters and disperses, like a drink of wine" (OCBP, p. 564). While Jarry was too independent to become a sycophant of Mallarmé and of the Symbolist *cénacle,* he was nevertheless indebted to it and to its leader. One of the most important influences they exerted on him was to form his lifelong attitudes against Realism and Naturalism. Under Mallarmé's tutelage, Jarry agreed that Realism is "a banal sacrilege of the true meaning of art." [2] At once he abandoned the sophomoric Romanticism which typifies much of his juvenilia; he now moved in new directions with Mallarmé's guidance.

Jarry began to think about manipulating the reader's mentality in order to rouse him or her to become actively involved in the creative process. This search is begun within the individual's imagination and is stimulated by the suggestions of the poet or dramatist. However, the creator must not give too many details because "To describe is to lose three fourths of the pleasure of the poem." [3] The extension of this theory is hermetic poetry, that is, the meaning or significance of the work is subterranean and can be found only by an intense effort by the reader to discover personal meaning or delight in the work. Jarry understood Mallarmé's concept very well when he asserted that "In a written work there is a hidden meaning, and the reader sees the hidden personal meaning and recognizes the eternal and invisible river and calls it *Anna Peranna*" (OCBP, p. 406).[4] Thus, both Mallarmé and Jarry arrive at the same goal of trying to engender a sense of the eternal or universal in the reader. This was no easy task, as Mallarmé attests, but Jarry undertook the trials, and the result was twenty-eight

experiments which he published as *The Records of the Black Crest.*
The several poems in this collection differ little from his previous
efforts either in style or message; the significant *études* are in prose,
a medium in which Jarry had done little before 1891. It was a wise
decision for him to change to prose because he had little chance of
gaining poetic fame in the face of Mallarmé's dominant position;
also, the latter's circle included others who were clearly Jarry's
superior in this genre. But the change to prose did not cause Jarry
much difficulty, and his earliest experiments are remarkably fluid
and facile.

Jarry's first Symbolist experiment was *The Report of the Terrible
Accident* (1891). Though not included in *The Records of the Black
Crest,* it had revealed the main intent of his work at this period
which was soon developed in *Being and Living, Phonograph, Opium,*
and *Funeral Songs,* and further extended in the "Lintel," which expresses one of Jarry's most celebrated concepts. The section begins
with a brief and innocent manifesto of literary freedom: it is absurd in literature to repeat the doctrines of various philosophers or
to present their concepts piecemeal (OCBP, p. 171). Jarry's clear
rejection of sycophancy is admirable, but his feelings are neither
new, revolutionary, nor brilliant. After establishing his aesthetic
liberty, he asserts that art should "suggest instead of stating," a
phrase which has been too widely cited as representative of Jarry's
aesthetics. While the sentence can be accepted for its Symbolist
quality, it is unmistakably only one statement in a kaleidoscope of
ideas, some of which are indeed of questionable validity. How,
then, is the reader to decide which to accept?

The first step in obtaining the answer is to construct a brief list
of some of the ideas:

1. "Suggest instead of stating; the phrase should be
directed toward a verbal crossroads" (OCBP, p. 172);
2. *"There is a constant relationship between the verbal phrase
and all senses"* (OCBP, p. 172);
3. The reader is "infinitely superior intellectually to the
writer" (OCBP, p. 172);
4. The writer creates at the "unique moment when he
sees EVERYTHING" (OCBP, p. 172);

5. "It is good to write a theory after the work, to read it before the work" (OCBP, p. 172);

6. "It is foolish to assert whether the written work itself [is] good or bad because at the moment of writing the writer has tried his best not to say EVERYTHING" (OCBP, p. 173).

Each "rule" is an aphorism, that is, a conclusion which invites the reader to inquire into its rectitude and then, if he wishes, to provide the necessary rationale. For example, Jarry says that the reader is "infinitely superior intellectually to the writer." Consideration of this phrase requires much introspection and self-evaluation on a reader's part, and the consequent difficulties are compounded by having to choose the writers with whom the comparison is made. Coleridge's "To a Young Ass, Its Mother Being Tethered Near It" demonstrates the point. It is a miserable work, and there are unquestionably many readers who, aware of Coleridge's inadequate performance in that poem, would indeed be his intellectual superior. But how should a reader measure himself against Aristotle and his *Ethics,* Baron d'Holbach and his brilliant achievement, *The System of Nature,* or Nietzsche and his magnificent *Thus Spoke Zarathustra?* How many people intellectually equal these great predecessors? By what criteria does one evaluate intelligence?

Once the reader has completed his analysis of that aphorism, he is invited to the next one and to repeat the process. But, arriving at the sixth, he finds that it directly contradicts the fourth. Which position should he accept? The reader has been placed at a "crossroads" from which only he can extricate himself. Consequently, he becomes an integral part of the creation of the essay, and it is at this point that Jarry shows most markedly the influence of Mallarmé, especially the emphasis on making the reader give the work of art an intimately personal significance. However, for Jarry, this self-analysis is more cerebral and cognitive than that of Mallarmé, and this difference will be important when Jarry creates *King Ubu.*

Another method of effecting this individualized art is juxtaposition, a technique which is, as Beausire rightly sees, "extremely important" to Mallarmé.[5] Jarry's first significant experiment in using this tool was *The Report Explaining the Terrible Accident.* It is a study in juxtaposing reason and irrationality, logic and absurdity, in order to generate within the reader a sense of reality's illogicality. *Opium* is another experiment in the same mold, but here Jarry juxtaposes images instead of counterpointing reality and fancy. A variation of the cascade of images occurs in *Phonograph.* Rather than using geographic references to guide the reader's rationality, as Jarry had done in *The Report Explaining the Terrible Accident,* or a phantasmagoria of scenes as in *Opium, Phonograph* is based on the technique of a recurring motif, like a record with a scratch on it.

These three experiments *(The Report Explaining the Terrible Accident, Opium,* and *Phonograph)* reflect Jarry's interest, like that of Mallarmé, in manipulating the reader's mind, and these works also show that Jarry was very quickly developing a striking technical skill in doing so. However, it is noteworthy that Jarry differs from Mallarmé in one significant point: he could not share his mentor's ascent from "the Void" and "the Nothing" in the "Overture" to *Hérodiade* into the Beautiful, the "Divine." [6] Jarry never sought, like Mallarmé, to guide the reader toward the realm of supernal Beauty or to make "ordinary existence disappear" into "the power of a second reality" (Beausire, pp. 28-29). Jarry's misanthropy did not allow him to accept this mysticism or metaphysical sensitivity. He was content to use juxtaposition to show how fragile are man's vaunted reason and grasp of reality, as well as how easily they are manipulated and confounded. Nor could Jarry share Mallarmé's enthusiasm for mankind. Except for a singular moment in *Faustroll,* Jarry was never able to conceive of man as anything but a primordial brute struggling for supremacy in the slime of life, or, as in *Days and Nights,* a beautiful creature brought to bay and slaughtered by social forces. The lessons Jarry learned from Mallarmé were significant in enhancing his technical repertoire, but they did not change his fundamental philosophical attitudes.

The Report of the Terrible Accident, Opium, and *Phonograph* are nondidactic, but Jarry was never very far from lecturing about his views of man and cosmos, and he increasingly found that the Symbolist technique of juxtaposing images and thoughts could be easily adapted to serve his misanthropic attitudes. *Being and Living* demonstrates how Jarry changed the techniques of using geographical references, cyclical motifs, or flights of hallucinogenic images to manipulating logic. It is a brilliant extension of Symbolist technology: rather than seducing the reader out of his rationality, Jarry uses logic to destroy logic.

Jarry's aesthetic concepts were further stimulated and enhanced by his acquaintance with Lugné-Poe, and as a result his aesthetics received direction and specificity which complemented and augmented the influence of the Symbolists. On October 30, 1894, Jarry began his formal relations with the director-producer who, at this time, was still struggling to establish his Théâtre de L'Oeuvre, which soon became of the most important theatrical crucibles in Paris. Although the two men might have met informally at either the salon of Mallarmé or that of the Vallettes, their definite contact was established when Jarry sent Lugné-Poe a copy of *Perhinderion* (1896), and shortly afterward a mutual friend, A. F. Hérold, introduced the two. Fortunately for both Jarry and the fame of Lugné-Poe, the secretary of the Théâtre de l'Oeuvre resigned in June 1896, and Lugné-Poe gave the job to Jarry. The arrangement was mutually beneficial: Lugné-Poe gained an eager worker who so zealously performed his duties that he was entrusted with many others, including publicity director, handyman, and minor actor. Jarry also gained a great deal from his association with Lugné-Poe and the Théâtre de l'Oeuvre. Once again he found himself in the center of a revolutionary group which sought to make the theater more relevant to the audience by producing Symbolist drama as well as non-French plays. For Jarry, this drama was an essential extension of his intimate friendship with Mallarmé and his circle as well as the concomitant evolution of his aesthetic theories. Now his lively but disciplined mind, precocious erudition, and acute curiosity served him well. He returned to a juvenile interest in the theater, learned many facets of it from the Théâtre de l'Oeuvre—including the pragmatic considerations of production—and integrated those experiences with Symbolism. Now he was properly tuned for another period of artistic explosion which resulted in six major essays on drama and a celebrated letter to Lugné-Poe. They, along with *King Ubu*, initiate one of the major developments of modern literature, the "theater of the absurd."

In "Theater Questions," Jarry asserts that dramatists should re-examine the philosophical foundations of drama and determine what makes drama a unique medium. While confidently maintaining that the characters in a play must be decidedly different from those in a book (OCBP, p. 415), he unfortunately does not elaborate. Nevertheless, his point is well taken: the question of the unique preserve of the theater and its function is seminal for modern drama because it serves to divorce drama from other art forms, a separation which was badly needed.

Instead of researching his own question, Jarry attacks the problems of the evolution of the theater and its relevance to modern audiences. Here is the artistic nihilism and revolutionary spirit which contributed markedly to the verve of modern drama. Jarry begins by arguing that there are various "theaters," each a product of its own time and culture; consequently, to attempt a transposition from one to the other can only end in failure, because "It is foolish to want to express new feelings in a 'preserved' form" (OCBP, p. 414). Several important issues arise, the first of which is the "crossroads" question: Is modern man psychologically different from the ancient Greek? Certainly the profound understanding of the human animal by Sophocles and Euripides allows them in such works as *Antigone* and *The Trojan Women* to speak powerfully to many who were opposed to the Vietnam War. Because of these plays the contemporary spectator is assisted in appreciating the cost of conviction as well as the seductive rationale for heinous deeds. Thus it would be erroneous to conceive of these two plays as having a " 'preserved' form."

However, Jarry has correctly seen that the past must never be a chain because man must be free to create anew. Ancient Greek drama was brilliantly adapted to its particular time and people, but as cultures evolve, so the dramatist must be free to change both form and content of a play in order to express that transformation. Thus the aesthetic standards and production techniques which were developed to make *Antigone* and *The Trojan Women* effective and meaningful might very well serve to desiccate the expression and creation of themes and styles which are meaningful to contemporary audiences. There is no question about the validity of Jarry's statement: art must never become "preserved"; it must always be fresh and vital (OCBP, p. 414). However, Jarry makes a concession to classical plays and their universal themes when he contends that they can be made "contemporary" by stripping away their " 'preserved' form"; again he fails to elaborate.

Jarry was unalterably opposed to historical plays, which he considered "really boring—useless" (OCBP, p. 414). Some of Shakespeare's work exemplifies the point. Who cares whether Richard II gave up his throne, thereby infuriating the Christian God? It is expecting too much for the contemporary to have a valid dramatic response to the Elizabethan king-God relationship. Similarly, except for the role of Falstaff, of what possible interest are the problems which beset the future Henry IV? Fortunately, monarchies today are so anachronistic that defending them is little more than an academic exercise.

Jarry was also constantly concerned with developing a literature which would be eternal and universal because, to him, true art is beyond the concept of time.[7] This fascination became a linchpin in his concept of "abstract" drama (OCBP, p. 411). Such a theater, he argues, would transcend history and allow all generations to "read without the effort of a translation something which may be as eternally tragic as Ben Jonson, Marlowe, Shakespeare, Cyril Tourneur, or Goethe" (OCBP, p. 411). His selection of plays is most unfortunate because Elizabethan theater is based for the most part on meaningless history or Christianity. Moreover, the dramatists whom he has chosen wrote verbal theater, and thus translations into foreign languages are required. Jarry's list of playwrights was primarily determined by his own linguistic ability with English and German, as well as by the necessity to select non-French plays in order to underscore his point to his French-speaking audience.

Well might Jarry mention celebrated names in the history of art, but he failed to detail his reasoning by showing those qualities which make their work "eternally tragic." His examples aside, there is no question but that Jarry was obsessed by this concept of the "abstract" and the universal, and his works are a series of experiments toward that goal. His most consistent technique was to use prologues, such as in *Haldernablou* and *Emperor Antichrist,* in order to state his cosmology and thereby elevate the work above the temporal—a questionable method because such didacticism falls far short of his goal of generating this awareness in the reader. A second and much more effective technique is the one used in *King Ubu*. The setting, the audience was told, was Poland, "a country so legendary and dismembered that it is Nowhere. . . . Nowhere is everywhere, as well as the country in which we find ourselves" (OCBP, p. 402). Poland, then, becomes a strikingly innovative symbol of universality, one with sufficient historicity that it falls within the learning of most Frenchmen.[8] Jarry's finest symbol is Ubu, and there is little question that Jarry gave him universal characteristics of being "an ignoble creature, which is why he resembles all of us" (OCBP, p. 402). His actions aside, Ubu is visually symbolic of the modern bourgeois, complete with paunch.[9] Jarry, then, has brilliantly selected a symbol which is functional for a very large segment of contemporary society because the individual spectator can see himself to the degree he is Ubuesque: middle class, well fed, satisfied—a buffoon.

The second quality of the "abstract" theater is that the play should bring the spectator into the creative process, which is a restatement of the crossroads thesis. Jarry's theory would have far-reaching consequences for the theater because he readily saw that the traditional definition of "spectator" was invalid. But his association with the Symbolists led him to see that the task of stimulating the spectator to enter into the creative process was not easily achieved. Jarry argues that the true theater is

> accessible only to those who feel themselves virile enough to create life: a conflict of passions more subtle than those known, or a character who is a new being. Everybody agrees that Hamlet, for example, is more alive than the ordinary man because he is more complicated with more synthesis . . . because he is a walking abstraction. Therefore, it is harder for the mind to create a character than for matter to create a man. (OCBP, p. 412)

This conclusion is a challenge to develop a theater meaningful to many people, but it soon proved to be the groundwork for his later retreat from democratic sensibilities, which occurred very shortly

after the production of *King Ubu*. He reacted to its defeat by rejecting his democratic views and condemning his critics for being unable to understand, let alone appreciate, what they had experi-
enced in seeing the play. His only possible choice was to withdraw
into élitism, which is precisely what Mallarmé had done. Consequently, his essays following the presentations of *King Ubu* are
marked by their castigation of the audience (OCBP, p. 417).

A major paradox of Jarry's thought reemerges. In his theory of
an abstract theater he spoke powerfully for literary freedom for the
artist and for the spectator-creator; however, his liberality con-
flicted with his didactic misanthropy. The latter attitude pre-
vailed. For instance, the spectator is allowed to relate intimately
with universals, but only in the directions and manner Jarry determined. Thus he was lying when he told the spectators at the première that they were "free to see in Mister Ubu the allusions you
wish, or, just a plain puppet, a schoolboy's deformation of one of
his teachers who represented for him everything in the world that
is grotesque" (OCBP, p. 399). Such a statement reflects the abstract theater, but Jarry's convictions were too deeply rooted to be
easily clipped; rather it was his misanthropy which kept growing
and blossoming, and the play should be viewed in that light. Jarry
confessed in "Theater Questions":

> I intended that, when the curtain went up, the scene in
> front of the public should be like the mirror in the stories
> of Madame Leprince de Beaumont in which the wanton
> saw themselves with horns on the body of a dragon, ac-
> cording to the exaggeration of their vices. It is not surpris-
> ing that the public should have been astonished at the
> sight of its ignoble other-self . . . : "eternal human im-
> becility, eternal gluttony, the vileness of instinct elevated
> into tyranny; the decency, the virtues, the patriot-
> ism and the ideals of those who have just dined well."
> (OCBP, p. 416)

Jarry readily saw that his concept of an abstract theater necessitated new attitudes toward all facets of drama. Some of his most
stimulating thoughts concerned revolutionizing décor. He began

by criticizing the prevailing concept of it as inadequate because it is a "hybrid, neither natural nor artificial" (OCBP, p. 406). He contends that when the producer tries to depict nature by using plants, shrubs, and the like he is doomed to failure because the setting would indeed be nature itself—and thus "superfluous" for the theater (OCBP, p. 406). Moreover, such "natural" décor must be rejected because a realistic setting does not spur the producer and spectator to use their imaginations. Jarry argues that the décor must, by its very nature, be symbolic, that is, "artificial," so that the audience can enter into the creative process and make the décor meaningful to them personally and individually.

Jarry's analysis of décor explains one of the most baffling aspects of *King Ubu*. Jarry focuses his attention on the backdrop, which is quintessential to fulfilling the spectator's "right to see the scene with a décor which agrees with *his* view of it" (OCBP, p. 406)—not easily achieved, as Jarry acknowledges. He first experimented with "heraldic" décors, that is, using a single shade of color to represent a whole scene or act (OCBP, p. 407). He rejected this technique because the color must be seen against a colorless background (OCBP, p. 407). His second experiment proved fruitful because he found that the proper background "can be achieved simply and in a way which is symbolically accurate by an unpainted backdrop or the reverse side of a set" (OCBP, p. 407). He became very excited at this discovery and suggested that the production of *King Ubu* have "a single stage set; a unified backdrop would be even better, thereby eliminating the raising and lowering of the curtain during the single act" (OCBP, p. 1043). Such a backdrop and décor, if "symbolically accurate," would permit each spectator to "see deeply that *part* [*of*] the backdrop which he wishes" (OCBP, p. 407). *King Ubu* demonstrates the point.

Recognizing that the décor for *King Ubu* was revolutionary, Jarry tried to explain it to the spectators in a short lecture before the curtain was raised at the première, but the audience was so noisy that only scattered phrases were heard. However, the text shows that Jarry forewarned the spectator that

> you will see doors open on snow-covered fields under blue
> skies, fireplaces decorated with clocks which split open

like doors, and palm trees growing at the foot of beds so that little elephants, standing on shelves, can graze on them (OCBP, p. 400).

Arthur Symons, who was present at the première, describes the scenery, which represented

> by a child's conventions, indoors and out of doors, and even the torrid, temperate, and arctic zones at once. Opposite you at the back of the stage, you saw apple trees in bloom, under a fireplace . . . through the very midst of which dropped in and about the clamourous and sanguinary persons of the drama. . . . On the left was a painted bed, and at the foot of the bed a bare tree and snow falling. On the right there were palm trees . . . a door opened against the sky, and beside the door a skeleton dangled.[10]

The backdrop allowed the spectator to focus on the part of it which he thought belonged to the production. For instance, at the beginning of the play when the Ubus are in their bedroom, the individual might very well concentrate on the bed, and thus stimulated, imagine the rest of the décor of a bedroom—perhaps his own. The clock might very well bring to mind his clock; the palm tree might engender a warm sense of tropical well-being; and the blooming apple tree suggests the delights of springtime. Thus enmeshed in the connotative importance of the "symbolically accurate" bed, clock, and trees, the spectator's mind would exclude the snow-covered fields and the skeleton. His imagination would be directed by "A correctly attired man coming onstage as in puppet shows, and hanging up a placard indicating where the scene takes place" (OCBP, p. 1043). Jarry was "certain" that such a placard "had 'suggestive' superiority" over any other aspect of the décor (OCBP, p. 1043). This technique would be especially helpful during the scenes when Ubu is fighting against the Czar because the placard informs the spectator the scene and he in turn might focus on the snow and skeleton and exclude the bed and trees.

Jarry also recognizes that the role and function of the actor must be largely transformed if the abstract theater is to be success-ful. At the outset it must be confessed that when Jarry uses the word "actor" he refers only to men, because Jarry was an un-qualified misogynist. He opposes the traditional view that young men's roles should be played by women because they would have more acting experience. He argues that this experience "is small compensation for the ridiculous profile and unaesthetic walk of women, or for the way the outline of their muscles is blurred by fatty tissue, odious because it has a function—it makes *milk*" (OCBP, p. 409). Moreover, "In light of the differences in intel-ligence [between men and women], if selected carefully (because the majority of women are common), the majority of young men, stupid though they be—with some exceptions—are superior, and they will perform the role adequately." If further proof is needed that women should not be allowed on the stage, then one has only to look at the English and ancient theaters because in them "one would never have dared give a role to a woman" (OCBP, p. 409).

The primary tenet of Jarry's attitude toward the actor is that the performer must "depersonalize" himself (OCBP, p. 403), lose his own personality and "become the entire body of the character" (OCBP, p. 407). He gives an example of his concept in "Inverse Mimeticism in the Plays of Henri de Régnier" ("Du Mimétisme Inverse chez les Personnages d'Henri de Regnier"; 1903): the char-acters "exude in some way their own unique atmosphere which could not exist in their absence. They live with muscles of stone, without being petrified. . . . They walk with a halo which marries their silhouette and swells it" (GC, p. 288). One way by which the actor can achieve this quality is by thinking in nonverbal terms. For example, the actor should use his body as a means of ex-pression, including "Diverse contractions and extensions of the fa-cial muscles . . . physiognomic movements, etc." (OCBP, p. 407). Jarry's concept of the actor's depersonalization and use of facial muscles proved to be fruitful for future dramatists; but he did not develop his own concepts by showing how the facial muscles and the body should be trained. Jarry was unable to do this because he lacked the expertise. His experience was limited to having some actors in his circle of friends and playing some minor roles in Lugné-Poe's company.[11]

Pressured by hopes of getting *King Ubu* into production, Jarry devised a more efficacious plan than training actors: masks. With them the actor would not have to train his facial muscles; instead, with a mask which encloses the actor's head, he becomes "the effigy of the CHARACTER" (OCBP, p. 407). However, the masks should not be like those in the Greek theater, which indicate only tears or laughter—in Jarry's opinion—but should depict the nature of the character: "the Miser, the Indecisive Person, the Avaricious Man" (OCBP, p. 407). Jarry saw that the mask is limited when compared with the flexibility of the facial muscles, which can be contorted. Such restrictions can be minimized if the actor nods his head up and down or moves it laterally so that he "shifts the shadows over the whole surface of his mask" (OCBP, p. 408). Consequently, lighting becomes crucial to Jarry's concept of the theater, but here again he fails to develop his thought and give practical guidelines. He terminates his very brief discussion of it by noting that the footlights should be considered as "a single point of light situated at an indefinite distance, as if it were *behind* the audience" (OCBP, p. 408). The comment is most interesting, but how can this effect be achieved? Again Jarry's lack of practical experience limits the practicability of his concepts.

Jarry's admonition that the actor should become "the effigy of the CHARACTER" reveals his interest in Symbolism, and as he began to synthesize his interest in it with his renewed affinity for the theater, he encountered a major problem for the Symbolist playwrights: How can actors effectively depict symbols? Jarry's initial solution was to follow the footsteps of Henri de Régnier, but Jarry quickly found another solution: puppets, specifically *guignol,* which is the slapstick genre of puppetry similar to Punch and Judy. As a youth Jarry received some puppets as a gift and, attracted to them, he subsequently made some more and produced shows in his home with the assistance of Charlotte and a friend, Henri Morin. When he arrived in Paris he found that puppetry had become a very sophisticated and respected genre. The Petit Théâtre des Marionnettes had pleasantly surprised many Parisians with its productions in 1888 of Cervantes's *The Watchful Guardian,* Aristophanes' *The Birds,* Hroswitha's *Abraham the Hermit,* and *The Mysteries of Eleusis* by Bouchor. Jarry learned of the Petit Théâtre because of his friend Henry Bauer's interest in the company, which began at least as early as 1890, when Bauer wrote about it in the *Echo de Paris*. Jarry, however, did not give serious attention to the dramatic possibilities of puppetry until he began to formulate his own dramaturgy, and when he extended his theories he quickly saw the essential relationships between puppets and symbols. It was a seminal integration for Jarry and a triumph for Western literature because Jarry saw one of the keystones of modern drama—the *Ubermarionette*. He explained the relationship concisely in a lecture he gave to a meeting organized by the editors of *La Libre Esthétique* in Belgium on March 22, 1902: "passive and rudimentary, [puppets] convey concisely and accurately the outline of our thoughts" (OCBP, pp. 422-23). His conclusion was now inevitable: Puppets as symbols could express the universal and eternal which lies deep within man. With this theory, Jarry showed not only his affinity to Symbolism but his ability to direct and adapt it for the stage.

Jarry's conclusions about the actor-puppet-symbol determine the rest of his aesthetics because he then embarked on a fruitful expedition to find techniques of advancing his concept of the *Ubermarionette*. For instance, Jarry thought that the costumes, exemplified by *King Ubu*, should avoid local color or chronology in order to help convey the impression of "something eternal" (OCBP, p. 1043). Ubu is to wear a charcoal gray vest and bowler hat, and have a cane always stuck in his right pocket. Such attire symbolizes the bourgeois who dresses conservatively and with the socially accepted ornaments. When Ubu ascends the throne (III, ii), he should be dressed in trappings which suggest royalty, such as "a hooded white cape resembling a royal overcoat." In the forest scene, when Ubu attempts to extract usurious taxes from the peasants, he is to wear "an impressive hooded overcoat and a hat with a visor and earmuffs," the latter suggesting the cold to which Ubu is going to subject the peasants. For the eighth scene, "A Camp Below Warsaw," which depicts Ubu going off to war, he is to wear "a cloak, a hat, a saber in his belt, a hook, scissors, a knife, always the cane in the right pocket" (OCBP, p. 403) to demonstrate his bourgeois fascination with war and patriotism, and the hook and scissors are symbols of his violent nature. Mother Ubu is to wear a "red hat, or a hat with flowers and feathers, [and] carry a shopping bag" (OCBP, p. 403) in order to show that she is a good bourgeois wife. During the plotting of the usurpation, she is to wear an apron (OCBP, p. 403) to underscore her function as a housewife who goads her husband into advancing his position, a lot with which many wives can immediately identify. Bordure is to dress "like a Hungarian musician, skin-tight, red. Large coat, long sword, well-worn Wellington boots, a tchapska with feathers" (OCBP, p. 403), which symbolize his military bearing as well as the various facets of his personality, such as servant of King Venceslas, sycophant of King Ubu, traitor, and servant of the Czar. Bougrelas is to be depicted as "a baby with skirt and bonnet" (OCBP, p. 404) in order to show how naive he is about the world, especially in his belief in "the right" and in a beneficent God.[12] The Czar is to be "dressed in black, wear a yellow sash, dagger, decorations, big boots. Have a bushy beard. Pointed hat like a black cone" (OCBP, p. 404); that is, be dressed in the accustomed trappings of royalty, yet wear a symbol of stupidity, the dunce's hat.

Jarry thought that "the actor must have a special *voice* which is the voice of the character he is portraying, as if the cavity of the mask's mouth could only speak as it does—as if the muscles of its lips were movable. And it is better that they do not move, and that the delivery be in a monotone" (OCBP, p. 409). The character, Jarry, says, should have a special "accent" (OCBP, p. 1043), implying that the discriminating spectator will find this "special voice," like the costumes and décor, stimulating to his creativity. For the première of *King Ubu*, Gémier took the voice of King Ubu from real life. He had confessed to Lugné-poe that he did not know how to depict Ubu's voice; Lugné-Poe suggested that Gémier "imitate the speech of Jarry." [13] The suggestion was accepted, but no critic commented on the imitation.

Jarry is also intimately concerned with the actor's movements, which, he advises, are always to be kept simple because, to him, unadorned expressions are "universal." Most pantomime is unacceptable to him because the mime frequently uses conventional, tiresome, and incomprehensible gestures. For example, in order to depict beauty and love, the mime moves his hand around his face in a vertical ellipse and kisses the hand (OCBP, pp. 408-9). A marionette demonstrates a "universal" gesture when it shows its amazement by reacting violently, such as hitting its head against the wings (OCBP, pp. 408-9).

Jarry's comments about puppets reflects his ambitious desire for the theater to reach a mass audience. His proletarian inclination reached its zenith in "On the Uselessness of the Theater to the Theater" ("De L'Inutilité du Théâtre au Théâtre"; September 1896) in which he advances the idea that in this age of traveling, the theater should be brought to the people, at least some plays "which are not too abstract—*King Lear,* for example" (OCBP, p. 410). The plays should be given in places which are not too far from centers of population, and "arrangements should be made for people who come by train." Jarry adds that "the places in the sun should be free and the few props could be carried in one or two cars" (OCBP, p. 410). Here is the seed for a proletarian theater or even "guerrilla" theater, although Jarry did not develop the idea.

"On the Uselessness of the Theater to the Theater" marks a turning point in several aspects of Jarry's thought. Fueled by the failure of *King Ubu,* he became bitterly antidemocratic and wrote "Theater Questions," which was published less than a month after the première of *King Ubu.* In this essay Jarry states that the audience is "illiterate by definition" (OCBP, p. 415). For example:

> The herd does not understand *Peer Gynt,* which is one of the clearest plays ever written; the herd does not understand Baudelaire's prose, the precise syntax of Mallarmé. The herd ignores Rimbaud, became aware of Verlaine only after his death, and is extremely afraid of hearing *The Smellers* [*Les Flaireurs*] or *Pelleas and Melisande* [*Pélléas et Mélisande*] (OCBP, p. 417).[14]

The public, Jarry continues, is what "the scientists call idiots . . . in which the senses have remained so rudimentary that they perceive only immediate perceptions" (OCBP, p. 417).

Jarry's antidemocratic sentiments should not obfuscate the value of much of his commentary. Of course the public is, generally, a moronic mass moved by football and breasts, a zombie driven by greed, a hyena yapping bourgeois platitudes. But Jarry should have asked himself why the audience is usually so stagnant, stultified, and unappreciative of significant art. Much of the blame needs to be placed elsewhere than on the shoulders of the spectators. For instance, most spectators today are conditioned to accept the ordinary and reject the innovative because of the opiate of television, the artistic wasteland of most schools, the emphasis on specialization and technical disciplines in universities, and so forth. Admittedly, these are major obstacles, but they need not be insurmountable. The hurdles should be considered challenges. To dismiss the public as ignorant and unsophisticated, as Jarry did, is a facile—and unacceptable—solution.

One of the central issues in Jarry's aesthetics is comedy, a theme which remained rather subterranean in his juvenilia. Some of his early works, such as the "Antliaclastes" series, show his ability to tease his classmates, and the "Bidasse" plays and especially *The Prospective Husband* exemplify how his comedic talents turned toward biting sarcasm. There is no doubt that he was quite sardonic in school, and Gide's description of him in *The Counterfeiters* demonstrates that Jarry was well known for the particular quality of his humor. The direction of his comedy was enhanced and channeled through a fortuitous relationship between Jarry and Henri Bergson (1859-1941).

Bergson's lectures at the Collège de France were enormously popular, and Jarry had opportunities to hear him there as well as at the *Lycèe* Henri IV, where Bergson taught from 1889 to 1898. Rich in ideas and scintillating in effect, Bergson had a seminal influence on much of French thought; but Jarry resisted much of Bergson's onslaught, and continued to form his own concepts. As a student he learned and grew; as a man he evaluated, accepted, and rejected.

Bergson published his theory of comedy as an extended essay, *Laughter (Le Rire)* in 1900. One of his fundamental principles is that comedy aims at the general, rather than the particular,[15] and Jarry agreed. He had long been concerned with such universals as the nature of man and the cosmos, to which the prologues of *Haldernablou* and *Emperor Antichrist* attest. This theme also surfaces in his "crossroads" theory in which Jarry aimed to draw generalities and then let the reader-spectator create the particulars which fit his own views and desires. As a consequence of this principle, Bergson concludes that the humorist must so symbolize the comic character that it strikes a sympathetic chord within the spectator's mind and body, making us "put ourselves for a very short time in his place, adopt his gestures, words, and actions" (Bergson, p. 148). His comments about deformity exemplify his point: *"In order to become comic, the deformity must be such that a person with a normal physique could successfully imitate it"* (Bergson, p. 18). For instance, "The reason that excessive stoutness is laughable is because it evokes an image of the same kind" (Bergson, p. 39). Here in Bergson's theory was the aesthetic foundation of Father Ubu's physiognomy. His rotundity, caused by his desire to gorge *à la bourgeoise* is frequently duplicated by those who have the money and position to be well fed; thus, the paunch becomes emblematic of them. The symbolic representation will be telegraphed to the spectator's mind, and if the projection is "symbolically accurate," the spectator will correlate the symbol with himself. In such a manner he confronts the crossroads. *King Ubu* demonstrates the point because in it Jarry shows the bourgeois' lust for "gut and pocket." The spectator is free to determine the extent of his own dedication to greed and gluttony.

Bergson notes that one way by which the dramatist can develop a sense of universality in the spectator "is . . . by showing us . . . several different copies of the same type" (Bergson, p. 126). This dictum surfaces in *King Ubu* when Jarry repeats the qualities of Ubu to a lesser degree in most of the characters which circle around him. For instance, Mother Ubu reflects the qualities of greed and ruthless ambition, which characterize Ubu, when she initiates the plot to kill King Venceslas; Bordure is likewise ambitious and murderous because he will serve anybody in order to gain his goals; and in a famous scene, the citizens of Poland, lusting after Ubu's gold, homicidally race each other. There are only two exceptions to the rule: Queen Rosemonde and Bougrelas, but they serve a very special function in the play.

One of the most important facets of Bergson's analysis of comedy is his discussion of puppets. Although Jarry had become familiar with puppetry during his Rennes years, he made no attempt to use them in a sophisticated manner or to incorporate them into his aesthetic theories until he heard Bergson, who saw that caricature can be "more lifelike than portrait" (Bergson, p. 20). This was an important point for Jarry because he now saw that through puppetry he could realize his artistic goals: he could be "symbolically accurate" with a puppet, thereby exposing reality and simultaneously engendering the spectator to relate directly to that revelation. Bergson's concept was truly a touchstone for Jarry as well as for future dramatists to whom Jarry showed new techniques of characterization, especially the *Ubermarionette*.

While Bergson proved enormously stimulating and provocative to Jarry, there were points of significant disagreement. An illustrative instance is Bergson's conclusion that a situation is humorous *"when it can be interpreted in two completely different ways at the same time"* (Bergson, pp. 73-74), a statement which closely approximates Jarry's concept of the artist putting the reader at a crossroads, thereby allowing each spectator to interpret the work independently. While some of his early works, such as *Phonograph, Opium,* and *The Report of the Terrible Accident* show that he was willing and able to create literature which could relate to an individual, the main thrust of his artistry, represented by *Being and Living* and *Haldernablou,* was to channel the reader's mind in order to force him to accept only one interpretation: the universe is malignant; people are degenerate brutes; and immorality is triumphant.

A second keystone in Bergson's analysis of comedy is that laughter must be "a kind of social *gesture.*" Bergson argues that "the fear which [laughter] inspires restrains eccentricities. . . . Laughter . . . pursues . . . a useful goal of general improvement" (Bergson, pp. 15-16). "Laughter is, above all, corrective . . . it must make a painful impression on the person against whom it is directed. Society avenges itself for the liberties taken with it" (Bergson, p. 150). Aristophanes and Molière demonstrate Bergson's point. Aristophanes uses comedy in *The Clouds* in order to ridicule Socrates' idealism, thereby showing what Aristophanes considered to be improper attitudes. Thus, his ridicule and denigration should be seen within a perimeter of optimism and didacticism. Such was also the case with Molière. In *Tartuffe,* for instance, he probes into the habit of a religious zealot, and the effect of the play is a positive one: beware, be suspicious, be reasonable. The play, then, is indeed "corrective." While Jarry agreed that comedy is to be painful, he certainly did not accept the "corrective" goal for it. Even in his earliest efforts at humor, he shows that he always considered it to be corrosive: to humiliate, ridicule, and degrade.

Bergson was the single most important influence on Jarry's concept of comedy; but most students of Jarry, notably represented by Marcel Jean, ascribe much of Jarry's humor to the influence of Rabelais. Jean thinks that Jarry was greatly indebted to Rabelais because Jarry's humor contains "the best of the verve of Rabelais by the use of incessant alliteration, equivocations [, and] esoteric etymologies." [16] These assertions are suspect. There is, of course, no question that Jarry knew Rabelais's work well, having studied him at a young age, probably as a student in Rennes, and assuredly during his sojourn at the *lycée* Henri IV. Moreover, some of his close friends, most notably Marcel Schwob, were devotees of Rabelais. In any case, it is inconceivable that a French student, especially one as precocious as Jarry, would not be familiar with this genius of French letters, whom one Frenchman calls "the father of our idiom" and an "epic brain." [17]

Both Rabelais and Jarry share numerous stylistic similarities, the most basic of which is their mutual interest in "esoteric etymologies." The reason for this parallel is that Rabelais and Jarry were widely read in mathematics, zoology, botany, among other scientific disciplines, and incorporated many scientific words and expressions into their vocabularies. Moreover, Rabelais and Jarry were profound students of Greek and Latin, and they manipulated these languages and infused them into their styles. Such similarity of interest led Jarry to borrow freely from his confrère. Caradec counts seventy-six Rebelaisian expressions in Jarry's work,[18] and Michel Arrivé considerably extends that list.[19] But such "esoteric etymologies" do not prove that Rabelais was a "dominant force" in the formulation of Jarry's humor.[20]

It is also questionable whether Jarry captured Rabelais' "verve;" because the two men were philosophically antithetical, and thus their interests were diametrically opposed. Rabelais, for instance, reflects the passions of the Renaissance, especially the middle and late fifteenth century and the early sixteenth century. Stimulated by the fall of Constantinople, the discovery of the New World, the revelations of Copernicus, the invention of printing, and the Protestant Reformation, many thinkers joyfully reconsidered many of the traditional assumptions about man, society, and cosmos. One such master was Rabelais, a titan of the Renaissance, a man fevered with "a thirst for new and ever widening horizons, for human freedom and the good life for all" (Putnam, p. 2). He is, Professor Putnam rightly concludes, "the humanist *par excellence*" (Putnam, p. 13). It is true that Jarry was also a widely read man and a profound thinker, but he was keenly aware that freedom is a myth. Man is enchained by his own sexuality, as Jarry exposes in *Messalina* and *The Supermale;* enslaved by his lust and greed, as *King Ubu* shows; and, as Jarry's juvenilia demonstrate, fated by the gods to suffer, weep, and die. The "good life"—impossible!

The famous episode of the Abbey of Thélème demonstrates the point. Rabelais gives considerable attention to the constitution of the Abbey's membership, which was limited to "only the pretty [women], the ones with good figures and sunny dispositions and only the handsome . . . good-natured men" (Vintage, p. 199). To Rabelais, these individuals, between the ages of ten and eighteen, are to be utterly free to "Do as thou wouldst" (Vintage, p. 200)! Rabelais had no fear that these people would be evil because, he felt, they had "a certain instinct and spur, which always impels them to virtuous deeds and restrains them from vice, an instinct, which is the thing called honor" (Vintage, p. 214). This conclusion is based, as Professor Putnam has correctly seen, on Rabelais's assumption that human nature is "potentially good . . . [Rabelais asserts] a faith in human progress and perfectibility that is at the heart of the humanist-Renaissance creed, the ideal of the free life, a dream that sees man, liberated from all mysticism and asceticism, walking upright in the sun and finding it a joyous experience" (Vintage, p. 37).

No one opposes Rabelais's optimism more persistently, more adroitly, and over a broader spectrum than Alfred Jarry. His work is a panorama of depravity—the result of people "doing as they wouldst"—killing, pillaging, and gorging. Those who are not similarly depraved, such as King Venceslas and Queen Rosemonde, are savagely and easily murdered. To underscore the primacy of evil, Jarry ends the play with Father and Mother Ubu gleefully anticipating their return to "sweet France" (OCBP, p. 397). If Ubu in Paris is a frightening thought, what would he have done at the Abbey!

Because Jarry differed so philosophically from Rabelais, the thrust of their humor is consequently quite different. Rabelais used humor to "correct," and his castigation of lawyers demonstrates the point. In Book II of *Pantagruel,* Rabelais recounts the legal arguments of two lawyers, significantly named Lords Kissarse and Suckpoop, which are nothing but illogical blather. The goal of such ridicule is to expose their superficial and inane logic in order to correct their behavior as well as to warn the reader to be wary. Not so Jarry. Jean Onimus succinctly concludes that in *King Ubu* "the humor is always congealed with horror." [21] Philippe Soupault agrees:

> For [Jarry], humor is above all cruelty, that is lucidity and sincerity. To be cruel, for Jarry, is to reject sentimentality, to oppose childish sentimentality with a clear attitude, without equivocation, it is also to attack prejudices. It is not a question of making something as much as to denounce. He does not seek to correct morality but to suppress it, be it good or bad.[22]

It is also suggested that Jarry was significantly influenced by Rabelais because Jarry spent more time on *Pantagruel* than on any other work. As early as 1897, shortly after the première of *King Ubu,* he began working on a stage version of *Pantagruel* in collaboration with his friend, Claude Terrasse, who had composed and played the music for *King Ubu.* But Jarry's interest in Rabelais, at least in this case, was colored by the fact that, by referring to *Pantagruel* as a "national work" in the subtitle (OCBP, p. 569), he was hoping to appeal to French national sensibilities in order to get it accepted for the Exposition of 1900. This version failed to get beyond a preliminary sketch, but the subtitle is illuminating. Jarry continued to work on this project because he hoped its production would bring him badly needed money, but he was forced to drop the project when Terrasse left it in 1905.

The first version, although only an outline, shows that Jarry never intended to remain faithful to Rabelais. For instance, he did not hesitate to include an episode between "The Old Dame" and Pantagruel. This episode was actually a vignette Jarry wrote to ridicule a friend's mistress, and his clumsy attempt to stitch it into *Pantagruel* shows both how anxious he was to use it and how little regard he had toward Rabelais's work.[23] Jarry carried his free interpretation of Rabelais's creation even further in the second extant version. Basically, the play is falsely named because Pantagruel's position as principal character is contested by Panurge, who has 307 lines to Pantagruel's 252. Moreover, Panurge dominates much of the action, such as his discussion with Pantagruel whether he should marry, and the scene on board ship during a storm when Panurge becomes terror-stricken. It is also noteworthy that Jarry only fleetingly refers to Pantagruel's ancestry, dropped all references to the Abbey of Thélème, skipped the story of Pantagruel's birth, deleted all of the scatological and sexual references in regard to Panurge, omitted the Dipsode-Amaurotes War, and all but the "sea scene" of Book IV. In Act I, scene vi, Jarry's second version takes a decidedly different turn from Rabelais's original. A Witch enters and tell Panurge that she is from the "Court of Miracles" and informs him that he is going on a long voyage [24] during which time Panurge will see "a beautiful princess" whom Pantagruel will marry (OCMC, VI, p. 104). The Witch's statement proves prophetic, and the ensuing story, about two thirds of the book, is extraneous to Rabelais's masterpiece. Brother John has a more expanded role than he does in Rabelais's work because in Jarry's hands he becomes a tool to ridicule Christian optimism by stating that "Pleasures are fleeting / And yield to bitter disillusion. Rejoice that you are going to leave this valley / Of tears and misery" (OCMC, VI. p. 97). Panurge parodies Brother John's advice, and this brings down the wrath of the Chorus, which now functions as a pack of devout yapping condemnation. A Bourgeois calls for Panurge to be punished for his sin—a rope is quickly called for as the forces of morality once again, blood-crazed like Lautréamont's dogs, bay for death in the name of an abstraction. Brother John terrorizes them by threats of excommunication, forces them to their knees, and then cows them into pardoning Panurge. The scene is clearly not Rabelaisian; rather it reflects Jarry's attack on

Christianity by showing the violence of these followers of the Lamb of Peace, their fear, meekness, and servility. Thus, what remains of Jarry's adaptation of *Pantagruel* is very little Rabelais and a great deal of Jarry.

Jarry was also influenced, both positively and negatively, by Aristotle. Jarry has been widely regarded as the progenitor of the avant-garde theater or, as it is sometimes called, "non-Aristotelian" drama. While there is little doubt that the battle of *King Ubu* signaled the emergence of different concepts and aesthetics of dramaturgy, the question remains as to the degree to which it is a revolt from Aristotle.

Jarry became acquainted with Aristotle's work through his prize-winning study of Greek, which began as early as 1888. His schoolboy essay, *A Letter from a Parisian Humanist to an Italian Aristotelian,* shows that Jarry admired Aristotle as a great man who should be honored for making contributions to the advancement of the Western mind. But there are no gods, as even the youthful Jarry recognized, and therefore he reasoned that others are free to contribute to or correct Aristotle's work. He followed his own advice, but his simplistic acceptance and rejection of Aristotelian dicta beguiles the profundity of Jarry's thought. He brilliantly appreciated Aristotle and concluded that many of his observations about art were valid to contemporary dramatists but that other conclusions must be rejected or remodeled.

Jarry was profoundly influenced by Aristotle's discussion of the goal of art and the role of characterization in obtaining it. Aristotle states that art is an "imitative process" [25] in which the artist depicts "men either better or worse than the average" *(Poetics,* p. 17). Aristotle was not concerned with "imitating" a particular individual; he focused on "universals." He concludes that art should be addressed to "what kind of person is likely to do or say certain kinds of things, according to probability or necessity . . . [;] it gives its persons particular names afterward" *(Poetics,* p. 33). Butcher correctly explains that "the whole tenor and purpose of *The Poetics* makes it abundantly clear that poetry is not a mere reproduction of empirical fact, a picture of life with all its trivialities and accidents." However, Butcher errs when he contends that Aristotelian "universals" represent "permanent and eternal facts." [26] The error illuminates a fundamental fact of Aristotle's aesthetics. Else has rightly seen that Aristotle did not use the term metaphysically; rather, "in so far as 'poetics' deals with universals at all it must be correlated with ethics and politics, or with rhetoric." [27] He succinctly concludes that these "universals" refer to "the *typology of human nature,*" that is, " 'what kind of thing such and such a kind of man will naturally say or do' under given circumstances" *(Else,* p. 305).

Jarry understood Aristotelian universals very well. While Jarry uses the play to present some facets of his cosmology, these concerns are peripheral. Jarry presents reality: Ubu represents the bourgeois's actions and attitudes rather than those of a particular individual. For instance, Ubu demonstrates that the bourgeois is motivated by "gut and pocket," calories and lucre. Homicidally egoistic, Ubu-bourgeois values "phynance" above life and humanistic morality. There is nothing "supernatural" about this depiction; it is all too natural.

Aristotle only tantalizingly refers to comedy in *The Poetics.* In spite of Professor Lane Cooper's brilliant attempt to reconstruct a theory of comedy from Aristotle's extant writings,[28] Aristotle's comments remain cryptic, but nevertheless his few remarks deserve notice. The principle of comedy, according to Aristotle, is "an imitation of persons who are inferior; not, however, going all the way to full villainy, but imitating the ugly, of which the ludicrous is one part. The ludicrous . . . is a failing or a piece of ugliness which causes no pain or destruction" *(Poetics,* p. 23). Certainly Ubu is ludicrous. His grotesque distortion of physique and comic actions, such as his brandishing a toilet brush in the "Banquet Scene," signals his buffoonery. However, there is no doubt that Ubu is a complete villain, which contradicts Aristotle's statement. Moreover, Ubu is not inferior; he is the embodiment of the modern bourgeois and of his dedication to paunch and pocket. Jarry's rejection of Aristotle's views of comedy is identical to Jarry's repudiation of the direction of Rabelais's humor: Aristotle could conceive only of people who viewed life with intense joy and delight, who were interested in how to live a full and rewarding life.

He remains an exemplar of his culture; it is a tribute to Jarry and a sign of the degeneration of contemporary life that he accurately depicted much of it.

Jarry found fertile ground in *The Poetics* to attack tragedy, and the result is that he did much to redefine it. His initial departure from Aristotle is over the purpose of tragedy. Aristotle argues that the plot should be structured in such a way that the person who hears and sees "the events unroll shudders with fear and feels pity at what happens" *(Poetics,* p. 40). Butcher remarks that "The emotion of fear is profoundly altered when it is transferred from the real to the imaginative world. It is no longer the direct apprehension of misfortune impending over our own life. It is not caused by the actual approach of danger. It is the sympathetic shudder we feel for a hero whose character in its essentials resembles our own" (Butcher, pp. 258-59; p. 259, n. 1). The reason for this sympathy— if not empathy—is that the playwright presents "the same practices in tragic actions as in everyday life" *(Poetics,* p. 52). This is precisely what Jarry did. He sought to generalize about modern man by utilizing a puppet whose characteristics could be individualized according to the imagination of the spectator. By this criterion, *King Ubu* emerges as an Aristotelian tragedy because Ubu, representative of modern bourgeois man, is pitiful because he is so disgusting and terrifying, so omnipresent and so omniscient. A transposition of terms shows how closely Aristotle's terminology describes King Ubu. Because Ubu represents "human nature in general" *(Poetics,* p. 43), and because his actions are "either . . . necessary [or] probable" *(Poetics,* p. 44), Ubu engenders a complex amalgam of "pity and fear" in the spectator.

Jarry also saw that the tragedy of modern man is decidedly different from Aristotle's concept because contemporary man struggles pitifully to survive in a malevolent cosmos. Well might the Ancient Mariner laugh in *The Albatross,* but there is nothing admirable in his humorous rejection of fate; in view of Death's victory, his mirth is ludicrous. Such is man: a buffoon goaded by instinct and directed by "the Celestial Bandit." The actions and antics of man, to Jarry, are tragic because of man's tears before the absurdity and injustice of life, and humorous because of the hopeless nature of his prison. As a result of this attitude, Jarry helped spawn a new literary genre, "tragicomedy."

Jarry demonstrated his rejection of Aristotle's discussion of tragedy by parodying it in *King Ubu*. Jarry judiciously chose *Macbeth* as his tool to show how humorous tragedy can be. Like Lady Macbeth, Mother Ubu goads her husband into regicide, but because Jarry did not accept Shakespeare's morality, Mother Ubu's machinations are delightfully successful. Similarly, Duncan, who was the portrait of King Venceslas, shows how vulnerable the weak and unsuspecting are, and his slaughter is an episode of buffoonery in *King Ubu*. Rather than generating "pity and fear," the characters are effective weapons for Jarry's comedic talents. The reference to Elsinor, Hamlet's castle, in the last scene of *King Ubu* summarizes much of Jarry's attitude toward Aristotle's concept of tragedy. Jarry is simply thumbing his nose at classical tragedy as he shows the Ubus engrossed in their plans for "sweet France."

While Jarry rejected Aristotle's views of tragedy, he was interested in some of Aristotle's observations about a play's structure. Jarry's critique is as insightful and stimulating as his analysis of Aristotle's statements about the function of art and of characterization. In terms of structure other than the beginning, middle, and end, Aristotle emphasizes that the events of the play should occur "either by necessity or in accordance with probability," because there must be no "illogicality in the web of events" (*Poetics*, pp. 35 and 44). Aristotle's criterion of "probability" is the basis of his rejection of the "episodic" plot, which he defines as "one in which there is no probability or necessity for the order in which the episodes follow one another" (*Poetics*, p. 34). Ostensibly, Jarry's organization of *King Ubu* would be different from Aristotle's admonition because *King Ubu* is a compendium of stories compiled by students and Jarry at the *lycée* in Rennes about one of their professors, which Jarry then embellished, refined, and retold. Thus, the play is a collection of episodes, but rather than functioning as separate and disjunct sections these units are unified by the actions and attitudes of Ubu.

Aristotle says that "a plot is not unified, as some people think, simply because it has to do with a single person. A large, indeed an indefinite number of things can happen to a given individual, some of which go to constitute no unified event; and in the same way there can be many acts of a given individual from which no single action emerges" *(Poetics,* p. 31). Aristotle's reservations are indeed noteworthy, but they are warning lights, not barriers to a master craftsman. Jarry safely navigated the narrows. He showed that a play can, indeed, revolve around an individual. Moreover, by conceiving the characteristics as representative of human beings rather than of a particular person, Jarry was able to present a unified plot and thereby expose possibilities for drama which Aristotle had underestimated. Admittedly, the episodes are loosely related in *King Ubu,* but they are consciously organized to expose the nature of Ubu, and each scene follows the preceding one in a manner which is easily understandable.

While Jarry followed some of Aristotle's dicta with surprising care, he took considerable liberty with others. Aristotle's view of language demonstrates the point. Aristotle was opposed to language which was "commonplace or low" *(Poetics,* p. 59), but Jarry was certainly not directing his work at the sophisticate, as was Aristotle in *The Poetics;* Jarry sought the jugular of the bourgeois, and in order to rip off his mask, Jarry exposes the language the bourgeois uses but hypocritically chastises others for speaking. Thus, while "shitr" in the Jarryesque form was not common, the basic word was. In fact Jarry selected one of the most functional and widely used expressions in the French language. By adding the notorious *r* to "shit," Jarry obeys Aristotle's acknowledgment that "newly coined words" can be brought into existence. He cites the examples of "sprouters" for "horns," and "supplicator" for "priest" *(Poetics,* p. 58), and he allowed "altered" or unusual words, that is, those which have been changed in any way which makes them different from "a given people's speech" *(Poetics,* p. 58). While Jarry deviated from Aristotle's rejection of "commonplace or low" language, he followed Aristotle's affirmation of "poetic license": "the extending, curtailing, and altering of words makes no small contribution; for being different from the regular form and thus varying the accustomed pattern, it will produce an effect of distinction, while at the same time by virtue of its overlapping with normal usage it will promote clarity" *(Poetics,* p. 59). "It is important,"

Aristotle continues, "to make fitting use of all the devices" *(Poetics,* p. 60). Jarry did precisely that.

The basic point of departure between Aristotle and Jarry is over the goal of art. Aristotle concludes that tragedy, "through a course of pity and fear," compels "the purification of tragic acts which have those emotional characteristics" *(Poetics,* p. 25). For example, " 'He who hears the tale told will thrill with horror and melt to pity at what takes place.' This is the impression we should receive from hearing the story of the *Oedipus."* [29] The intricacies of Aristotle's meaning are of no concern here because Jarry rejected the entire concept of catharsis. He had no intention of relieving the spectator's emotional or intellectual discomfort at seeing *King Ubu;* in fact, Jarry was dedicated to intensifying the spectator's awareness of life and human nature and to castigating the spectator for his bourgeois attitudes of lust for power, inhumane drive for money, and crass hypocrisy. The difference between Aristotle and Jarry is seen in the ending of *Oedipus the King,* which Aristotle praises far more than any other play, and *King Ubu.* The former play ends positively. The chorus in the last lines of the former play forces the observer to think about Oedipus, the man "Who knew the famous riddles [of the Sphinx], and was a man most masterful. . . . See him now." [30] The Chorus, speaking in the first person singular like a knowledgeable observer of the play, states the lesson that a reasonable person should learn: "Count no mortal happy till he has passed the final limit of his life secure from pain" (Sophocles, p. 100). The spectator exits having learned a lesson of life and knowing that Apollo still reigns. *King Ubu* gives no such comfort and assurance. This play ends on a frightening note for the Parisian audience: the Ubus are off the coast of France and anticipating their return to "sweet France" where Father Ubu will become Secretary of the Treasury—hardly a prospect to relieve "pity and fear."

Butcher correctly notes that "The fundamental thought of Aristotle's philosophy . . . is Becoming not Being" (Butcher, p. 160) because "art is concerned neither with things that are or come into being by necessity nor with things that do so in accordance with nature." [31] Although the dramatist might, as a tool to gaining the "Becoming," depict events and people "the way they are said or thought to be" *(Poetics,* p. 67), Aristotle never forgot that a work of art should have a rational purpose; specifically, a play should be written so "that a greater good may come about or a greater evil may be averted" *(Poetics,* p. 69); consequently, didacticism is inescapable. Not so for Jarry. He was immune to what man might "Become" because, to him, man is continually "present." Thus, Jarry makes no attempt to show man the dangers of life so he can avoid them and thereby improve himself or his condition. Jarry was constantly concerned with what is and exists rather than what might be or should be.

Aristotle thought that one of the finest ways to teach was for the protagonist, who is of high station, to fall. Ubu, ex-King of Aragon, Count of Sandomir, and King of Poland, is a person of eminence, but from the very first word he shows his true colors. Granted that he falls from his throne, but his descent is never depicted as a disaster, nor does Ubu regret the loss of his crown because he is too busy enjoying the sea voyage and anticipating the joys of being Secretary of the Treasury in Paris. There is no reason for the spectator to doubt that he will succeed admirably. Ubu, then, "falls" from a cave in Lithuania into Paris.

The most revolutionary deviation Jarry made from the theories of Aristotle was in the area of organization of the play. Aristotle observes that a play should be "whole," that is, it should have a "beginning, middle, and end" *(Poetics,* p. 30). He then proceeds to define each term: a "beginning is that which does not necessarily follow on something else, but after it something else naturally is or happens" *(Poetics,* p. 30). Butcher rightly comments that the beginning must be "the natural sequel of something else. Still it must not carry us back in thought to all that has gone before" (Butcher, p. 280). Jarry blatantly disregarded Aristotle's dictum. In the opening scene the Ubus are in the middle of a fine family argument. The spectator is not given any information as to the reasons for the heated discussion, but he quickly becomes privy to the argument as Mother Ubu chastises her husband for not killing the King and usurping the throne. Because the opening line is not a "natural sequel," the beginning does not meet the Aristotelian criterion.

Jarry's most flagrant violation of Aristotle's observations about structure occurs in the last few scenes of *King Ubu*. Aristotle defines a proper ending as "that which naturally follows on something else . . . but nothing else after it" *(Poetics,* p. 30). *Haldernablou* marks the first time that Jarry rebelled against this dictum. The last scene focuses on Haldern's brutal killing of Ablou, which completes Haldern's cycle because he has moved from earth to the supernatural and then back to earth; purified, he returns to his ethereal regions. The cycle, however, will reactivate the subterranean forces, and he will be drawn earthward again. Thus, there is no Aristotelian ending to the work.

Even the poorly executed ending of *Emperor Antichrist*'s "Terrestrial act" shows that the ending of *Haldernablou* was no mistake because Jarry had consciously rejected Aristotle's suggestion long before *King Ubu*. In *Emperor Antichrist,* Ubu is portrayed as overthrown and desolate, dreaming that to "grab money and drink yourself to death. . . . That's happiness for the Master of Finance" (OCBP, p. 323). Unfortunately, the bourgeois audience sees him as a besotted beast, an inebriated Polyphemus who has been overthrown and reduced to a sad state. While this ending summarizes the driving forces of Ubu, it destroys the intent of the play by allowing the spectator to reject Ubu. Nevertheless, it is clear that Ubu will awaken—and there is no doubt that he will continue his march. Jarry considerably refined the ending in *King Ubu*. In the final version the Ubus are anticipating new and rewarding experiences in France. With such a firm promise of yet more action to come—perhaps more interesting than the play itself—the work can hardly be considered "ended" in the Aristotelian sense.

Jarry's aesthetic concepts are characterized by an astute knowledge of the literary revolution of his epoch. With his extraordinary erudition, he was able to learn much from his fellow rebels, and yet he had the personal fortitude to continue walking his solitary and independent path. As a result, he made significant contributions to modern drama. Jarry saw that the theater is a distinct medium which requires specialized attitudes and techniques, not just reworked prose or poetry. His suggestions about the visual aspects of the dramatic presentation are remarkable, and his comments concerning the relationships between the spectacle and spectator have proven farsighted. Even his undeveloped views of the training of the actor and various technical aspects of production have been provocative even for that genius of modern dramaturgy, Antonin Artaud, who, in homage to Jarry, named his great experiment in the theater after him.

With his aesthetic concepts firmly in mind, Jarry completed his experiment in drama, *King Ubu*. Not only was it a platform from which he proclaimed his philosophical attitudes, but the play was a crucible in which new forms of the theater were tested and watched. Literary history has shown that the experiment was an enormous success, but its initial defeat left Jarry embittered. He did not live to see *King Ubu* honored as one of the great creations of modern literature.

Notes

1. The first part was published as "The Island of Ptyx" ("L'Ile de Ptyx") in *The Gests and Opinions of Doctor Faustroll, Pataphysician,* Book III, Chapter 29. The work also appears in the *Almanach of Father Ubu* (1899). See OCBP, pp. 564f.
2. Haskell Block, *Mallarmé and the Symbolist Drama* (Detroit: Wayne State University Press, 1963), p. 84.
3. Cited in J. Huret, *Enquête sur l'Evolution Littéraire . . .* (Paris: Fasquelle, 1913), p. 60.
4. The quotation is from Ovid's *Fasti,* Book III, 1. 654: "I am a nymph of the calm Numicius. In a perennial river I hide, and Anna Perenna is my name."
5. Pierre Beausire, *Mallarmé, Poésie et Poétique* (Lausanne: Mermod, 1949), p. 172. Hereafter cited in the text as "Beausire."
6. Stéphane Mallarmé, Letter to Cazalis, May 14, 1867. See Henri Mondor, *Vie de Mallarmé* (Paris: Gallimard, 1941), p. 237.
7. Alfred Jarry, *La Chandelle Verte,* ed. Maurice Saillet (Paris: Le Livre de Poche, 1969), p. 566. Hereafter cited in the text and abbreviated as "GC."
8. Poland was partitioned among Russia, Prussia, and Austria, and consequently there was no country of Poland until about 1919. During the uprising of 1830 against Russia, about ten thousand Poles fled to France, a wave which was enhanced by the revolt of 1863. Russia decided to russify Poland at this time: all self-government was crushed, in 1869 the Polish language was outlawed in the schools, and in 1873 all of the judicial system was "russified."
9. Notice should be given to the spiral on the paunch of Ubu. Cirlot

describes the spiral as "A schematic image of the evolution of the universe." See J. E. Cirlot, *A Dictionary of Symbols,* trans. Jack Sage (New York: Philosophical Library, 1962), p. 290.

10. Arthur Symons, *Studies in the Seven Arts* (New York: E. P. Dutton, 1907), pp. 373-74.

11. The most important role Jarry played was that of the Old Courtier Troll (Dovre-Master) in *Peer Gynt.*

12. Jarry wrote to Lugné-Poe that he had found the proper person to play the role of Bougrelas: a thirteen-year-old boy who was "very handsome" and "intelligent enough" for the part. Moreover, he thought that this boy would "excite the old ladies" and cause scandal. See OCBP, pp. 1049-50.

13. Aurélien Lugné-Poe, "La Parade," *Acrobaties* (Paris: Gallimard, 1931), vol. 2, p. 176.

14. A three-act play by Charles Van Lergerghe.

15. Henri Bergson, *Le Rire, Essai sur la Signification du Comique* (Paris: Presses Universitaires de France, 1958), p. 125. Hereafter cited in the text and abbreviated as "Bergson."

16. Marcel Jean and Mezei Arpad, "Jarry et le Tourbillon Contemporain," *La Nef* 7 (February-September 1950), p. 189.

17. Etienne Pasquier; cited in the Portable Viking edition of *Rabelais,* ed. and trans., Samuel Putnam (New York: The Viking Press, 1946), p. 3. References to this translation will be cited as "Vintage," and references to the introduction by Professor Putnam will be cited as "Putnam."

18. François Caradec, "Rabelais dans l'Oeuvre de Jarry," *Cahiers du Collège de 'Pataphysique,* no. 5 (1954), pp. 43-47.

19. Michel Arrivé, *Les Langages de Jarry, Essai de Sémiotique Littéraire* (Paris: Publications de l'Université de Paris, 1972).

20. Legrand-Chabrier, "De Gargantua à Ubu," *Gaulois,* November 5, 1921, p. 2.

21. Jean Onimus, *Face au Monde Actuel* (Bruges: Desclée de Brouwer, 1962), p. 117.

22. Philippe Soupault, "Confrontations: Alfred Jarry," *Cahiers de la Compagnie Madeleine Renaud-Jean-Louis Barrault,* nos. 22/23 (May 1958), p. 178.

23. "The Old Dame" was later successfully included in *The Visits of Love.*

24. Alfred Jarry, *Oeuvres Complètes* (Monte Carlo: Editions du Livre, 1948), vol. 6, p. 103. Hereafter cited in the text and abbreviated as "OCMC."

25. Gerald F. Else, trans., *Aristotle: Poetics* (Ann Arbor, Michigan: University of Michigan Press, 1970), p. 15. Hereafter cited in the text as *"Poetics."*

26. S. H. Butcher, trans. and ed., *Aristotle's Theory of Poetry and Fine Art*

(New York: Dover Publications, 1951), p. 184. Hereafter cited in the text as "Butcher."

27. Gerald F. Else, *Aristotle's Poetics: The Argument* (Cambridge, Mass.: Harvard University Press, 1957), p. 305. Hereafter cited in the text as "Else."

28. Lane Cooper, *An Aristotelian Theory of Comedy* (New York: Harcourt, Brace and Company, 1922).

29. Francis Fergusson, *Aristotle's Poetics* (New York: Hill and Wang, 1961), p. 18.

30. Sophocles, *Oedipus the King,* trans. David Grene, in Charles Alexander Robinson, Jr., ed., *An Anthology of Greek Drama* (New York: Holt, Rinehart and Winston, 1962), vol. 1, p. 164.

31. Elder Olson, "The Poetic Method of Aristotle: Its Powers and Limitations," in William H. Handy and Max Westbrook, eds., *Twentieth Century Criticism, The Major Statements* (New York: The Free Press, 1974, p. 137.

3.

The Monster Marionette:
Father Ubu

Félix Hébert graduated from the prestigious Ecole Normale Supérieure in 1853, and his dissertation in physics made him a progenitor of modern atmospheric science. He is better known, however, as the prototype of King Ubu.

Professor Hébert became a physics teacher at the *lycée* in Rennes where he was so odious to the students that they contrived stories ridiculing him, and Jarry readily contributed. Unfortunately, there is no documentation as to what he borrowed and created. The issue was inconsequential until Charles Morin wrote a letter (December 17, 1897) to Jarry's friend Henry Bauer in which Morin claimed to be the author of *King Ubu*. Bauer's reply glossed over the issue, and Morin chose not to press it. There the matter rested until 1921 when Charles Chassé reiterated Morin's claim, and the rekindled argument has drawn much attention. Chassé's scholarship is highly respected, and his exposé was motivated by his honest interest in correcting literary history with regard to the authorship of *King Ubu*, but Noël Arnaud successfully argues that Chassé was duped by Charles Morin's machinations.[1]

Chassé states that *King Ubu* is the work of Charles Morin and his brother, Henri, although Charles in his letter to Bauer claimed to be the only author. According to Chassé, the Morin brothers wrote a play about one of their Rennes professors between 1885 and 1886 and had finished it by October 1887—one year before Jarry came to the *lycée*. Charles was certain of the date of completion because he began his preparation for the Ecole Polytechnique shortly afterward and, he said, "I certainly had other things to do than concern myself with such foolish things as this play."[2] Chassé accuses Jarry of taking the play as his own, although Charles Morin magnanimously adds that he sees nothing wrong in what Jarry did because Charles and his brother wanted to be "completely anonymous,"[3] but Charles had forgotten his letter to Bauer claiming authorship.

In order to give credence to his claim, Charles gave some details about the "original" manuscript, which, he said, was written in a thirty-page notebook which was an illustrated catalogue of a fossil collection (Chassé, *D'Ubu Roi*, p. 34). It is unfortunate that Morin could not produce the notebook; it would be a wonder to see. *King Ubu* in the *Tout Ubu* edition is ninety-six pages of twenty-seven lines of ten words each, and the Bibliothèque de la Pléiade edition is forty-eight pages of ten words to each of the forty-one lines. Thus, the penmanship of the Morin brothers must have been minute indeed. Unfortunately, this notebook was lost, and there is no corroborative evidence of its existence. However, the Morin brothers said that they edited a copy of *King Ubu* in 1907-8 in order to reproduce an "exact copy" of the play. To do this twenty years after the première is, as Arrivé rightly notes, "a feat of a truly prodigious memory" (OCBP, p. 1142).

In order to attack Morin's claim to authorship of *King Ubu*, Rachilde recounts the story that Paul Fort had a copy of the play which Jarry had corrected, and she adds that this text was well marked and that some of the addenda were quite new (Rachilde, pp. 105-6). Unfortunately, according to the story, Franc-Nohain destroyed it because he thought the manuscript was an unimportant "acting copy" (Lot, p. 46). Although there are witnesses that the manuscript existed, the veracity of this evidence should be carefully assessed in the light of Jarry's friends trying to defend him rather than presenting the truth. Moreover, Fort claims that the text of *King Ubu* hardly interested Jarry and that he was even going to burn it,[4] but Charles Guérin, the painter Ulman, and Fort published it *"against his will"* (Fort, p. 52). Fort continues: the reason for Jarry's displeasure with the play is that he recognized that the text was disorganized, but "During the night, and without Jarry, we put the scenes in a little more logical order, and this order just happened to be miraculously good. Thus we condemned to immortality Father Ubu, Mother Ubu, Captain Bordure and all the Boorans" (Fort, p. 52). Fort's commentary is not consistent with known facts about Jarry and the play. There is no doubt about his fascination with the Ubu myth, as shown in his frequently telling stories about Ubu, and he published some of these tales, revised the *"ur-Ubu"* text extensively, and then included the vast majority of the play in *Emperor Antichrist*. Hardly the acts of a person who did not want the play published. Moreover, the organization of the play corresponds so closely to Jarry's aesthetic theories that it is indeed doubtful if Fort made any noticeable contribution. Fort's comment is also suspect because it is most unlike Jarry not to give credit to those who helped him. In this case it was Marcel Schwob, who helped edit the manuscript of *King Ubu*, and in appreciation Jarry dedicated the play to him.[5]

While each side draws relatively even in defending its claims to authorship of *King Ubu*, Lugné-Poe offers a compromise. In 1922 he argued that "Whether Jarry did or did not principally participate in the creation of *King Ubu* is of no importance. . . . Schoolboy farce or social satire, what difference does it make! It is the result which is interesting." [6] There is no reason to question the validity of this assertion, but it is likewise clear that it begs the responsibility of determining authorship.

The right place to start this inquiry is with the known and accepted facts of Ubu's history. First, no one contests Charles Morin's assertion that he and his brother had written a play, entitled *The Poles*, at the *lycée* in Rennes in 1885-87. Although this play no longer exists, there is no question that this was the *"ur-Ubu"* text. The protagonist of the play was Professor Hébert, whose mannerisms and pedagogy were unending sources of humor to the students. They above all ridiculed his physiognomy: he was "a short, obese man with a porcine face, small eyes," [7] with a pale face and a blond mustache (Hertz, p. 73). In "The Paralipomena of Ubu" Jarry describes Professor Hébert as "an animal, especially the porcine face, and the nose looks like the upper jaw of a crocodile, and his dress made him resemble the brother of that most aesthetically horrible marine creature, the crab" (OCBP, p. 467). The most pronounced facet of his physique was his enormous paunch, which he enhanced by eating candy, petits fours, and other bonbons (Chauveau, pp. 40-41) which he carried in his pockets. In short, he looked like a huge insect (Hertz, p. 73). In class, Professor Hébert was known for "the tenacity of his malice and the baseness of his wickedness" (Chassé, p. 19).

Not content with writing poem, plays, and narratives ridiculing Professor Hébert's appearance and mannerisms, the students began to imagine highly fanciful stories about his "exploits." The Morin brothers joined in the ridicule, and one of their additions to it was *The Poles,* which they undoubtedly finished before Jarry arrived in Rennes. Henri showed the play to Alfred in the winter of 1888, about a year after Charles had left the school. Jarry was drawn to it because of his friendship with Henri and his own detestation of Professor Hébert, whom Jarry considered to represent "everything in the world that is grotesque" (OCBP, p. 399). Jarry also gravitated to *The Poles* because of its satire and iconoclasm, two themes which were beginning to surface in his own work. One of its earliest discernible facets is the joy of ridiculing authority figures, one of which—as shown in the "Bidasse" series—was the teacher. A few months before going to school in Rennes he wrote a short play, *The Opening Day of Fishing,* which is based on satire and ridicule. Thus, he was mentally and artistically ready for the "Hébert" experience, and for *The Poles.*

Delighted with the satire Henri had shown him, Jarry decided to produce it at the Théâtre des Phynances, which was a company of puppeteers, comprised of Jarry, his sister Charlotte, and Henri Morin. Jarry adapted Morin's play for puppets after Jarry received some of these toys as a holiday gift (Chassé, p. 19). He also made the sets for the production, for which he was qualified because of his award-winning skill in drawing, and he also spoke the role of the protagonist. Charlotte was later to publish two poems,[8] but her slight literary importance rests solely on designing the puppet of Ubu, which she did after she saw Professor Hébert pass in front of their home and was at once inspired by his physique. The original performance was in December 1888 in the attic of the Morin house; but the company later moved to the Jarry apartment.

Jarry took *The Poles* with him when he went to Paris in 1891. His infatuation with the Ubu myth was enhanced by the reception he received in various *salons* he frequented where he was well known for his stories about Ubu. Although there is no precise record of the tales he told, he no doubt invested new ones or at least drastically revised the old episodes because it is most unlikely that schoolboy farces would have been sufficiently entertaining to the Parisian literati, let alone garner a reputation noted even by Gide. Although this was a period of striking intellectual and artistic production, Jarry found time to revise *The Poles* several times, retitle it (Chassé, pp. 37-38) and created the definitive name for Professor Hébert. Most scholars have assumed that the name evolved from Hébert to Ebé, Eb, Ebouille, Père Heb, and finally Ubu. But this explanation is not convincing because the evolution of the sound changes is an illogical movement from shortening the sounds to lengthening them, adding a word, and then completely transforming the word. Charles Morin notes that the new title "sounds better than Heb," but his rationale is indeed suspect: he argues that the name "Ubu" "evokes better the idea of the owl" (Chassé, pp. 37-38). There is no question that Jarry was infatuated with owls and used owl imagery, but Morin is not convincing because the owl has nothing whatsoever to do with the play. Another erroneous view, held by J.-H. Sainmont, is based on the assumption that Jarry selected it for poetic reasons: Jarry had parodied a national and liturgical hymn, which would later become the basis of the "Song of the Debraining," which initially ended with the line "Hurrah, cheeks of the butt, long live Father Ebé" ("Hurrah, cornes-au-cul, vive le père Ebé"). Sainmont reasons that Jarry had to change the name from Ebé to Ubu for purposes of rhyme (OCBP, p. 1148). This is a doubtful explanation. Why would Jarry change the name of his major character just for one rhyme? In fact, there is one notable occurrence when just the opposite took place: Jarry changed Ubu's name in *Ubu Cuckolded* to "Ubé" for purposes of rhyme (OCBP, p. 500). The most plausible explanation for the name is offered by Perche, who suggests that the origin of Ubu's name is *ybex,* a Latin word for "vulture" which Jarry slightly altered.[9] Perche's conclusions most certainly describe Jarry's deeply felt attitude toward Professor Hébert, and the expression also reflects Jarry's interest in language and his delight in modifying it.

Jarry's first known utilization of the name Ubu under his own signature was in *Guignol* (1893). The specific name of this section is *The Uninvited Guest (L'Autoclète),* and it represents a watershed in the transition from *The Poles* to *King Ubu.* Several facets of Ubu's personality in *The Uninvited Guest* show that by 1893 Jarry still had not completely freed the Ubu myth from being a schoolboy farce. For instance, Ubu appears similar to the descriptions given of him in Rennes: huge, with a paunch so enormous that he finds a doorway "minuscule," and he is surprised that he can get through it (OCBP, p. 181). However, his physiognomy is not correlated to an attack on the bourgeoisie. Ubu's corpulence has no content, no philosophic or societal direction; his remarkable physique expresses simply and solely the understandably superficial and awkward sarcasm of a schoolboy about one of his teachers. Similarly, Ubu is called the "ex-King of Poland and Aragon," [10] but these references have no relationship to Jarry's later concept of universality, and thus the titles are only sophomoric references devoid of philosophical significance. Moreover, Ubu's expression, "pataphysics" (OCBP, p. 181), is a play on Professor Hébert's frequent reference to "our physics"; the term has no relationship to its later definition. The last point to reflect the schoolboy nature of *The Uninvited Guest* is that Ubu's opponent is Achras, a name the students at Rennes devised for another of their teachers. Mr. Périer.

The Uninvited Guest shows that Jarry was still oriented toward some of the Rennes stories about Professor Hébert, but it also demonstrates that Jarry was not married to *The Poles* and was able to graft his special brand of misanthropy onto the Ubu myth. The first step was to drop all references to Ubu's pedagogic origins and to give him more sophisticated qualities, such as an insufferably self-centered personality. He demonstrates this attribute when he abruptly informs Achras, using the royal first person plural, that "your house is agreeable to us and we have decided to install ourselves here." Achras is about to remonstrate, but Ubu silences him with the statement that he will allow Achras "to dispense with the gratuities" (OCBP, p. 182). Thus, in terms of at least one comic technique, which would be quintessential to *King Ubu,* Jarry had developed Ubu beyond the Rennes years, including *The Poles.*

Jarry also considerably develops Ubu's personality by splitting the character into Ubu and his Conscience. Ubu carries his Conscience in his valise, and when it appears it is covered with cobwebs because, as Ubu observes, "it doesn't serve us very often" (OCBP, pp. 182-83). Conscience pleads and reasons with Ubu not to kill Achras, who Ubu feels has insulted him in his "own house." Conscience argues that "it is unworthy of a civilized man to return evil for good" (OCBP, p. 183). He notes that Achras is very brave and inoffensive and is a "poor man incapable of defending himself" (OCBP, p. 183). Fatal observation! Immediately Ubu seizes upon the salient point: Achras is helpless. "Thank you," Ubu says to his Conscience, "We will kill Mr. Achras because there is no danger, and we will consult you more often because you know how to give better advice than we could have believed. Get back in the bag!" (OCBP, p. 183). With the decision to kill Achras, Jarry exposes his contention that right and wrong do not exist, and the vaunted conscience, quintessential to most Christian moral precepts, might very well aid evil. Jarry's fundamental principle about human existence is that it is governed by only one law: "Do What You Will But Don't Get Caught!" With that aphorism, which emerges in *The Uninvited Guest,* Jarry took the first step in developing that incarnation of the modern bourgeois—Father Ubu. The depiction of the triumph of evil is most assuredly not new to Jarry's thought; it was, in fact, one of the earliest themes to appear in his juvenilia. Thus, one of the central points of *The Uninvited Guest* is very much a part of Jarry's intellectual development, and his ability to integrate this pessimism with buffoonery was to be expected from their paralleling each other throughout much of the early work.

The Uninvited Guest shows that Jarry was quickly converting the Ubu myth into his own tool, and very shortly, with *Emperor Antichrist,* any claim of Morin and Chassé should be rejected because Ubu then belonged completely to Jarry. The utilization of Ubu in *Emperor Antichrist* comes at a significant moment in the evolution of Jarry's thought because that work follows *Haldernablou,* the pivotal drama of the 1894-95 period in which Jarry elaborates his cosmology, and it is in the "Terrestrial" act of *Emperor Antichrist* that the integration of the Ubu myth takes place. Except for several modifications, the "Terrestrial act" is *King Ubu.* However, it is noteworthy that in *Emperor Antichrist* Jarry's "black humor" is fully developed and coupled with other major themes in his philosophy: atheism and irreligious attitudes, excoriation of bourgeois platitudes, ridicule of conventional concepts of morality, exposing the baseness of human nature, and applauding the triumph of evil. All of these threads of his youth are firmly woven together in this section of *Emperor Antichrist,* and because of the unique nature of the warp and woof it is clear that, as with *Emperor Antichrist,* there can be no question that Ubu is completely Jarry's creation.

Following the appearance of the *Emperor Antichrist* version of *King Ubu,* Jarry revised it once again and published a final full-length theatrical version of it, entitled for the first time *King Ubu,* in *Le Livre d'Art* (Spring 1896); it appeared as a book in June 1896. The text, then, was readily available at least six months before the première (December 10, 1896), so that those who were to attend had ample opportunity to study the play carefully. Jarry requested permission to produce the play from Henri Morin—significantly not from Charles—a request which exposes Jarry's thoughtfulness and respect for a friend. Henri gave his consent, and Ubu soon marched over the plains of Poland, the steppes of Russia, and literary history.

Enter Lugné-Poe, who at this time was valiantly trying to keep the Théâtre de l'Oeuvre going. The director-producer was trapped in the dilemma of wanting to produce new and innovative works and at the same time having to make his presentations financially successful. Fortunately for Jarry, Lugné-Poe's productions had not earned sufficient money, and thus he was receptive to Jarry's suggestions that he produce a play which Jarry had written and which could be produced cheaply. In the celebrated letter to Lugné-Poe of January 8, 1896, he lists how masks would be used, simplified décor, number of actors reduced, and so forth. It is unknown which influenced Lugné-Poe more, the revolutionary nature of the dramaturgical ideas or the low production costs, although subsequent events strongly suggest the latter was the deciding factor. Lugné-

Poe's zeal for *King Ubu* waned shortly after the initial decision, and he began to reconsider the advisability of the production; but Rachilde, who had long been able to reason with him, answered his reservations, and he relented. Then Ubu came to life for two nights, but literary history shows that one night was quite enough!

The theater was full,[11] including the notable drama critics of the day. The presentation was delayed a few moments while Jarry addressed the audience. He sat behind a table covered with a heavy sheet of wrapping paper. Rachilde, who was present, depicts him as "a small swarthy man, whose clothes were too big, hair plastered down like Bonaparte, pale face and somber eyes, inky-black eyes, eyes the color of a pool of water" (Rachilde, p. 71). He began by apologizing for the hasty production, which did not allow time for the construction of Ubu's "real mask" (OCBP, p. 400). He also applauded the "subtle talent of Monsieur Gémier," who was playing Ubu, and then talked about some of his own theories of drama, although few of his comments were heard because of the restlessness of the audience. When he finished, he picked up the table and left. The overture began. Jarry originally conceived of an orchestra of sixteen musicians, the principal instruments being the timpani and trombones—"to cover up the cat-calls" [12]—as well as "oboe, concert clarinet, deep bass . . . flageolets, German flutes, concert flutes, [bassoons and coronets], sackbuts . . . [horns], green Provençal flutes, bagpipes . . . kettledrums, drum, bass drum [and] grand organ" (OCBP, p. 1147). Financial reality forced him to be more modest: at the première the "orchestra" was reduced to a piano played four-hands by Claude Terrasse, who composed all of the music for the play, and his wife. From time to time Terrasse left the keyboard in order to bang a pair of cymbals.

After the overture, the curtain rose, and Gémier stepped forward and spoke his first word, "Shitr!" The battle began! The anti-Ubuists played upon the word,[13] and the supporters called the opposition "idiots" and accused them of not being able to understand Shakespeare and of having rejected Wagner, which is a reference to Wagner's dismal reception in Paris. When the house lights were turned up in an effort to restore order, several spectators were seen shaking their fists at each other. The uproar was so great that Gémier could not be heard, so he stopped for about fifteen minutes

(Rachilde, p. 80), then improvised a little jig, which he ended with some buffoonery. The ruse worked, and it brought about a truce—until the next time "the word" was used. It was used twenty-eight times.

The première was more than the opening of a controversial play: it was a literary civil war. With the first word, Jarry marched to attack the bourgeois sense of decency and propriety, for which he had no respect whatsoever. At one of the receptions of the *Mercure de France*, Jarry remarked, "Taste! Shit on good taste!" Some scholars, represented by Perche (p. 78) and Morin (Chassé, *D'Ubu Roi*, p. 40), think that the word "shitr" originated during Jarry's schoolboy years. Morin says that "the word" was a means of circumventing parental displeasure with swearing. "Don't forget," he admonishes, "we were still quite young; thus, we decided to put an 'r' in it." [14] This explanation is hardly convincing. Surely no parent could be so gullible as to be fooled by a child saying "shitr" instead of "shit."

J. H. Levesque has correctly seen that by using "shitr" Jarry was deliberately trying to scandalize the spectators.[15] In fact, the first word was designed to offend, and by warping it Jarry signaled that its utterance was no accident. Essentially, Jarry had taken one of the favorite French expressions and catapulted it onto the stage, which was an audacious act considering that convention did not permit its dramaturgical use. But such a restriction was hypocritical and limiting, as Jarry clearly recognized: Who were the bourgeoisie to dictate to the creator? The only right which Jarry accepted was freedom, and in this specific case freedom meant that the dramatist should use whatever vocabulary he thought appropriate.[16] In retrospect the battle over "shitr" seems petty, but in terms of literary history Jarry had struck a blow for artistic freedom, because with that one word Jarry had considerably liberated the vocabulary of drama. Professor Wellwarth has correctly concluded that "With that incredibly simple yet explosively destructive word, Jarry changed the whole course of the future dramatic continuum. Indeed, the theater would never be the same." [17]

The flagrant use of "shitr" announces Jarry's intention to penetrate forcefully and profoundly beneath bourgeois hypocrisy and explore the nature of this dominant force in Western culture. He concludes that the most basic bourgeois instincts are those centered around the waist. Thus, it is appropriate that gluttony is one of Ubu's most important vices. No wonder that Mother Ubu inveigles Ubu to usurp the throne by assuring him that as king "You will be able, dear . . . to eat very frequently" (OCBP, p. 354). Nor is it surprising that Ubu unites the conspirators at a "splendid meal" (OCBP, p. 355); but, glutton that he is, Ubu cannot wait for the guests so he samples extensively from the table, including a roast chicken and a fillet of veal (OCBP, p. 355). He eagerly anticipates the rest of the menu: "Soup Polonaise, raston ribs, veal, chicken, dog pâté, Pope's Nose of Turkey, [and] charlotte russe" (OCBP, p. 356.)

The second of the bourgeois instincts is the desire for "phynance." By using the promise of enriching himself, Mother Ubu astutely lures Ubu into assassinating the King (OCBP, p. 354). His inflamed greed beclouds any sense of morality, which is exemplified by his reaction to the question of the nature of justice. Ubu replies that "We shall proceed to the finances" (OCBP, p. 372). His mind is lucid and analytical, and he sees quite clearly that in order to gain money, he must kill; therefore, he does so. Totally dedicated to acquiring *phynance,* human life has no significance, and Ubu readily and easily throws people into the "Debraining Machine." Like the bourgeois, he grabs "phynance" with a ruthlessness and efficiency that a banker or industrial magnate could easily envy.

Jarry shows that the lust for money is not limited to Ubu; it is a universal facet of mankind regardless of how it is papered over. A dramatic example is provided when Ubu, in order to cement his monarchy, offers gold to the citizenry. How the citizens fight over it! The bloodbath is so extraordinary that Ubu overcomes his own greed and orders more gold to be thrown to the "herd" so he can watch the battle (OCBP, p. 367). No wonder he refers to them as "friends" (OCBP, p. 367), a comment which poses the baseness of human nature and its dedication to "phynance."

The third of man's basic instincts is the genital, but in this regard there is an unexpected occurrence in *King Ubu.* In *Haldernablou* (July 1894) and *The Visits of Love,* parts of which he was writing while working on *King Ubu,* Jarry very frankly discusses many facets of human sexuality, such as homosexual and heterosexual love, prostitution, and so on, but *King Ubu* is surprisingly chaste. Chassé asserts that the reason for this is that Jarry did not write the play (Chassé, pp. 24-25). However, the section of *The Visits of Love* entitled "At the Fiancée's" provides the key to understanding this facet of *King Ubu.*

In this brief cameo Jarry shows that marriage is primarily the result of parental insistence rather than personal sentiment (OCBP, pp. 876-77). The woman is trained is to be a "shark" trying to trap the male in her net of allurements, including stimulating the man sexually and giving him the impression of sexual experience yet remaining chaste (OCBP, pp. 874-75). All the ensnarements are exposed if the male makes direct vigorous sexual advances, according to Jarry, which force the female to drop her façade and confess that *"love is not the business of honest people"* (OCBP, p. 877). That conclusion is Jarry's fundamental assessment of marriage: it is an emotional and sexual wasteland. "At the Finacée's" becomes the pattern for Jarry's view of marriage even in such a late work as *Messalina,* and such is the case with *King Ubu.* The connubial relationships of the Ubus are devoid of affection: marriage is a bog where powerful personalities contend for supremacy, unite for mutual advantage, and clash for individual advancement. This picture of marriage compliments the picture of Homo Sapiens drawn in *King Ubu,* and Jarry has rightly deleted any discussion of sex and marriage because he would have been forced to deal with its complexities, and the ensuing presentation would have detracted from the thrust of *King Ubu.* He was, of course, acutely aware of the problems of sexuality, and he examined them extensively in *Haldernablou, The Visits of Love, Messalina,* and *The Supermale.*

In the sanctum sanctorum of the bourgeoisie stands the pedestal and bust of Woman. Jarry yanks her off the dais and drags her into the mire along with everybody else. Few men equal Jarry in misogyny, which he frankly confessed to Rachilde: "We don't like women at all" (Rachilde, p. 59). It first appears in *Haldernablou,* in which a homosexual affair is beatified and the Mother is reduced to passive acquiescence (OCBP, p. 222). Jarry's attitude toward women became increasingly condemnatory, and when he wrote

King Ubu his misogyny was fully matured. The first time he portrays Mother Ubu is when she is goading her husband into being
ambitious for the crown of Poland by asking the basic and blood-
thirsty question: "Who's stopping you from slaughtering the whole
family and putting yourself in their place?" (OCBP, p. 354). Only
then is he stirred into action, and Mother Ubu, dressed as a housewife in her apron, gives support and praise to her husband when
she rejoices over his decision to kill the king: "Oh, great! You're a
real man" (OCBP, p. 354). There are repeated instances when the
spectator might reconsider his initial appraisal of her because she
frequently observes how disgusting Ubu is, but she never objects to
his activities on the basis of principle; she criticizes him for his
methods. Lest the audience have any respect for her, she too uses
"shitr," a sign of her Ubuesque nature, which she clearly manifests
when, after seeing her husband off on his "Czar hunt," she grasps
the opportunity: "Now that that fat baboon has left, let's look after
our own business, kill Bougrelas, and grab the treasury" (OCBP, p.
378).

Jarry depicts the bourgeoisie so brilliantly that *King Ubu* becomes a textbook on how to succeed in the bourgeois moral and
philosophic climate. Jarry begins by stripping away the hypocrisy
of the "Puritan work ethic," and proves that success is not gained
by hard work and innovative ideas, which are mere platitudes and
rationalizations—sop for the bourgeois aspirant! Triumph is
achieved by being more ruthless than others. For instance, Ubu
easily overpowers the Nobles and then turns to the Magistrates,
and their objections are facilely overruled by Ubu, who immediately orders them thrown into the Debraining Machine (OCBP,
p. 371). The Financiers likewise protest Ubu's tactics, but the Financiers end like the Magistrates (OCBP, p. 372). Ubu lets nothing stand between himself and his goals: neither class, government
nor financial moguls. He acts with a zest which a John D. Rock-
efeller or a Joseph Kennedy might well admire.

Jarry appears to treat the Peasants differently because they act
upon their protestations by rebelling. But lest anyone think that
Jarry was praising them for their courage, he immediately shows
that they do not revolt in order to gain their freedom; they reject
Ubu because he tries to grab too much "phynance" from them. At

first they denigrate themselves by begging him for mercy (OCBP, p. 374), but they soon learn that it was foolish to have expected any compassion from him. "So that's how it is," they rightly conclude (OCBP, p. 374). At once they switch allegiance, and proclaim Bougrelas "by the grace of God, King of Poland and Lithuania" (OCBP, p. 374). Well might the people scathingly reject Ubu, but "Liberty, Equality, and Brotherhood" have nothing to do with their revolt; they are as amoral and "phynance-oriented" as Ubu. To add insult to injury, Jarry pictures the Peasants clamoring for Bourgrelas, which literally means "that wretch" *(ce bougre-là)*.[18]

As his juvenilia demonstrate, Jarry was concerned with cosmological questions at a surprisingly young age. In *The Deluge,* which was written when he was fourteen, for instance, he shows how the gods almost playfully punish man, not with a slap or spank, but with agonizing death. His concept of a malignant cosmos reappears in *Haldernablou,* and the idea of a good-evil cycle was included in *Emperor Antichrist* in which he concludes that the Antichrist, represented by Ubu, must inevitably reign. Unfortunately, the postulate is defective because he does not defuse the logical extension that "good" will inevitably follow "evil," a problem which Jarry solved in *King Ubu.* He began by excising two thirds of *Emperor Antichrist,* including the Prologue and "Heraldic" act, an artistic necessity which must have been anguishing because of his propensity for prologues. However, this deletion was a superbly simple solution to a very difficult obstacle. Instead of allowing the reader to contemplate the return of the "good," as in *Emperor Antichrist* or a besotted Ubu, in *King Ubu* Jarry intensifies "evil" by forcing the spectator to see the Ubus anticipating their landing in France. Thus, the cosmos clearly favors the Ubus by improving their station.

Jarry also makes his point about the malignant cosmos when he ridicules the practice of praying to saints. For instance, King Venceslas decides to go to the military review unarmed, and immediately Queen Rosemonde and Bougrelas, sensing danger for him, call upon "God and the great Saint Nicholas" to protect him (OCBP, p. 362). But to no avail: he is butchered even as he appeals to the "Holy Virgin" (OCBP, p. 363). Similarly, the Queen prays for God to defend her as she is being attacked (OCBP, p. 363), but she too is slaughtered. In order to intensify the insult to Christians, Jarry proves that the converse is not true. Ubu exemplifies the point when he learns that the Czar of Russia is going to kill him. Immediately he calls upon "St. Anthony and all the saints" to protect him, and he even promises to burn a candle for them (OCBP, p. 377). Naturally, he is protected, although he immediately forgets his promise. Ubu also prays to God in the "Cave" scene when he thinks he is being attacked by the Bear, and the prayers are indeed answered: he is "saved." True, his two henchmen kill the Bear—but the spectator sees demonstrable proof of Ubu's relationship with God. How can the spectator deny that if there is a God, He favors Ubu?

Jarry's cosmology clearly places him at the antipodes of Christianity, and he continues the assault on it by deprecating the traditional concept of morality, especially in the primacy of the right. Jarry shows that right and wrong cannot be viably distinguished. Ubu demonstrates the point. As he struggles to retain the throne of Poland, Mother Ubu asserts that "young Bougrelas has the more righteous case" (OCBP, p. 369), but Ubu impressively and convincingly replies: "isn't the bad right just as valid as the good right?" (OCBP, p. 369). This twist of logic, which is reminiscent of *Being and Living,* places the spectator in a quagmire from which he must extricate himself, and the task is not easy. Cultural conditioning has prejudiced the Western mind to accept the Christian morality, that is, Ubu's logic is wrong, yet Jarry places reality before the spectator. Which is he to accept?—What he has been conditioned to believe, or what he sees on the stage?

The wasteland of evil in *King Ubu* is broken by the honorable Bougrelas. He proclaims, as Ubu, who has just killed Venceslas and is now advancing toward the Queen, that "I will defend my mother to the death" (OCBP, p. 364). There is no question of his bravery, but she is killed anyway and he is spared. Jarry has anticipated the audience's sympathy for this young man, and it is for this reason that Bougrelas's name is significant. Jarry traps the spectator in a "crossroads." He sees a courageous person, who is dressed to "excite" the ladies, called a rather derogatory name. Which sense organ is the spectator to believe, sight or hearing?

Jarry clearly saw that optimism, the bourgeoisie, and Christianity are integrated, and that to attack one is to insult the others. The triumvirate represents a fearful army to confront, one which requires a courageous analysis of the foundations and keystones of Western culture. It is a tribute to Jarry's fortitude, independence, and intellect that he not only unhesitatingly undertook the necessary task but followed his analysis through to its completion. He recognized that the bourgeois, the dominant force in much of modern life, is living behind a moral and intellectual façade of protective hypocrisy. Jarry sounded the tocsin that the bourgeoisie will no longer be allowed the security of their dishonest luxury; and Jarry's attack consequently forced him to assault anew his old enemy, Christianity, because it is the "nuclear glue," the moral chain, which holds the society, including the bourgeoisie, together. There was no doubt in his mind that the Christian cosmology would have to be rejected, and man must be ready to accept the truth: "God is dead." The Age of Absurdity was born, and Jarry became its High Priest.

Jarry saw that the expression of the absurdity of life required new forms, and one of them was the establishment of black humor as a viable dramatic technique. Its caustic and nihilistic quality not only exposes the nature of the bourgeoisie, optimism, and Christianity, but it also shows that these concepts result in the tragedy of life, which is so grievous that men can only laugh at it. Helpless and effete, he is ruled by buffoons and clowns, like Ubu, within a malignant cosmos.

Jarry's concept of absurdity also required a new dramatic structure. Many Aristotelian postulates were unworkable because, to Jarry, Western art no longer shares Aristotle's assumptions about life and its relationship to art. The need for Jarry was clear, but his concepts were not readily recognized or accepted, a fact which caused some of the furor over the première of *King Ubu*. Mille, for instance, condemned the form of the play, which, he says, is "the most incoherent, the most disorganized, the craziest piece ever written." [19] Not at all! There is indeed method to Jarry's madness! The mistaken impression focuses on the episodic structure, and the key to understanding its rationale surfaces in a statement Jarry made in January 1894: "I prefer that the theater be the unfolding

of a dream, like purple streamers" (OCBP, p. 1003). Jarry had long
tried to capture this dreamlike quality in such works as *Phonograph,
The Report of the Terrible Accident,* and the superb *Opium* in which the
images cascade and intertwine in a subconsciously organized
dream sequence. *King Ubu* is in this tradition. Jarry meant the
episodic structure to weaken the spectator's grasp of reality, which
is composed of bourgeois-Christian platitudes, and to induce a
semidream state. But, as he had done in *Being and Living* and *Funeral Songs,* he did not want the spectator so stupefied that he could
not follow the marked guideposts which enabled him to extricate
himself by relating to the pictures which Jarry had drawn of the
feebleness and falsehood of traditional bourgeois-Christian beliefs.
Thus, the structure of *King Ubu* is strange because it is not primarily directed toward the spectator's rationality; the episodes are
effective building blocks of a dreamlike state.

Such was *King Ubu.* At the end of the presentation Gémier came
forward to center stage, took the mask from his head, "and this
time, with a clear voice rolling like thunder and drums, imperially,
like Hercules entering the Augean stables, shouted 'Shittrrr.' Then
he said proudly: 'The play which we have just presented is by
Monsieur Alfred Jarry' " (Rémond, p. 668). This public homage
was thoughtful and welcomed, but the names of Jarry and Ubu
would not soon be forgotten.

The form and content of *King Ubu* gave the critics much ground
to march and countermarch, and Jarry expected this reaction, but
his naiveté and enthusiasm led him to misjudge the strength and
resilience of the opposition. He quickly found that the battle over
King Ubu did not end with the première. That proved to be only
the initial clash. The real contest moved to the newspapers, and
the defenders and attackers of *King Ubu* quickly withdrew in favor
of two champions: Henry Bauer, a close friend of Jarry and critic
of *Echo de Paris,* and Henry Fouquier, the reviewer for *Le Figaro* and
spokesman for the detractors of the play. Bauer rightly and astutely argues that the play

> is an uncommon farce [with] immoderate tone, tremen-
> dous vulgarity, truculent fantasy overlaying the biting
> and aggressive verse, overpowering with the haughty

scorn for men and things; it is a philosophico-political pamphlet with jaw stuck out, which spits in the face of traditional chimeras and fabricated masters. . . . It is, finally . . . an original and discordant cry in the concert of the usual. (Chassé, p. 13)

He continued his wholehearted and insightful support of the play in subsequent articles and concluded his defense with the assurance that

From this huge and strangely suggestive figure of Ubu blows the wind of destruction, of inspiration for contemporary young people, which overthrows the traditional respects and scholarly preconceptions. And the type will remain. (Chassé, pp. 16-17)

But for Fouquier, *King Ubu* presented an ill wind blowing through the Parisian theatrical scene, and while pretending to support the avant-garde movement, he solemnly warned the public that "Every sincere friend of progress is obligated to defend it against those who destroy it and make reactionaries by the violence of their foolishness." [20] It was clear to him that *King Ubu* was indeed foolish! The contest between Fouquier and Bauer was over a fundamental aesthetic issue: What constitutes progress in the arts? The rancorous discussion became very personal, but since then the tirades have subsided and other people have taken the field. They have not only substantiated Bauer's conclusion but have extended it. Morot-Sir, for instance, agrees with Bauer that *King Ubu* is "not simply the apparition of a new character in the cultural universe, it is a new . . . means of expression." [21] Leonard Pronko has rightly concluded that "With *King Ubu*, Alfred Jarry may be said to have founded the avant-garde drama, for it is the first modern play reflecting the anarchy of the author's double revolt against the society in which he lived and the more or less set forms of the realistic and naturalistic drama." [22] Others, to be certain, had reacted against their culture's stultifying and frequently homicidal nature, and much of the revolt centered around Lugné-Poe and the Théâtre de l'Oeuvre, but it was Jarry who extended these re-volts into a systematic revolution.

The cost of his revolution was great to Jarry. Lugné-Poe, who was never an ardent supporter of *King Ubu*, reassessed his position not only toward the play and Jarry but toward the direction of the Théâtre de l'Oeuvre. He published his conclusion in a public letter:

> Of the eight plays this season, five were written by for-eigners and three by Frenchmen. The five translations were unanimously, or almost unanimously, praised by the public and the press; the French works, however, were given scant attention and were briefly reviewed in the press. The only conclusion is that these works are without interest, and that our country is impoverished in original dramatic production. . . . [Except] for the five admirable plays of Maurice Maeterlinck, [mystical themes] have produced nothing, from the dramatic point of view. . . . The Oeuvre will produce only the works of foreigners.[23]

The implications of Lugné-Poe's statement were shocking to Jarry and his friends in the revolutionary phalanx, and they, too, published an open letter to answer Lugné-Poe's charges. They rightly note that

> The Oeuvre, on the contrary, has gained by the produc-tion of French and foreign plays, from the movement of ideas which have arisen . . . and from the writers whom M. Lugné-Poe has not evaluated. (Robichez, p. 395)

The open letter was signed by twelve people, among them were Romain Coolus, Paul Fort, A. F. Hérold, Gustave Kahn, Pierre Quillard, Rachilde, Henri de Régnier—and Alfred Jarry! But, de-spite such judicious reasoning, the insult remained, and the doors of the Théâtre de l'Oeuvre were now closed to Jarry and to many of his friends who had also experimented in Symbolist theater.

The exchange of letters places Lugné-Poe in a questionable light. He had long been regarded as the patron of Symbolist and avant-garde drama, but the fact is that he quickly divorced himself from the revolutionaries after the "Ubu massacre." Perhaps he did not want to alienate desperately needed financial supporters; perhaps he was not as revolutionary as is generally thought. In any case, hindsight shows that he made a mistake because his career never regained the stature it once had. But the revolutionaries lost a man who had been of considerable help to them, and now they would be hard pressed to find a medium for their dramaturgical experiments. Jarry lost the most because his meteoric dramatic career was extinguished. He was to die a decade later almost forgotten, and his masterpiece would not reappear on the stage for a quarter of a century. Bitterly confronting reality, Jarry left the theater and never seriously returned to it; and whereas other genres were to benefit greatly from his creativity and brilliance, the theater had lost one of its most ingenious, courageous, and revolutionary minds.

The Ubu legend was too deeply enmeshed in Jarry's personality to be quickly discarded, although he gave only sporadic and cursory attention to it after 1897. The decline of his interest in the Ubu theme is frequently overlooked because, to judge from *Ubu Cuckolded* and *Ubu in Chains,* it seems as if he had a vast creative effort in mind, an "Ubu cycle" or an "Ubu trilogy." This interpretation is given credence by Ubu's name in the titles as well as by the publication of the plays together.[24] But these observations are misleading. Jarry never conceived of the three as an integral unit. It was not until 1899, after *Ubu in Chains* had been written, that he thought of publishing the three plays together (OCBP, p. 521).

The second play of the so-called "Ubu saga," *Ubu Cuckolded,* clearly exposes the error of the "Ubu trilogy" concept. There are certain similarities because the play, like *King Ubu,* had its genesis in Jarry's Rennes years as a schoolboy farce about Professor Hébert and Priou, the star of *The Pickled;* like *Poles,* it, too, was presented at the Théâtre des Phynances in Rennes. It was initially called *Onanism, Or The Tribulations of Priou,* but the title was soon

changed to *Ubu Cuckolded, Or The Archaeopteryx,* although the subtitle is frequently deleted.[25]

Ubu Cuckolded is putrid, made more so by its proximity to *King
Ubu.* The play is damned by its organization. Jarry's juvenilia show
that he had serious problems sustaining plot and action, which
explains why many of his creations are so brief and undeveloped
that they are hardly more than sketches. As he became more sophisticated, these episodes frequently became charming vignettes
or effective units in a phantasmagoria of images and logic, as in
Being and Living and *Opium,* or in capturing a dreamlike state of
consciousness, represented by *King Ubu.* But *Ubu Cuckolded* quickly
recalls the trials and errors that preceded this achievement. In
writing it, Jarry stitched together vignettes and scenes written at
various times and on various subjects during his Rennes years.
Consequently, the scenes are frequently so disjointed in content
and style that their relationships are vague and confusing. This
was a disastrous method of composition, and only a consummate
craftsman could rescue such a play. *King Ubu* shows that Jarry did
indeed develop the necessary technical expertise, and some of his
later prose, such as *Days and Nights* and *The Supermale,* prove that
his mastery of organization in *King Ubu* was neither accidental nor
dependent upon the help of Marcel Schwob, who helped him edit
King Ubu. But *Ubu Cuckolded* remains lackluster because of Jarry's
redirected energies as well as the trials and tribulations following
King Ubu's reception.

Some of the Rennes stories included in *Ubu Cuckolded* are several
choral odes by the Boorans, a story about Ubu being cuckolded, a
revised version of Achras and his polyhedrons, and a few anecdotes
about a fellow student. There is a clear need to synthesize these
tales and characters, which Jarry attempted to do in the first act by
using a thematic organization, but he was unable or unwilling to
effect the necessary miracle. As a result, the play represents the
pitfalls Aristotle had foreseen: because "there is no probability or
necessity for the order in which the episodes follow one another"
(Else, p. 34), the work is doomed from the outset.

The basic reason why the organization of *King Ubu* is successful
is that Jarry developed Ubu's personality quickly and accurately,

and, on this secure foundation, could develop the subsequent episodes. This expertise is missing in *Ubu Cuckolded,* as the introduction illustrates. Instead of assaulting the spectator as in *King Ubu, Ubu Cuckolded* opens with a choral ode by the Boorans rejoicing over the Debraining Machine and Ubu. Rather than providing necessary identification and elaboration, the play's development is at once inhibited by the entrance (scene iii) of a flying archaeopteryx and four lines later (scene iv) by Mother Ubu denouncing Ubu for having "devoured" her son, the archaeopteryx. Mother Ubu giving birth to an archaeopteryx? [26] That strains the credulity of any spectator! Jarry is attempting to use the well-tried technique of having the characters, such as the Boorans and Mother Ubu, expose salient facets of the principal's personality before he appears on the stage. However, the attempt fails when the Soul of Father Ubu enters, states that he is "the soul of the paunch" (OCBP, p. 495), and then confesses his regrets over not having fathered the archaeopteryx with its qualities of "chiroptera [bats], leporidae [hares and rabbits], raptors [birds of prey], palmipedes [web-footed animals and birds], Pachydermata, and swine" (OCBP, p. 495). Jarry intends for the audience to realize that Father Ubu admires various qualities which these animals and birds represent, although the vocabulary is, once again, too technical. Moreover, the Ubuesque characteristics of ducks and rabbits are unclear, and the contradictions among bats, rabbits, and elephants are inescapable. Such terminology reflects Jarry's youthful fascination with scientific expressions, which recalls *The Pickled* with its talking fetuses. Such expressions are too esoteric for the ordinary spectator; however, the episode's initial audience comprised science students with whom Jarry shared common interests and attitudes. Thus, the specialized vocabulary might well have been humorous to schoolboys, but to the mature spectator it is foolish and nonproductive.

Another malfunction of the organization of *Ubu Cuckolded* is the pale and insipid portrait of Ubu, which does little to unify the episodes. Except for the Ubu-Achras section of the first act in which Ubu shows his insufferable and amoral personality, he is depicted as a bumbling buffoon devoid of the black humor which characterizes Jarry's mature depiction of him. The vapid portrait of Ubu is reflected in the last two scenes of the work in which Ubu

announces that "the play has gone on long enough," and then
engages in a silly conversation with Achras in which Ubu concludes that a crocodile "must be a whale" but corrects himself: "it
is really a snake! A rattlesnake at that!" (OCBP, pp. 516-17). This
aimless banter allows the spectator to reject Ubu easily and completely as a fool. This error is akin to the mistake in the ending of
Emperor Antichrist in which the spectator dismisses Ubu as a sot.[27]
Subterranean to Ubu's ridiculous dialogue is his greed and amor-
ality, but these themes are not adequately sustained, and Jarry
never correlates Ubu's buffoonery with an attack on the bourgeoisie. The most promising moment for making this linkage
comes when Ubu abuses his Conscience, but the incident quickly
degenerates into inconsequential dialogue. Jarry was too young
and centered about the Rennes student group to see the implications of the Ubu-Conscience motif as a tool to expose the bourgeois
mentality.

Except for the Ubu-Conscience episodes, the closest Jarry comes
to iconoclasm in *Ubu Cuckolded* is his superficial ridicule of Achras's
specialization in polyhedrons, which he could easily have con-
verted into a satire on academia. Priou's difficulties with his baccalaureate examinations could have been expanded into a fine
ridicule of students, professors, and the education industry. The
brief comment on policeman's shoes could have become a platform
for comments on the police, whom Jarry detested; and the Priests
in *Onanism* could have become a forceful statement about organized religion, but the latter theme is deleted in *Ubu Cuckolded* and
the former is immediately forgotten. Every possibility for significant comedy was overlooked in Jarry's myopic view of his Rennes
experiences. The years in Paris added essential perspective to those
tales, but he did not use that experience to develop *Ubu Cuckolded.*

It is regrettable that the Ubu-cuckolded theme is not immediately introduced nor, once presented, quickly developed. The
first mention of it is at once followed by Ubu's regrets over the
paternity of the archaeopteryx (OCBP, p. 495) and his respectful
mention of Mother Ubu's name (OCBP, p. 495). He then proceeds
to speak about his sons and daughters, who will also be staying in
Achras's house. The tantalizing reference to Ubu's family, especially to the children, who are "terribly sober" and "terribly well

raised" (OCBP, p. 407), whets the spectator's anticipation to see the Ubu offspring—especially in light of Mother Ubu's remarkable ability to spawn an archaeopteryx. But the issue is dropped as suddenly as it was raised, and it never reappears in Jarry's work. He does not return to the subject of cuckoldry until very late in the second act when Ubu confides to Achras that he has "learned that Madame Ubu, our virtuous wife, is deceiving us shamelessly" (OCBP, p. 499). At once Ubu comes to a surprising conclusion which might well have become the rationale for the play: "cuckoldry . . . implies marriage without which it is not, so to speak, valid; the sacrament of cuckoldry, in our opinion, can take place in the church or city hall." The delightful logic is dismissed at once as Ubu turns to a more personal problem: the cuckold "has ridiculed us at the same time, sir, with the fathering of an archaeopteryx" (OCBP, p. 499). The cuckold motif does not recur until Act V, scene ii, in which Mother Ubu comes to a window to greet her lover, but the occasion serves only to tease Prayou, whose name is spelled differently in this play, and for the Boorans to pummel him (OCBP, pp. 512-13). Meanwhile, Mother Ubu greets her lover, now identified as Barbapoux, but the voice of Ubu is suddenly heard, and thus begins a tiresome slapstick scene of Mother Ubu trying to hide her paramour (OCBP, p. 514). Finally, the lover is caught, and when he insults Ubu by announcing that he fears neither the Shit Pump (which is not working) nor the Debraining Machine, Ubu replies that "By my green candle! I'm going to rip out your eyes . . . reject of humanity" (OCBP, p. 516). The inept references to Barbapoux, who was not introduced previously, shows the disorganization of plot and character, and the reference to the Shit Pump helps to date the episode as part of Jarry's juvenilia, probably as early as the "Antliaclastes" plays of 1888.

With little of Ubu and the Ubu-cuckolded motif, what is left? The play's principals, the Boorans, named Crappot, Flygog, and Fourzears. The term "booran" originated in a Jarryesque modification of *palot*, meaning a boorish and coarse individual driven by base instincts. Jarry never explains their origins, how they came to serve Ubu, and why they do so, but their customary function is to be a gang of thugs terrorizing people into giving money to Ubu. They also act as a chorus, an artistic technique Jarry frequently used in his juvenilia. He usually had trouble with this device, however, and the Chorus in *Ubu Cuckolded* is no exception because it fails to underscore any significant didactic quality in the play or to control the spectator's responses. The only information that the Boorans impart is about Ubu's greed, but their commentary is so superficial that it is mostly ineffective. Many of their odes are so childish and insipid that they could be humorous only to school-boys; consequently, the lines add little or nothing to the play.

Although the play abounds in faults, some of Jarry's themes periodically protrude from the mire. The most outstanding quality of Ubu is his greed, which is exemplified by his primary title of "lord of Phynance." But, instead of the superb depiction of Ubu's lust for lucre in *King Ubu*, the spectator is subjected to the vapid action of Prayou, attired as a man of means, confessing that he has only 3,700 francs but he has to pay 80,000. The nature of the debt is not stated, but he is terrified that because he cannot pay, he will have to go through the "Squeeze-Blood-Out-Of-A-Turnip" Machine in the Place de l'Opéra—and the price for each session is 15,000 francs (OCBP, pp. 507-8).

Scatological references, which are characteristic of Ubu, also appear in *Ubu Cuckolded,* but they lack the excitement and shock of those of *King Ubu.* One instance of such language appears in Act III when Achras and Prayou decide to flee to Egypt, but before they escape Prayou must purchase some shoes. The cobbler specializes in "Shit Stompers" (OCBP, p. 510). "Here," he demonstrates, "is one for newly dropped turds, here's one for horse droppings, here's one for the meconium of a child in the cradle, here's one for the poo-poo of a cop, here's one for old nanny goat crap, here's one for the stool of a middle-aged man" (OCBP, p. 510). The extended discussion underscores Jarry's infatuation with scatology, but he still had to refine the technique and give the language dimension by carefully integrating it into the major themes of the play. The expressions in *Ubu Cuckolded* reflect the natural inclination of a youth entering manhood to use salacious terms, and the ensuing naiveté is ludicrous and without redeeming value.

Ubu Cuckolded, then, would quickly be excused as the work of a youth if it were not for its title and placement in Jarry's corpus. There are parts of it which Jarry could have polished, but he was not inclined to do so and subsequently left the project in its dismal condition. He did not return to the Ubu theme until September 1899. By then he had written *Days and Nights* and *The Visits of Love*, translated *Pope Joan*, revised *Pantagruel*, and finished both *Faustroll* and *Absolute Love*. Despite his other literary achievements, he continued to be rankled by the reception accorded *King Ubu*. Rather than overtly excoriating the critics in an essay, as he had done immediately after the première, he tried another stratagem to administer what he hoped would be the coup de grâce. The result was his last serious play, *Ubu in Chains (Ubu Enchaîné)*, which he wrote between May and September 1899. It is a rather clever piece, but his anger had not yet sufficiently cooled to permit him the necessary control and perspective to create another masterpiece.

Ubu in Chains was designed to be the antipodes of *King Ubu* (OCBP, p. 1211) in order to ask the detractors of *King Ubu* what they thought of Ubu in this play where he is diametrically the opposite of the former depiction of him. Instead of ascending a throne, Ubu announces that "I am not capable of acting like everyone else [; therefore,] I am going to enslave myself" (OCBP, p. 430). He leaves no room for doubt: "No one is going to keep me from my slavish duty. I am going to serve without mercy" (OCBP, p. 435). He soon gets an opportunity to demonstrate his new attitude when he meets Eleutheria and her uncle, Pissale, also known as the Marquis of Grandair. Ubu decides that he is going to prove how subservient he is by polishing Eleutheria's feet, although she is not wearing shoes. That makes no difference to him. Pissale begins to protest, but Ubu "throws himself" on him and kills him in an orgy of "stupid brutality" (OCBP, p. 435). There are numerous graphic examples of Ubu's savage servitude, and all of them exemplify Jarry's contention that Ubu represents human nature, which is constant. The slave, then, like the King or bourgeois, is a primordial brute wallowing in the brackish slime of life.

Jarry brilliantly seized upon the transformation of Ubu's character to attack social revolutionaries, and the result is some of the most telling and memorable scenes he ever wrote. Many of Jarry's friends, such as Félix Fénéon, A. F. Hérold, Camille Mauclair, Pierre Quillard, and Henri de Régnier were anarchists, and some fought duels to defend their independence: Octave Mirbeau, one; Catulle Mendès, five; Henry Bauer, one; Jean Moréas, four; and Henri de Régnier, one. The question of anarchy was very much in the cultural climate of France at this time, as witnessed by the bombing of the Palais Bourbon on December 9, 1893; Laurent Tailhade, a member of the Théâtre de l'Oeuvre, lost an eye in a bomb blast at the Foyot Restaurant; and Carnot, the president of the republic, was assassinated on June 24, 1899. Moreover, Jarry's friend, Fénéon, was arrested on April 26, 1894, for anarchist activity. Credence was given to this allegation when mercury and detonators were found in his possession, although he was acquitted during the trial. Jarry, then, was reacting to these acts, debates, and duels, and much of *Ubu in Chains* is aimed at questioning the results of that liberty for which people were so ardently fighting. Certainly he shared with the anarchists the common ground of needing freedom—perhaps Jarry more than most of them—but he used his freedom to denounce the doctrines of progress and utopianism.

Ubu in Chains was a platform from which Jarry launched his attack on liberal hopes of freedom. The opening volley begins very quickly in the play (Act I, scene ii) when a corporal marches three "Free Men" on a parade ground. Since "it's our duty to be free," they recite, they disobey orders together (OCBP, p. 430). For example, when ordered to "Fall in," they "Fall out" together; when commanded to "Fall out," they "Fall in" and march off en masse—"all the time avoiding marching in step" (OCBP, p. 431). Thus imbued with "freedom," they are easily regimented. Moreover, they clearly enjoy their enslavement, a delight which Corporal Pissweet exemplifies when he announces that "we are free to do what we want, even to obey, to go anywhere we want, even to prison. Liberty is slavery" (OCBP, p. 457). To add insult to injury, no one takes advantage of their conformity; their existences are without direction or meaning until they have a chance to pursue "phynance" (OCBP, p. 454). While Jarry continues to castigate man for his greed, his basic point is powerfully made: like the elixir of Alaodine in *The Old Man of the Mountain,* the drug "revolution" is doomed to enslave people; the myth of freedom and happiness is an opiate concealing chains.

Jarry's attack on the revolutionaries is one of the very few comments he made about social change. His superficial treatment shows how inadequate his knowledge was of economics, politics, and social revolt. His ignorance of disciplines other than literature and art was now severely restricting and marring his artistic efforts because he had little idea of the causes of social change, and without this quintessential understanding he was unable to attack the revolutionaries effectively. Instead, Jarry had to be content with ridiculing the conduct of the "Free Men"; his comments, while frequently clever, are hardly penetrating or incisive. Had Jarry known more about revolutions, he could have shown how they can prostitute the idea of freedom or how doublethink can be used to warp concepts.

Artistically, then, *Ubu in Chains* is markedly superior to *Ubu Cuckolded,* but not the equal of *King Ubu.* The most noticeable improvement over *Ubu Cuckolded* is the command of organization. Jarry handles the episodes confidently and effectively, and the development of the "Liberty is Slavery" motif is superbly interwoven with the Ubu-enchained theme. Moreover, the episodes are well paced, and the action within them is stiking, thereby making the play move quickly and with considerable interest, especially when coupled with effective utilization of the characters. The reason for Jarry's success with the organization and characterization is that he did not depend upon schoolboy stories about Ubu and then have to revise and integrate the material. This play began as the work of a mature artist who constructed a tool to work his will against his detractors. With that goal in mind, he was able to marshal his forces.

Although there are many admirable facets to *Ubu in Chains,* it failed all the same; one reason is that Jarry allowed his resentment of the critics to interfere with gaining the necessary perspective on the subject. For instance, at the beginning of the play Ubu steps forward and says—nothing! His wife chastises him for having forgotten "the word," but he replies that "I don't want to say that word anymore; it brought too many disagreements upon me" (OCBP, p. 429). The comment is meant to chastise the critics for their zealous condemnation of "shitr," but the effectiveness and judiciousness of the technique are certainly questionable. There is no doubt that the deletion of scatological references is an unfortunate retreat from Jarry's former revolutionary posture. He failed to see that he played into the hands of his enemies because by failing to use common expressions he has done just what they wanted—to keep the vernacular off the stage.

Jarry also attacks the critics for misunderstanding *King Ubu*. He uses a reference to the famous toilet brush of *King Ubu* to have Ubu comment that "we have more experience now, and we observe that what makes little children laugh risks making grown-ups afraid" (OCBP, p. 438). There is no dispute about the difficulties ensuing from *King Ubu*, but Jarry's rationale for the play's reception is hardly convincing. First, to suggest that many of his difficulties came from the principal character waving a toilet brush on the stage is an unjust simplification of the issue. Second, Jarry tries to insult the critics by accusing them of being so unsophisticated that they could not distinguish between a children's puppet show and a mature presentation. His remarks are, of course, fallacious. Jarry had anticipated trouble with the reception of *King Ubu* and had devised an escape route for himself when with disarming innocence he announced to the spectators just before the curtain went up that "you are free to see in Mr. Ubu as many multiple allusions as you wish or a simple puppet . . . of [a] professor" (OCBP, p. 399). But the content of the play belies such a choice; the façade quickly and easily collapsed because it fooled no one. Jarry keeps up this untenable apologia, nevertheless, in *Ubu in Chains*, especially at the end. Ubu is on a galley, ordered there by Soliman the Turk, who reminds the audience of Ubu's greed, which is so great that Soliman wants to deport Ubu as quickly as possible (OCBP, p. 461). Safely aboard the slave ship, Ubu announces that "I do not remain less than Ubu in chains, slave, and I will no longer give orders. I will be obeyed much more" (OCBP, p. 462). The logic is rather obtuse, but he assures his wife that she should not be concerned about their destination: "It will certainly be a country . . . worthy of our presence." Now the world is Ubu's domain—and he is being transported "in a trireme with a fourth bank of oars" (OCBP, p. 462). More oars for more speed so that all people can look forward to the rapid arrival of the Ubus. It is true that this continuing "ending" of the play allows Jarry a parting slap at his critics by proving to them that, in spite of their demeaning comments, Ubu is greater than ever. Literary history has, of course, proven Jarry correct. But the ending is nevertheless an artistic disaster. In *King Ubu* the last scene of Ubu anticipating Paris is an affront to the Parisian bourgeoisie, but in *Ubu in Chains* the French spectator could leave the theater relieved by the departure of Ubu for other destinations—a grave mistake on Jarry's part.

The three years between *King Ubu* and *Ubu in Chains* was a period in which Jarry moved very quickly away from drama, and consequently *Ubu in Chains* reflects his lack of interest in the theater. There is no sign that he meant this play to continue the artistic iconoclasm of *King Ubu*, to construct new guidelines, or to substantiate old ones. All of the excitement of formulating new theories about décor, costume, gestures, voice, masks, and the like is gone in *Ubu in Chains*. What remains is a rather ordinary play which could very well be narrative drama because there is nothing in it which makes it uniquely theatrical. By the standards of *King Ubu* and its letters and essays, it is reactionary. Also missing in *Ubu in Chains* is the "crossroads" thesis. It is difficult for the spectator to relate to Ubu in any way because he is removed from any point of common contact with the audience' experience. It is expecting too much for the spectator to see something of himself as a slave trying to polish the feet of a shoeless girl. However, the sedate and apathetic bourgeois can enjoy the ridicule of the revolutionaries. Is this a desirable reaction for Jarry to allow the enemy to have? Is it not possible for the bourgeois to find truth in the Arabic aphorism that "The enemy of my enemy is my friend"? Jarry—an enemy of anarchists and friend of the bourgeoisie? But Jarry ignored such a possible interpretation in his zeal to be victorious over the critics of *King Ubu*. It was most unfortunate that Jarry let critical reactionaries affect him. What did he expect to accomplish by attacking them? *Ubu in Chains* is certainly better than *Ubu Cuckolded*, but that was scant reason to expect *Ubu in Chains* to be produced because Jarry now had few friends in the theater, especially after the rupture with Lugné-Poe. Without an audience there could be no satisfactory victory.

Ubu in Chains is Jarry's last major presentation of Ubu, but he did not completely give up the Ubu stories. They had been with him since his schooling in Rennes, and they accounted for much of his notoriety in various Parisian salons. As a result, Jarry sporadically returned to Ubu and wrote various "Almanacs" (1899 and 1901), which contain calendars according to Father Ubu, "Useful Knowledge Gathered by Father Ubu," several short scenes with the Ubus, a long list of characterizations of his friends, an homage to Mallarmé, the articles for the "Grand Order of the Paunch," a sketch of *Pantagruel,* and a "Song to Make Blacks Redden with Embarrassment and to Glorify Father Ubu." Except for *Ubu Cuckolded* and *Ubu in Chains,* the most serious efforts to utilize Ubu were devoted to adapting *King Ubu* for puppets, the first version of which was a full-length production in 1901 at the "Théâtre des Pantins" in Paris. The puppets were made by Pierre Bonnard; two of the voices were those of Louise France, who had played Mother Ubu in the original cast, and of Fanny Zaessinger; [28] Claude Terrasse played the piano once again. There were fifty spectators, including Mallarmé, Valéry, Pierre Louÿs, Régnier, and Debussy. Jarry returned to the Ubu theme for the last time in 1901 when he condensed *King Ubu* and *Ubu Cuckolded* into a two-act puppet play called *Ubu on the Mound (Ubu sur la Butte),* which was performed at the "Théâtre des 4-Z' Arts" and published in 1906.

There are two significant changes in this completely *guignol* version, the first of which occurs at the beginning. As in *Ubu in Chains,* Jarry rejected offending the spectator at once as he had done in *King Ubu.* It opens with a prologue in which Guignol observes that "There are more people here than in the entire city of Lyons," and thus he must be at the "4-Z' Arts" (OCBP, p. 631). The ensuing conversation between Guignol and the Director is insipid, the slapstick is inane, and the songs idiotic. Jarry returns to using scatological references in this play, and "the word" is mentioned several times as well as the infamous toilet brush. Except for dropping several scenes, the most important of which is the Citizens chasing and killing each other for Ubu's gold, the play very closely follows the text of *King Ubu.* The Ubu-cuckolded motif is grafted on to Act II, scene ii, but the theme is quickly dropped. The "Cave" scene is reduced to a battle between Ubu's general and the Bear—the Bear wins and leaves the stage with the general in its mouth.

Another major transformation of the Ubu theme occurs at the end of the play. Shortly after the Bear exits, Father and Mother Ubu decide to leave for France (OCBP, pp. 651-52), but Bougrelas unexpectedly enters and announces "Not yet!" After citing Ubu's crimes, he has the ex-King of Poland arrested and orders the police to take Ubu to Paris and put in "a slaughterhouse where he will be debrained for all his crimes" (OCBP, p. 652). The finale is sung by the company: "Let us trust in Providence, Heaven always rewards virtue. . . . Virtue is its own reward" (OCBP, p. 653). Jarry could hardly have been serious in this didactic ode; but the ending is no mistake because Jarry has prepared the spectator early in the play for the triumph of Justice when, after the death of the King, the Souls of the Ancestors enter and one of them tells Bougrelas that he is entrusted with their vengeance. He then gives him a sword and tell him that "you will not rest until it has struck down the usurper" (OCBP, p. 638). In *King Ubu* the charge is significantly forgotten, but in *Ubu on the Mound* the spectator sees that the promise of the Ancestors is fulfilled and thus "order is restored."

Ubu on the Mound ends on a tone and message which would have been inconceivable just a few years before. Ubu had been sold to the marketplace and now became a support of the hated bourgeoisie and their morality. Of what must have Jarry been thinking? Perhaps he wanted to gain access to puppet theaters, which had indeed interested him for years; perhaps he sought to avoid controversy, which had been so costly to him and his friends, especially when it was clear that the conservatives ruled the literary scene. His feelings and rationalizations aside, his decision about Ubu in *Ubu on the Mound* is treason to the literary and philosophical revolution.

Thus the history of Ubu comes to an ignominious end, not with a bang, but with a decided whimper: foolish and ludicrous in *Ubu Cuckolded,* castrated and prostituted in *Ubu in Chains,* deranged and despoiled in *Ubu on the Mound*—a pitiful demise for one of the great characters of modern literature. Now Jarry's fertile mind and creativity were active in other areas, and soon he would produce some of his finest achievements and most memorable contributions. Another great period was now before him. For him King Ubu was dead; enter Doctor Faustroll, Pataphysician.

Notes

1. Noël Arnaud, *Alfred Jarry D'Ubu Roi au Docteur Faustroll* (Paris: La Table Ronde, 1974), p. 132. Hereafter cited in the text and abbreviated as "Arnaud."
2. Charles Chassé, *Dans Les Coulisses de la Gloire: D'Ubu Roi au Douanier Rousseau* (Paris: Editions de la Nouvelle Revue Critique, 1947), p. 132. Hereafter cited in the text and abbreviated as "Chassé."
3. Charles Chassé, *D'Ubu-Roi au Douanier Rousseau* (Vanvers: Editions de la Nouvelle Revue Critique, 1947), p. 104. Hereafter cited in the text and abbreviated as *"D'Ubu Roi."*
4. Paul Fort, *Mes Mémoires, Toute La Vie d'un Poète* (Paris: Flammarion, 1944), p. 58. Hereafter cited in the text as "Fort."
5. Pierre Champion, the biographer of Schwob, dismisses *King Ubu* as "a schoolboy joke" and Jarry as "a quaint, mad character who diverted Schwob from his studies and priggish nature" (pp. 104-5). Questionable conclusions. It is hardly likely that Jarry would dedicate a work to a person unless there were significant reasons for doing so. Schwob must have been a very special person to Jarry. There were reasons why these two men should enjoy each other: both were precocious, brilliant in foreign languages, and superb in vernacular French and regional dialects; moreover, they shared a mutual circle of friends at the *Echo de Paris*. Schwob's health forced him to leave Paris for extended periods after 1900, and it is interesting to speculate what assistance he might have given to Jarry. No letters have been discovered between the two men. See Pierre Champion, *Marcel Schwob et Son Temps* (Paris: Grasset, 1927), pp. 104-5.
6. Aurélien Lugné-Poe, *L'Eclair*, January 10, 1922, pp. 90-91.
7. Paul Chauveau, *Alfred Jarry, Ou La Naissance, La Vie, et La Mort du Père Ubu* (Paris: Mercure de France, 1951), pp. 40-41. Hereafter cited in the text and abbreviated as "Chauveau."
8. She used the pseudonym suggested by her brother: "C.-J. Kernec'h de Coutouly de Dorset." This name was partly based on the mother's maiden name. See OCBP, p. xliii.
9. Louis Perche, *Alfred Jarry* (Paris: Editions Universitaires, 1965), p. 50. Hereafter cited in the text and abbreviated as "Perche."
10. In "The Erotic Gestures of Monsieur Ubu, Master of Phynances" ("Les Gestes Erotiques de M. Ubu, Maître de Phynances"), Ubu is referred to as having been king of Greece (OCBP, p. 520). The silly little story is about Ubu taking a bath, and when he is naked he looks like a hippopotamus. Many of Ubu's titles are based upon a particular literary context rather than on a philosophical system.
11. Pierre Des Gachone, *L'Ermitage* 13 (1897), pp. 59-60.
12. Letter to Hérold November, 13, 1896. See OCBP, p. 1056.

13. Some of the expressions were "congre, mangre, crochon, sigre, trrourr du crull, outre boufrre, bouffresque." See Georges Rémond, "Sur Jarry et Autres," *Mercure de France* (April 1955), p. 666.

14. "Merde" becomes "merdre," or "shit" becomes "shitr." See Chassé, p. 40.

15. Jacques-Henry Lévesque, *Alfred Jarry* (Paris: Seghers, 1951), pp. 39-40. Levesque is supported by Georges Rémond, who recalls Jarry saying before the première that the scandal of *King Ubu* will be "greater than that of *Phaedra* or *Hernani.*" See Rémond, "Sur Jarry et Autres," p. 664.

16. *King Ubu* contains many commonly used salacious expressions, but the epitome is "shitr."

17. George Wellwarth, *The Theater of Protest and Paradox, Developments in the Avant-Garde Drama* (New York: New York University Press, 1967), p. 14.

18. Perche, *Alfred Jarry,* p. 74. Michel Arrivé suggests that the name means *bougre-las,* meaning *sodomite passif.* See OCBP, p. 1151.

19. Pierre Mille, *Anthologie des Humoristes Français Contemporains* (Paris: Delegrave, 1925), p. 427.

20. *Cahiers du Collège de 'Pataphysique,* nos. 3-4, p. 85.

21. Edouard Morot-Sir, "Apparition de l'Humour dans la Littérature Française au XXe Siècle," *Bulletin de la Société des Professeurs Français en Amerique* (1970), p. 38.

22. Leonard C. Pronko, *Avant-Garde: The Experimental Theatre in France* (Los Angeles: University of California Press, 1962), p. 4

23. Jacques Robichez, *Le Symbolisme au Théâtre: Lugné-Poe et Les Débuts de l'Oeuvre* (Paris: L'Arche, 1957), p. 394. Hereafter cited in the text and abbreviated as "Robichez."

24. Reference is made to *Tout Ubu,* which was published by the Librairie Générale Française in Paris (1962). This fine edition contains the three *Ubu* plays.

25. *Ubu Cuckolded* was not published until 1944. See OCBP, p. 1187, for a fine chart showing the different sources and changes in the evolution of *Ubu Cuckolded.*

26. An archaeopteryx was a prehistoric flying reptile. It was about the size of a crow and had combined reptilian and birdlike claws. Only two specimens have been found. Mother Ubu maternally speaks of it as being "0 m 25 long, 0 m 30 with feet extended, 0 m 05 in diameter, 0 m 25 in wing span, 0 m 08 earnes [sic] 0 m 04 tail." See OCBP, p. 494.

27. This point supports Arrivé's contention that *Ubu Cuckolded* was written closer to 1894 than 1890. See OCCBP, p. 1185, n. 1.

28. She is one of the characters in *Days and Nights.*

4.

Brilliance in Darkness:
Ecce Homo

Paris—at the end of the century! The Impressionists were in full flower, the Symbolists were well established, and the anarchists were active. But encompassing everything was the series of scandals which permeated the fabric of the culture. Coming in the wake of the disasters of the Franco-Prussian War and the Paris Commune, the scandals so inflamed Frenchmen that only World War I offered effective balm to their feelings.

The first of the great affairs was the Panama scandal (1892-93). Many people, including members of the Jarry family, had been induced to invest in the Panama Canal Company because of its publicity and government support. However, the scandal began when the truth spread that many members of both houses of the national legislature as well as many people in the press had accepted bribes in order to give the appearance of viability so that people would invest in the company. The ruse was successful, but when the company collapsed the financial loss was great and widespread throughout French society. Billfold and bank account have often proven stimuli for the evaluation of governmental reliability and integrity, and such was the reaction of Frenchmen to the Panama scandal.

The loss of confidence in the government was greatly intensified by the Dreyfus affair (1894-1906), which was so grave that the French government almost collapsed. The details of the complex affair are of little importance here; suffice it to note that some military documents were obtained from the German military attaché in Paris which showed that a member of the French General Staff was probably giving information to the Germans. Capt. Alfred Dreyfus, a member of the Staff and a Jew from the Alsace-Lorraine region between France and Germany, was arrested on September 24, 1894, charged with treason, given a secret court-martial, convicted on questionable evidence, condemned to life imprisonment, and sent to Devil's Island in French Guiana. Dreyfus claimed innocence, and the case exposed bitter social, economic, and political schisms in French society. One phalanx was the French army, which wished to conceal its incompetence and corruption, including forgery and concealment of information. Among the army's bedfellows were the anti-Semites. Because of the Franco-Prussian War, many Frenchmen of the Alsace-Lorraine region had moved south, including many of German heritage and Jewish religion. The influx was especially noticeable in Paris, and many anti-Semites saw Captain Dreyfus as a scapegoat for their prejudice. The army was also supported by chauvinists, who, hating the Germans because of the humiliating defeat of France, felt that the army had to be unconditionally supported. Many reactionary Catholics allied with the anti-Dreyfusards because of their fear of the "Red Specter" on the political Left, which was seen as inimical to the resurgence of Catholic political power. These groups were opposed by the socialists and republicans, who eventually won the battle and exonerated Dreyfus, but the contest was bitter and left marked scars for decades.

Jarry was not interested in the political, economic, or social aspects of the scandals, but they did fuel his iconoclasm. The involvement of the army inflamed his instincts to criticize, expose, and defeat. The Dreyfus case had flushed his hated enemy from murky labyrinths camouflaged by medals, ribbons, and flag. Now he sought full measure of revenge for his own experiences with military dehumanization; one result was *Days and Nights (Les Jours et Les Nuits)*, which he finished in April 1897 and published the following month.

Days and Nights is the story of Sengle [1] who, after his induction into the army, finds his refined personality challenged, stunted, and eventually conquered by omnipresent regimen and authority. He quickly learns that "Discipline is the fundamental force of the army," a dictum which requires that the individual submit his will to others and become an automaton (OCBP, p. 763). Obey and never question: rules and orders are sacred, and the slightest infraction of them brings unreasonable punishment. Sengle, for instance, is quickly sentenced to thirty days in prison because he did not salute the flag, which is a requisite but meaningless display of patriotism.

The absurdity of the military is fully reflected in its most humane facet, the medical corps. Jarry's attack on it serves also as an opportunity to disparage another of his favorite targets, doctors,[2] whom he depicts as being ghoulishly inept. In an exaggerated example, a patient has one leg seven centimeters shorter than the other, but the doctor chastises him for trying to "annoy him" and prescribes a "vomitive" (OCBP, p. 774). Another soldier is brought to the hospital with a gunshot wound in the abdomen. After examining him the doctor concludes that "Nothing can be done. Impossible to extract the bullet. Perforated abdomen. . . . The only thing to do is to let him die." After the soldier's death, an autopsy shows that the diagnosis was incorrect and that the man's life could have been saved with "a simple dressing" (OCBP, p. 776).

The refined nature of Sengle is crushed by the military, and his denigration and death represents the organizing theme of the work. While the antimilitary theme of *Days and Nights* unifies the work, Jarry wove other concepts into it which he formulated in response to the scandal of Oscar Wilde, who had been arrested in London in 1895 for "posing as a sodomite," although the charges were subsequently changed to numerous counts of illegal sexual acts. The complex case was initiated by the Marquess of Queensberry, who was convinced that Wilde was defiling and debasing his son, Alfred Lord Douglas, who was Wilde's very close friend. Wilde's subsequent trials and imprisonment received widespread publicity. For the prurient, the Wilde case teemed with tantalizing references to male homosexuality, transvestites, dens of sin, panderers of boys, champagne dinners to lure youths into lascivious acts, homosexual love letters, and passages from a "pornographic" book, Wilde's *The Picture of Dorian Gray* (1890). For the intellectual there were probing questions about the nature of the artist and his art, the relationship of his work to society and its mores, the selection of audience, and many problems of literary criticism.

Wilde's name became well known in Parisian literary circles during his three-month sojourn there in early 1893. He met Hugo, Verlaine, Mallarmé, Gémier, Zola, Daudet, Degas, and Pissarro, among others. He wrote his *Salomé* in French, which was published in Paris on February 6, 1893 and reviewed by Jarry's friends, Marcel Schwob and Pierre Louÿs. Wilde's association with the Parisian literati prepared them for his *cause célèbre*, which was further publicized by Douglas when he visited Paris. He, too, became an intimate of the avant-garde. *La Revue Blanche,* to which Jarry frequently contributed, published some of Douglas's poetry and one of his articles on Wilde's case (June 1, 1896),[3] and he seriously considered publishing some of Wilde's letters to him in the *Mercure de France,* where the subject of male homosexuality was well known after Rachilde published her sensational novel *Monsieur Vénus* in 1889. There is little doubt that the Parisian literati supported Wilde, and Lugné-Poe's presentation of *Salomé* in February 1896 was an overt sign of sympathy. Jarry became aware of Wilde's case and its intellectual and cultural ramifications, not only from his membership in the avant-garde, but because Douglas was frequenting the same artistic and social circles. It was likely that the two men met in one of the literary salons in 1896, and Jarry subsequently brought Douglas to the Théâtre de l'Oeuvre. Jarry met Wilde on May 19, 1898, through the auspices of a mutual friend, Henry Davray, who was Wilde's translator into French as well as the translator of H. G. Wells's *The Time Machine,* which later stimulated Jarry to write a part of *Faustroll.*

Many issues in the Wilde case attracted Jarry, but he focused on Wilde's claim that his relationship with Douglas was platonic rather than sexual, that is, a unique friendship between two very intelligent and sophisticated men. Jarry incorporated Wilde's argument into his own concept of "adelphism," which is fundamental to *Days and Nights*. He defines "adelphism" as a joining with a friend in true comradeship of such intensity that the past is relived as present. It is wonderful, Sengle observes, "to live two different moments of time in one moment" (OCBP, p. 750). This synthesis is quintessential to *Days and Nights,* which depicts the disintegration of this unity.

Jarry's statement of "adelphism" comes as no surprise; several of its foundation stones were laid in *Haldernablou,* and Jarry subsequently expanded and refined them in *Days and Nights.* For instance, he again contends that true friendship is a male preserve, a point which is made early in *Days and Nights* when Sengle recalls escorting two ladies with his "adelphic" friend, Valens. The two men speak infrequently to the women "because [Sengle and Valens] can more intelligently speak to each other" (OCBP, p. 748). Jarry's explanation of this interpersonal relationship is inadequate: they "do not speak to each other because they understand each other well enough to be together" (OCBP, p. 748). Another parallel between "adelphism" and *Haldernablou* is that the relationship between the two men leads to a cosmic sensitivity. Ablou, for instance, experiences Beauty as a consequence of his coupling with Haldern, and Sengle concludes that there is "no astral body more golden or whiter" than his friend (OCBP, p. 748). But there is a difference in the emphasis given to sex because in *Haldernablou* Jarry presents homosexuality as a way of gaining this elevated state of mind, but the sexual motif is not so explicit in *Days and Nights.* By giving scant attention to sex, Jarry is able to highlight other bonds of affection between the two men, but he is most convincing when he describes Sengle's physical attraction for Valens, an emotional and intellectual affinity which exposes the sexual rather than platonic foundation of this friendship.

Jarry intertwines his concept of "adelphism" with his detestation of the army in order to expose the forces which operate upon the refined individual and crush him. Jarry brilliantly uses Sengle to epitomize the point. Initially, the army's regimen forces Sengle to surrender his memories of his enriching relationship with Valens. Shortly after his induction, Sengle thinks that his friend has left France for India, a place so distant that communication is difficult and infrequent (OCBP, p. 767). Reduced to being philosophical about his friendship with Valens, he reasons that it is necessary to know a refined soul in order to judge one's own in relation to it (OCBP, p. 769). Thus, Valens becomes just a concept for Sengle rather than reality, and soon he cannot even remember what his friend looked like; he can only recall parts of Valens's body (OCBP, p. 767). The past for Sengle, including his pleasant thoughts of his friend, becomes a source of sorrow (OCBP, p. 771).

Sengle seeks many ways of escaping his enemies in order to retain his individuality and continue his "adelphic" friendship, but each method fails. He first attempts to use the night to remember his "adelphic" friend because the day is dominated by the military. His attempt is an illusion, a mirage of freedom, and he quickly finds that "night" and "day" are ultimately the same. He recalls one night when he smoked hashish in which his soul's elevation reached the state of some Chinese whose heads become physically separated from the body (OCBP, p. 750). The scene is based on a translation of a thirteenth-century Chinese work called "Leao of the Flying Heads" in which the Leaos, a particular group of Chinese, "have heads which sometimes fly away by cutting a red circular line around the neck, thin like a silk or hemp thread . . . the heads, which disappear during the night, return in the morning" (OCBP, p. 1241).[4] Sengle envisages himself having this ability, a theme which is of little importance until the end of the work.

Signaling the decline of Sengle, this hashish vision metamorphoses into a grotesque scene which is counterpointed to his relations with Valens. Many of the characters in this scene are borrowed from Jarry's personal life: Lord Douglas, for instance, appears as Bondroit; the painter Léonard Sarluis is Raphäel Roissoy; Maurice Cremnitz is Moncrif, Fanny Zaessinger is probably the young girl Huppé, and Ernest La Jeunesse is the Jew, Severus Altmensch (OCBP, pp. xxxiv-v and 1242).[5] Huppé sees Sengle and tells him that "it would be nice to see and have [your] body" (OCBP, p. 750). Sengle changes the subject by suggesting that it would be comical to see Severus Altmensch naked and ascertain if enough of his foreskin has been removed "to make him a eunuch or just enough to mark him as a Jew" (OCBP, p. 750). Huppé agrees, and while Sengle pinions Severus's arms, she removes his pants. The lengthy description of Severus's nude body leads to brief descriptions of those of the others: Severus with an enormous paunch; the twenty-four-year-old Freiherr Suszflache is "only a back and living stomach"; Roissoy has "a very effeminate body like Leonardo's John the Baptist"; Bondroit is rather handsome; but Valens's physique is like the sun and moon, "the most chaste" of all of them (OCBP, p. 751).

The failure of the "artificial paradise" of hashish is followed by a more natural means of hallucinating: illness and fever, which is Sengle's second technique of escaping from the military. Again Sengle remembers his friend, but the thought is brief and is restricted to his beloved's hair and face, which are the color of "yellow gold and of an electric sun or of a round lighting bolt" (OCBP, p. 775). The scene changes and Sengle envisages Valens and himself swimming in the city's natatorium. Jarry repeats the sun imagery when he describes the road to the swimming pool, which is gilded and the flowers and sun are golden (OCBP, p. 778). Such a picture provides an excellent backdrop for the descriptions of Valens's faunlike physique, which Sengle notices when Valens bends down: "his dense muscles of his back laugh with nine delicate vertebrae. His golden tawny chest strikes the flat water, and where his thighs meet each other—browner than the sides" (OCBP, p. 779). However, Jarry punctures the idyllic scene with the death motif, which is represented by an ecclesiastic whom Jarry equates with hell (OCBP, p. 779). This theme is intensified when Sengle's hallucinations metamorphose into scenes of the army, a scalped soldier, a vision of the arterial and venous parts of the heart, the sight of a dissected heart of a gastropod, an Egyptian crocodile embalmed in a glass case, and then a picture of a preserved fetus and two-week-old stillborn children. All these death images culminate in Sengle feeling that blue, nonareated blood is beginning to swell the extremities of his body (OCBP, pp. 784-86).

No longer able to form a hallucinatory vision of Valens either through hashish or fever, Sengle moves to the third stage of his degeneration, which proves to be a vilification of Jarry's old enemy, Christianity. Sengle forms an intellectual substitute for adelphism by conceptualizing Saint Anne, whom he conceives of "as a double astral body, sun and moon," which is a cosmic synthesis reminiscent of Valens (OCBP, pp. 798-99). Following his newly found religion, Sengle seeks confession, during which the priest asks about his health and the ordinary sins of a soldier, such as drunkenness, visiting bawdy houses, and swearing. However, such "sins" hardly apply to Sengle. Christianity, therefore, is inapplicable to him.

Sengle's continued decline is exemplified by his last hashish experience. He recalls taking the drug with two other men, and while the drug permits them to escape from the notion of time and distance (OCBP, p. 823) and then expand their minds toward the sun and moon, which are Jarry's symbols of cosmic synthesis, the men are limited to the small room in which they take the drug. Jarry further depreciates their hallucinations by citing parts of their ridiculous conversation (OCBP, pp. 821-23 and pp. 826-28). The idyllic scene of the sleeping hashish users concludes with the death motif, in this instance the moon, "dispenser of death" (OCBP, p. 829), shining into the room.

In the last visionary scene, which is caused by remembrance rather than hashish, fever, or Christianity, Sengle reexperiences his happiness with his friend, but his memories serve to show how much he has been spiritually enchained and polluted by the army (OCBP, pp. 833-35). Sengle's despair is so great that he knows escape is foolish because all of his visions terminate in images of death. He writes to his friend and ends the letter with a sincere hope that "you become very ill" in order to escape the nightmare of the army (OCBP, p. 830). The theme is elegantly underscored by counterpoining Sengle's situation with his remembrances of Valens's kiss and "the reviviscence of the last walk . . . which was like the celestial music of the spheres" (OCBP, p. 834).

The subtitle of *Days and Nights* is that it is *A Novel about a Deserter,* and now the meaning becomes clear. Awash in the army, Sengle can only "grope in the night toward his Self, which has disappeared" (OCBP, p. 835). In a brilliant metaphor, Jarry tells the story of Sisyphus, who is sentenced by "the Eternal" to try to carry a heavy and uneven rock to the top of a mountain (OCBP, p. 816). The task is seemingly impossible, but Sisyphus, "who was a very wise man" (OCBP, p. 817), outwits "the Eternal." But man is not like Sisyphus; thus, he must submit to God's homicidal nature.

Sengle therefore is condemned to the military and the destruction of his self. Now the work returns to the theme of the Chinese with the "flying heads": Sengle lets his mind fly away; the military experience breaks the cord; and his mind fails to come back from "overseas" (OCBP, p. 837). Thus, he deserts the army—and why should he remain in it? The day is the same as night—visions of the magnificent and the sublime have become the hellish realm of daylight. Day and night, the assault on individuality and refinement continues until the unique and the sophisticated are overwhelmed and crushed.

The militarists cannot, of course, understand Sengle's intellectual and spiritual feat; they are content with a death certificate, which, like the other activities of the doctors, is false. The report notes that Sengle had "heart trouble . . . , was an excellent soldier (not a single punishment)," and "had never given signs of mental trouble" (OCBP, p. 836). His spiritual problem is called "acute mania" (OCBP, p. 836), caused, according to the report, by "some very heavy plaster falling off a wall and hitting him on the head as he worked at his desk, giving his brain a severe shock, which our investigation has substantiated" (OCBP, p. pp. 836-37). With superb execution of the technique he used in *Funeral Songs,* Jarry ends the work with an abrupt sentence which impels the reader to question what he has just been told. Jarry recalls that Sengle had read about the Chinese whose heads would fly "overseas" (OCBP, p. 837), which invites the reader to analyze the army and Sengle's relationship to it.

Philosophically, *Days and Nights* restates Jarry's pessimism, and in this regard there are few surprises: the rejection of Christianity, the inevitability of evil's triumph, the dehumanization of man, and so on. However, one of the most admirable facets of *Days and Nights* is the range of Jarry's artistic technique. The scenes in the hospital show his acerbic nature; the hashish episodes effectively capture a nightmarish quality; and when he describes Valens, Jarry shows a rarely seen sensitivity and compassion. Fortunately, Jarry became adept at expressing understanding and sympathy, and this ability makes some of his later works, such as *Messalina* and *The Supermale,* rich, powerful, and convincing.

One of the most striking attributes of *Days and Nights* is the organization. The technique of integrating the Dreyfus and Wilde motifs is the most complex and ambitious Jarry had attempted, and it shows considerable development and sophistication. The length of *Days and Nights* is also noteworthy. Now he was generating the ability to handle long creations which allows for greater penetration of more sophisticated concepts than were possible in his short poems, plays, and stories. This development of Jarry's artistry was an essential steppingstone to *Faustroll, Messalina,* and *The Supermale.* But his evolution was by no means complete. His mind was capable of formulating very complex and abstract ideas which his artistic abilities did not yet allow him to express effectively. For instance, in *Days and Nights* he discusses the nature of friendship, its relationship to the development of the individual, and the influence of the military on the sophisticated personality. Any one of these concepts would have been worthy of extended treatment, but Jarry did not adequately explore them. "Adelphism," for instance, needs more than a brief definition and several comments. Jarry also has trouble with some of the episodes, which are so intense and compact that they seem divorced from the rest of the work. The description of the grotesque hashish experience exemplifies the point; the reader is not adequately reminded that this episode is but one part of an organized and unfolding presentation. In other cases, such as the attack on the doctors, the examples are so exaggerated that the reader rejects them as being unreal. There is also a question whether Jarry has tempered his disdain for the army adequately so that the work could become more than just another antimilitary novel. There is no doubt that Jarry could have easily extended the subject matter to include the relationship between the individual and society, acceptance and rejection of Christianity, and methods of escapism. Rather than give a profound treatment of these concerns, Jarry is content to subordinate them to his attack on the army, a decision which unfortunately limits the work.

Days and Nights, in spite of its flaws, is, as Arnaud rightly concludes, one of Jarry's finest books (Arnaud, p. 364); ironically, it also marks the end of Jarry's professional relationship with Vallette and the *Mercure de France.* Vallette concluded that he could not continue to publish Jarry's works because they had never been profitable. Moreover, both Vallette and Rachilde thought that Jarry's creations were becoming increasingly incomprehensible if not pornographic. Jarry understood the situation and did not let Vallette's commercialism hinder their friendship. He searched for another publisher, and Rachilde kindly put him in contact with Pierre Fort, who specialized in publishing semipornographic works; it was he who published *The Visits of Love (L'Amour en Visites;* 1898).[6]

The publication history of *The Visits of Love* also adds to its misunderstanding. Fort's professional interest in erotic literature does not mean that *The Visits of Love* should be considered, as Chassé maintains, a catalogue of "erotic experiences" (Chassé, pp. 25-26). Eroticism would certainly be unexpected in Jarry's works because there is nothing in his letters, writings, or remembrances of him to suggest that he was interested in this literary genre. On the contrary: to focus on eroticism would have distracted the reader's attention from the iconoclastic nature of the work, and this is the reason why Jarry correctly stops far short of writing sensuous literature. For instance, in "Manette," Lucien visits a celebrated prostitute, but the scene ends as the two are about to couple, her commenting on his sexual inexperience, and then a depiction of the moon shining in the windows "in large drops of amber" (OCBP, p. 849). Hardly titillating!

The Visits of Love is a collection of vignettes and stories which Jarry had written as early as 1896 when he finished *The Old Man of the Mountain.* The principal group of episodes ("Manette," "Manon," "The Old Dame," "The Great Lady," "The Little Cousin," "The Fiancée," and "The Doctor") are loosely related by the same character, Lucien; however, the predominant unifying force of the collection is the theme of love, which allows Jarry to incorporate "non-Lucien" stories, such as *The Old Man of the Mountain,* "Fear's Visit to Love," "The Muse," and "Madame Ubu." [7] Lebois sees *The Visits of Love* as an autobiographical account of Jarry's sex life,[8] but this assessment is indeed suspect. There is no question that Jarry included incidents from his life in his works, such as *Haldernablou* and *Days and Nights,* but in each case the material can be documented. With one exception, "The Old Dame," this cannot be done for *The Visits of Love;* moreover, many of the episodes contradict known aspects of his life. For instance, the first episode deals with Lucien's visit to Manette, a prostitute, but there is no record that Jarry ever had sexual relations with a woman. Nor was he ever engaged, which is the subject of the sixth story, "The Fiancée." It can be argued that these episodes might be Jarry's vicarious wish fulfillment, but this is unlikely because *The Visits of Love* is a mocking exposé of love. The work is, then, another manifestation of Jarry's iconoclasm and nihilism, not of his subconscious.

The Visits of Love is neither autobiographical, with the exception of "The Old Dame," nor inordinately sensuous; it is an analysis of various manifestations of "love." "Fear's Visit to Love" underscores the absurd nature of love, which is represented by Love's three-handed watch, the first hand of which "notes the hour, the second marks the minutes, and the third—always stationary—shows my indifference" (OCBP, p. 882). This attitude is also reflected in Love laughing at Fear's trepidation, and Her chastisement of Him elicits His frigid comment that "I am loved. That's enough for me" (OCBP, pp. 882-83). But those who love Him are of little interest, and He frankly admits that "I don't think very much about the love-bitten who knock at my door" (OCBP, p. 883).

Because love is absurd, Fear's travel and travail to reach Him can only be ridiculous and tragic. She had to cross a boulevard which was "deserted to infinity, and I walked along a huge wall so high and so long that only the tops of trees could be seen" (OCBP, p. 882). Becoming fearful before the insurmountable obstacles which She had to confront alone, She raised Her head "in order to look for God" (OCBP, p. 883), although She confesses that She does not believe in a deity (OCBP, p. 883). Love rightly states that the search for God is "Absurd. Absurd. Absolutely. Absolutely" (OCBP, p. 883). The same can be said of the expedition to find Him! The rest of Fear's trip is so grotesque that it is similar to a hashish hallucination: "Suddenly the clear water of the sky spins between two roofs and disappears carrying off the stars—all the stars. I was no longer free, my feet were rooted to the earth" (OCBP, p. 884).

Jarry also closely connects love with death, which is by no means a new theme in his work. The motif first surfaced in *Haldernablou,* and "Fear's Visit to Love" is a variation of it. Fear walked along a wall on Her erratic way to Love, and She sensed that behind the wall there was a cemetery (OCBP, p. 882), and later She admits to Love "That it was in your hallway of unhappiness that I had a foretaste of death" (OCBP, p. 884). Although She does not die, She experiences spiritual putrefaction when She fully realizes that although She is in love, Love has no affection for Her (OCBP, p. 888).

Jarry's concept of male supremacy often reappears in *The Visits of Love,* and "The Visit to Manette" epitomizes the theme. Lucien braves a trip through a den of thieves to come to Manette only to find that she wishes to practice her profession. She asks him to leave, but he categorically states that "I have decided to go to bed here tonight—and not to sleep. . . . Take my clothes off" (OCBP, p. 847). It quite quickly becomes apparent that his boorishness is a cover for his sexual inexperience, which becomes obvious when he stammers that he learned about sexual intercourse at school because "First, it develops the muscles. It is excellent for the health! Oh, you won't be the first. . . . I've had eight women before you" (OCBP, p. 847). Although she sees through his act, she quickly yields to him.

Manette's submission to Lucien demonstrates Jarry's contention that a woman is a "cunning animal, deadly, completely stupid" (Chauveau, p. 137), a mindless robot which cannot resist the magnetism of the male. But women, as Jarry recognized, are neither defenseless, weak, nor subservient creatures; they are hunters laying traps and snares for the male. Manette, for instance, "uses a particular pomade smelling of putrified roses" (OCBP, p. 847) in order to lure men to her bed; Manon, "princess of the sidewalk," is "very alluring in her chemise" (OCBP, p. 853); and the "Old Lady" hypnotizes Lucien with her handkerchief, which is scented with "a discreet perfume of good taste" (OCBP, p. 867). And men fall into the traps! Lucien demonstrates how easily they stumble, fall, and are ensnared by such bagatelles as perfume and a handkerchief. The men, then, are as base as the scent bearers and handkerchief wavers.

To Jarry, women are also extremely vain and romantic, a point which he demonstrates in "The Old Dame." Lucien visits the "Old

Dame," who loans him a book, and four months later he dusts it, preparatory to returning it unread, when a note falls out. It is a love letter to him, and its tone and phraseology are ridiculously romantic and antiquated:

> It was for us that the Trojans died in order to keep Helen—Beauty; that the Romans submitted to the barbarians—brutality; that the Indian, after centuries of meditation, discovered Nirvana. . . . Come, our time is near. Come, I will give you time and eternity. . . . Come, and you will reign; come, and I will carry you into boundless space. . . . Come, and you will be the Conqueror. (OCBP, pp. 859-60)

Lucien subsequently visits her, and during his conversation he learns that she washes with vaseline in order "to preserve the delicacy" of her skin, and buys only cheap false jewels "because they have more reflection than true stones" (OCBP, pp. 862-63). Her conversation is so romantically banal that Lucien falls asleep.

"The Old Dame" is more than just an attack on the vanity and romanticism of an aging woman; it is the only autobiographical episode. The piece is a caricature of Berthe de Courrière, the mistress of Jarry's friend, Remy de Gourmont, with whom Jarry had founded *L'Ymagier*. Courrière was born in Lille in 1852, came to Paris when she was twenty, and subsequently made the acquaintance of Cléfinger, a noted sculptor who introduced her to art circles. Following his death, she associated with Huysmans and inspired his novel *Là-Bas;* in 1892 she met Remy de Gourmont and influenced his work. Her pretensions and nymphomania irritated Gourmont's friends, although his eyes were closed by love to their criticisms. One of the friends enlisted Rachilde in a practical joke. The scheme was to hint to the "Old Dame," as she was called, that Jarry was deeply in love with her; the plan was realized, and, as expected, she in turn made romantic overtures to Jarry. She even wrote a letter to him which expressed her affection. This letter became the pattern for the love note in "The Old Dame." When her advances were exposed, she was ridiculed, and Gourmont ended his friendship with Jarry. The story, although insensitive, shows the quintessential nature of a facet of sex and how it can lead people into preposterous situations.

The universal nature of human sexuality and its dominance over rationality surfaced quite early in Jarry's work, and Jarry returns to it in *The Visits of Love*. Jarry depicts "The Great Lady" as a woman whose high social standing and consequent haughty air (OCBP, p. 865) not only divorce her from reality but lead her to believe bourgeois moral platitudes. Specifically, she is lost in her devotion to the unhappiness of the "morally abandoned children" whom she thinks she protects (OCBP, p. 867). But she, like Haldern, finds that her "Pure Thoughts" evaporate before the power of the "subterranean," that is, sexuality. The fragility of her attitude is shown when Lucien becomes hypnotized by her handkerchief and her perfume, falls on his knees, and confesses his love for her. Then he feels the duchess's arms nervously encircling his shoulders like "two supple tentacles of an octopus" (OCBP, p. 869). As she passionately kisses him on the ear and mouth, she murmurs that "The impertinence, my dear, is not in showing [your love]—but in having dared to say it" (OCBP, p. 869). The point is repeated in "The Doctor," in which Jarry discusses the sexuality of nuns. He suggests that their imitation of the lily is a façade, because if they were in the presence of a man they might very well have lustful thoughts (OCBP, p. 881).

The Visits of Love primarily focuses on sexual love, but Jarry is also interested in other forms of it, such as the artist's devotion to his work. Jarry's analysis results in "The Muse," which is one of the most sensitive and pathetic episodes in *The Visits of Love*. Jarry depicts the artist quickly learning that the gardens of the Muse are filled with great tombs, and She tells him that "Only the dead are here" (OCBP, p. 889). The death motif is suspended by a depiction of the artist joyfully reaching Her domicile, and, while having brought many presents for Her, She nonetheless encourages him to depart and closes the door on him. His persistence leads him to evaluate his work, which has proven to be very conservative in technique. He decides that "It is time to invent new rhythms" (OCBP, p. 890). Unfortunately, Jarry does not develop this tantalizing thought. Instead, he continues to discuss the artist's fate: telescoping time, Jarry shows that the poet's efforts lead him to catch cold, the vehicle of his death. He falls asleep and dreams of the Muse, who opens the door and appears almost nude. The poet's excitement and desire for Her is mollified when he realizes that she is blind, emblematic of the absurd manner by which She bestows Her gifts. Her inconsistent nature is shown by Her previous rejection of him, yet as he dies She weeps over him. It is at this moment of death that he has his greatest insight into the nature of art: "death is not eternal . . . death . . . is . . . plagiarizing" (OCBP, p. 893).

Jarry's analysis of love was not restricted to *The Visits of Love;* his correspondence about the publication of this work shows that he wanted to expand it, but the editor insisted on a smaller volume. The latter won the skirmish, and as a result Jarry deleted some episodes, such as *Absolute Love (L'Amour Absolu;* 1899). To Rousseaux, Jarry emerges in this work "as one of the champions of Luciferian poetry. . . . *'Absolute Love* is the book of Genesis and the Passion according to Alfred Jarry—something like the Old and New Testaments reduced to the size of a poem or a history of fifteen short episodes.' " [9] This assessment is too enthusiastic. *Absolute Love* is indeed "Luciferian," but there is scant reason to suspect that Jarry intended so vast a canvas as to restate the Bible. Clancier is much closer to the purport of the work when he concludes that *Absolute Love* is a "novel of metamorphoses, of the mutations of love—and of eroticism" (Clancier, pp. 154-55). The elements of truth in the views of Clancier and Rousseau are easily synthesized: *Absolute Love* is yet another of Jarry's satires on Christianity, one that concentrates on the love roles which Mary had to perform.

The subject matter is most interesting and promising, but Jarry failed to bring the potential to fruition because the episodes wander from subject to subject with little development or integration. For instance, the attack on God rightly belongs at the beginning of *Absolute Love* in order to provide an adequate backdrop for the subsequent episodes, but the subject is not treated until Chapter 12. As is frequently the case in Jarry's writing, the particular episode can be strikingly effective, and this is the situation with Jarry's discussion of the Christian God. Jarry cleverly reasons that "Only God . . . can, knowing *the Truth,* perpetually and in a perfect and varied way, *lie"* (OCBP, p. 950). The result of God's deception is chaos, in which man is continually tripped by the nefarious God. Well might one plead "Lord God, Have pity on us" (OCBP, p. 929), but He has all too frequently demonstrated His callous disregard for man's supplications. Unfortunately, Jarry detracts from the effectiveness of his thesis by presenting a phantasmagoria of logic and assertion which is unsuitable to the purport of the section. As a result, the reader is confused and bewildered, and consequently the impression of a very interesting point is limited.

The first two of the fifteen episodes, "Let There Be Darkness" and "The Christ-Errant," function as an introduction. The reader is informed that the time has come for the arrival of Jesus, whom Jarry calls "Emmanuel God" (OCBP, p. 920) because "Emmanuel" was the original name of Jesus (Isaiah 7:14) and means "God with us" (Matthew 1:23). Rather than being a figure of joy, for Jarry, Emmanuel is a symbol of the Apocalypse: His death signals the forthcoming destruction of man in the Last Judgment and the subsequent engulfment of the earth by fire (OCBP, pp. 923-24). The concept is an interesting one, but Jarry does not adequately develop it. Too many people have had the picture of Jesus as the Lamb of Love inculcated and infused into their minds for them to consider that, theologically, Jarry is correct. Essentially, this is the same position that he stated in *Emperor Antichrist,* but because the assault on Jesus in *Absolute Love* is inadequately organized and developed, it is not the equal of the former work.

By mixing and blending the biblical myths of Moses and Jesus, Jarry finds a rich mine for humor, but here again the tale is too far removed from the knowledge of the average person, who really is not concerned about the story of the naming of the animals, for instance, which is the subject of one of Jarry's biblical tales. Instead of Adam, Emmanuel-God helps name the animals "in light of what they do, the accidents of their orthopedics, and their resulting appearance" (OCBP, p. 931). But "The sight of terrifying beasts caused the little Emmanuel-God to tremble for two days" (OCBP, p. 932). It is highly questionable whether this technique of synthesizing biblical stories is valuable, since the few people who know the creation myth would balk at this deviation in naming the beasts. Moreover, the references to such animals as "rakirs" and "rastons" originated during Jarry's schooling in Rennes, and his willingness to include these terms in *Absolute Love* shows his reluctance to cast off his childish pranks.

Jarry's warping of the Old Testament and the New Testament frequently becomes too imaginative. The presentation of Joseph exemplifies the point. Jarry transforms him into a Breton notary. In this position he does not have to do manual labor, Jarry assures the reader. Lest anyone have the slightest admiration for the man's achievements, Jarry quickly adds that "Joseb," the Breton form of "Joseph," could hardly read or write (OCBP, p. 929). The principal point is valuable: Joseph was an illiterate; thus denied access to great literature, art, and philosophy, he probably remained a desert-roaming boor. It is, of course, miraculous that God would select this kind to be the "father" of His only son when He could just as easily have chosen an educated Greek. But the ways of God are hard to understand or justify.

In the section entitled "The," Jarry attacks Jesus' supposed education, a subject which might well have been delightful and piquant, but it drifts into the inconsequential. Jarry explains that Jesus, at the age of four, went to school in the city, and because all the boys were still dressed like little girls, Jesus uses the feminine definite article when referring to them: *"La* Mecquerbac, *La* Zinner, *La* Xavier [sic]" (OCBP, p. 933). Charlotte notes that Jarry is recounting an actual occurrence from his own school days (OCBP, p. 1261, n. 1). Jesus' experiences allow Jarry to attack the educational system, with its emphasis on the child learning useless facts and the teacher's omnipresent tyranny. The result is a charming episode, but it is questionable whether it belongs in this work, which is ostensibly about Mary, and moreover it is highly probable that Jarry had indeed gone so far afield in his attempt to ridicule Jesus that the result has no effect.

One of Jarry's most interesting techniques is to change the place of Jesus's activity from the Holy Land to Brittany; and judging from the dialect the characters speak, the specific region is the Lampaul area (OCBP, p. 928). The effect is very striking, and by divesting the characters of the geographical aura which has been impregnated into Western man's thoughts about Jesus, Mary, and Joseph, Jarry is better able to ridicule them. A very clever technique, but while brilliant in conception, it fails utterly because he does not develop it. As it remains, it is sophomoric.

Jarry's presentation of Mary is commanding in conception, but it too is disappointing in execution. He conceives of a triune Mary: the Mother of God, wife of Joseph (Varia), and the Virgin—a "very pure Jocasta" (OCBP, pp. 924-25). Jarry utilizes these functions in order to ridicule much of the underpinnings of Christianity, and the subsequent interplay of the tripartite Mary is the strongest part of the work. However, the superb episodes fade into a scene in which Jarry depicts Jesus trying to seduce Varia while she begs for His mercy (OCBP, p. 943), although Jarry immediately adds that "For God to pity would mean the abdication of His divinity" (OCBP, p. 943). Pitiless, Jesus continues his aggression, but Varia bounds to the wall and grabs a sword. What might have been a very promising theme quickly becomes mediocre when Emmanuel, "Naked, arms rigid . . . crucifies himself on the shroud made from the bed" (OCBP, pp. 944-45).

It is regrettable that Jarry was unable to bring *Absolute Love* to fruition because his insights into various facets of Christian love are promising and need exploration. Such inspection was well suited to his talents and sense of humor, but, except for a few charming vignettes, Jarry failed once again to integrate the episodes because he allowed his zeal in ridiculing Christianity to impede his perspective on his work. Consequently, many scenes strain the credulity of the reader, and other episodes are so obtuse or abstract that they fail to communicate. *Absolute Love* is flecked with intriguing items, but the work hardly commands respect or interest.

Although better constructed than *Absolute Love, The Cut of Love (Par la Taille;* 1900, p. 1906) also fails to merit much attention. It, too, satirizes how love beguiles and befuddles men into unjustified egotism. The two principal characters, the Hunchback and the Giant, fall in love with the same girl, and Jarry presents their suffering the "pains of love." Much to the stupefaction of the two men, the girl loves another, an Ordinary Man (OCMC, VI, p. 233). Certainly the subject matter is suitable for comedy, but Jarry's treatment is disappointingly amateurish. The verses are in-

sipid and recall his poems written in St. Brieuc; the rhymes are
stilted and hackneyed, and the buffoonery certainly requires a
defter hand than Jarry's in order to make it effective. The result is
a play which is rightly overlooked and best forgotten.

Jarry's analysis of love in *The Visits of Love, Absolute Love,* and *The
Cut of Love* is hardly noteworthy because of the superficial treatment of the subject. Too frequently Jarry is content with cameos or
brief expositions rather than sustained analysis. Moreover, he is too
often concerned with his attack on Christianity rather than con-
centrating on love. The result is some excellent commentary on
Christianity, but parts of the presentation are frequently irrelevant
to the announced subject. Moreover, his humor sadly lacks the
scintillating quality which he had previously shown. Certainly the
black humor of *King Ubu* is missing, and the aggressive and youthful abandon, which are so clearly present in that work, do not
surface in the statements of love. Thus, while there are a few moments of glitter in *The Visits of Love, Absolute Love,* and *The Cut of
Love,* these efforts are generally lackluster and mediocre.

The post-Ubu period was indeed productive for Jarry. Not only
did he react to the reception of *King Ubu,* but he finished *Days and
Nights,* and worked on *Faustroll;* in 1898 he published *The Visits of
Love, The Little Almanac,* and parts of *Faustroll* (Chapters 6 and 10-
25) in the May issue of the *Mercure de France* and later in *La Plume*
(November 15, 1900); on December 5 he finished the first draft of
The Cut of Love, and the next day he began to supervise the printing
of *The Little Almanac,* which appeared at the end of the month;
and he finished the first act of *Pantagruel* and the Prologue in November 1898. Thus, the period was very productive for Jarry, and
a very happy one, too, perhaps the most rewarding time of his life.
He and the Vallettes and others rented a large house at Corbeil in
1897, and Jarry promptly named it "The Phalanstery." He became infatuated with canoeing, and his other sports included bicy-
cling and fishing. He so refined the latter that he was able to fish
for chickens with a string and hook from a tree which overhung his
neighbor's chicken yard. He also had opportunity to maintain his
proficiency with pistols, and his frequent practice required that he
buy gunpowder by the hundred-pound keg. His exploits with his
pistols became legendary and anecdotal, but his most notorious

deed was his using the apples in his neighbor's tree as targets for pistol practice. When the neighbor's wife complained of the obvious danger to her children, Jarry assured her that if a child were killed, "We will make others with you" (Rachilde, p. 141).[10]

In January 1899 "The Phalanstery" disbanded, and in May 1899 Jarry moved into a house in La Frette with the Vallettes where he stayed until November, and it was here that he wrote *Ubu in Chains.* In early 1900 he moved into a house along the Seine near Coudray, where the Vallettes were then living. The building where Jarry lived was

> an old shed where the mules of the mariners were kept ... the shed, open to all the air currents, became a bedroom, a playhouse, and a kind of bar for fishermen. . . . When one entered one walked alternatively on broken glasses and fish heads. There were drawings on the walls [as well as] circus placards, and jars of gray flowers or bouquets of thistle or blackberry bushes. It was indeed picturesque . . . "Can I sweep your reception room, Father Ubu?" [Rachilde asked]." Then Jarry showed me the beautiful panorama which spread out from his door: "What sweeps, Ma-dam-mah?" "That which blows, Father Ubu." "Good! When a storm blows at night, we will open our door and the crosswind will take care of [the dust and dirt]" (Rachilde, pp. 188-189).

Nearby was a cabaret for sailors where Jarry went for two years and never paid his bill. He reasoned that

> the patrons of this bistro do not dare to complain to me about the large sums I owe them . . . because they know very well that they would lose my business if they demanded payment. But if I stay two days without coming to drink my absinthe, they would not hesitate to cut my throat. I drink in order not to pay what I owe them.[11]

Jarry's contentment is fully reflected in *The Gests and Opinions of Dr. Faustroll, Pataphysician (Gestes et Opinions du Docteur Faustroll, 'Pa-*

taphysicien; p. 1911), the work which dominates his post-*King Ubu* period and which remains the zenith of his mature intellectual and artistic abilities. Whereas *Days and Nights* is clever and thoughtful, and *Messalina* and *The Supermale* sensitive and insightful, *Faustroll* is a pyrotechnical display of erudition, a virtuoso performance of artistic technique, a methodical exposition of what Jarry considers to be man's fundamental philosophical dilemma.

Faustroll has had an uneven reception. Lebois speaks for a considerable number of Jarry scholars when he concludes that *Faustroll* is a "confused bric-a-brac, a garage sale of sparkling and sordid things, the rendezvous of all the finest and the most original of Jarry's thoughts" (Lebois, p. 176). Arrivé agrees and calls *Faustroll* "the most disconcerting" of Jarry's works because of its complexities "and the apparent incoherence of its structure." He concludes that at times "it seems impossible to establish the slightest relation between some of the sections." For instance, he asks what could be the relationship between a voyage "from Paris to Paris by Sea"; the islands visited "representing in reality a literary, artistic, and musical universe . . . ; [a] pseudo-rigorous definition of 'Pataphysics'; descriptions of imaginary tableaux; [and] aberrant calculations . . . about 'the surface of god . . .' " (OCBP, pp. 1216-17). The reactions of Lebois and Arrivé are indeed understandable, but *Faustroll* is not a "confused bric-a-brac"; it is unified according to principles with which Jarry had long experience. Thus, while there is no doubt that *Faustroll* is the most complex of all of Jarry's works, he was nevertheless in complete control of his material.

A second source of the misunderstanding of *Faustroll* is the inordinant attention given to the concept of Pataphysics. [12] Professor Wellwarth views it as epitomizing much of Jarry's philosophy. "Jarry," Wellwarth reasons, "rebelled against all things, both physical and metaphysical, to the point where he had to invent a 'reality' beyond the physical and metaphysical worlds—and thus the calculated insanity of Pataphysics came into being." Thus, Wellwarth continues, Pataphysics is a manifestation of "the ultimate rebel who insisted on building up his own real world after completely rejecting all existing reality" (Wellwarth, pp. 3-4). Wellwarth has astutely seen the nature and extent of Jarry's revolt, but Jarry's nihilism was complete: his work is dedicated to destroying nonrealistic concepts, never to creating one. Roger Shattuck views Pataphysics as "an inner attitude, a discipline, a science, and an art, which allows each man to live his life as an exception, proving no law but his own." [13] This "existential" view is interesting and attractive but inaccurate. Shattuck also sees *Faustroll* as being "the final expression of all of Jarry's attitudes.[14] This conclusion is too enthusiastic and indeed suspect. Chauveau agrees with Shattuck, and like several other scholars he uses Pataphysics as a tool to interpret many of Jarry's previous works (Chauveau, p. 125). The charm and uniqueness of Jarry's concept has proven to be an opiate. In reality, Pataphysics is only a small part of *Faustroll*. It is one of forty-seven chapters in the work, two pages out of seventy-seven in the Bibliothèque de la Pléiade edition—two pages out of the thousands Jarry wrote.

There are two keys to understanding *Faustroll* on the title page. The first is Faustroll's name, which is a synthesis of Faust and troll.[15] The name succinctly represents one of Jarry's conclusions that man is an earthbound creature capable of the Faustian search to know the mysteries of the universe. This attitude is hardly new in Jarry's work; he had outlined the dilemma of man's dual nature in *The Second Life, Or Macaber* and *Haldernablou.* He expanded the theme in his early experiments in toying with the reader's rationality in order to engender in him a sense of elevation and recognition of "universals," such as human lust, greed, and imbecility. The theme is the foundation stone of *Emperor Antichrist* in which he shows that "Man is the mean between Infinity and Nothing" (OCBP, p. 280). The concept is also an integral part of *King Ubu* where Jarry exposes man's nature—and the spectator's ability to understand and react to "universals." Jarry considerably refined and extended the concept of protoplasmic man being able to formulate abstractions in *Faustroll*, which focuses on the Faustrollian dualism central to artist and scientist alike, represented by the subtitle, *Neo-Scientific Novel*, the second key. The thesis of *Faustroll*, then, is that man is trapped inextricably in an unending duality, fated to bound between the terrestrial and the ethereal, rebound between art and science, eternally ricochet between truth and fiction. The line of demarcation between these alternatives is sometimes very difficult to discern, as Jarry demonstrates in the work, but his analysis and presentation of the quintessential problem allows him to probe and critique many theories and assumptions of Western thought.

Briefly, *Faustroll* is the story of a fanciful voyage made by three people: Dr. Faustroll, a bailiff named René-Isidore Panmulphe, and a servant called Bosse-de-Nage. The work begins with Panmulphe trying to serve a summons on Dr. Faustroll for failure to pay his rent. Panmulphe, which means "All Snout," is a denigration of the bureaucrat who, obsessed with paper, stamps, and legal technicalities, officiously tries to enforce the laws and responsibilities of the bourgeois infatuated with "law and order." Fortunately, Panmulphe's mundane vision proves useless when confronted by this counterpart, Dr. Faustroll, who is a fanciful being:

> born in Circassia in 1898 . . . at the age of sixty-three . . . which he kept all of his life, Dr. Faustroll was a man of medium height . . . yellow-gold complexion; he did not have a beard except for sea-green whiskers, like those in the portrait of King Saleh; the hairs of his head were alternatively . . . dirty blond and jet black, [an] auburn ambiguity which changed with the sun; his eyes were two pools of ink . . . with golden spermatozoa in it. (OCBP, pp. 658-59)

Jarry continues by describing Faustroll's clothing and then notes his hands, especially the right index finger upon which he wore many emerald and topaz rings—"piled up . . . to the fingernail . . . the rings were kept from falling off by a molybdenum pin screwed into the ungual phalanx bone of the finger" (OCBP, p. 659). This technique of juxtaposing reality and fantasy in *Faustroll* closely resembles the method of *The Report of the Terrible Accident.* For instance, the unreality of Faustroll's "sea-green whiskers" is counterpointed to the assertion of reality, in this case reference to King Saleh, and then the place of birth is juxtaposed to his date of birth, which is also the year when Jarry recopied the manuscript of *Faustroll.* The duality of Faustroll's dress also exemplifies the technique of counterpointing imagination and science. Faustroll's rings, for instance, are attached in a scientific manner, replete with references to the specific metal used and the bone to which the screw is attached.

After establishing the dualism, Jarry proceeds to show that the distinctions between reality and fantasy are frequently difficult to discern. The point is made with regard to literature when Panmulphe lists Dr. Faustroll's twenty-seven "Equal Books," which includes a volume of Poe translated by Baudelaire, Coleridge's *The Rime of the Ancient Mariner*, Galland's translation of *The Thousand and One Nights*, Lautréamont's *The Chants of Maldoror*, *Verse and Prose* by Mallarmé, Rabelais, *The Illuminations* by Rimbaud, Verlaine's *Wisdom*, *Voyage to the Center of the Earth* by Jules Verne, and *King Ubu*. Poe's *The Raven* exemplifies Jarry's point. The poem is, of course, intentionally fanciful, as Poe explains in *The Philosophy of Composition*, but the force and verve of the poem drive the reader to "suspend his disbelief" and accept the world of imagination as reality. Lautréamont demonstrates another aspect of the blurred line of demarcation between fiction and reality when he uses the bizarre and macabre *The Chants of Maldoror* to demonstrate facets of man and nature, such as man's lust for absolutes, his pleasures in being cruel to others, the absurdity of life, and the malignancy of the cosmos. Where, then, does reality end and imagination begin? Jarry ends the list of "Equal Books" with Verne's *Voyage to the Center of the Earth* to show how realistic fiction can be.

Jarry proceeds to examine in Chapter 6, "The Doctor's Boat, Which Is a Sieve," how science can be so revolutionary that it might be considered fictional. Such was the work of Charles Vernon Boys (1855-1944), a British scientist whose essay "Soap Bubbles and the Forces Which Mould Them" (1890) [16] is a famous analysis of surface tension. This study resulted in extraordinary experiments which almost defy imagination. For instance, Faustroll remarks that by using Boys's findings, webbed sacks have been invented which can hold water but which are porous to air and steam, and he speaks of his "confrère," F. De Romilly, actually boiling water in a pan, the bottom of which was gauze mesh (OCBP, pp. 663-64). With the communication of this scientific information, Jarry then extends it into the realm of fiction. He first experimented with this technique in an essay he wrote to supplement H. G. Wells's *The Time Machine*. Jarry knew the novel well because it was translated into French by his friend, Henry D. Davray, and it appeared in the December 1898 and January 1899 issues of the *Mercure de France*. Wells was interested in presenting various conclusions about human nature, and he omitted some technical aspects of the time machine; Jarry furnished this information in the February 1899 edition of the *Mercure de France:* "Dr. Faustroll, 'Commentary for the Practical Construction of a Machine to Explore Time.' " ("Commentaire pour servir à la construction pratique de la machine à explorer le temps;" December 1898). As he had done in *The Report Explaining the Terrible Accident*, Jarry intersperses numerous references to facts throughout the essay in order to give it a tone of scientific veracity. For instance, he logically discusses the interrelationship of time and space, elaborates the qualities of the time machine, describes its construction, and then gives various calculations for its movement through time (OCBP, pp. 735-43). He uses the same technique of packaging fantasy in science when he presents Faustroll's boat, which is constructed "according to" Boys's scientific principles: the boat is twelve meters long and

> is shaped like an elongated sieve. The mesh is open enough to let a large pin pass through; and the entire sieve has been dipped in melted paraffin, then shaken in such a way that this substance . . . while covering the woof and warp, has left the holes—approximately 15,400,000—open. The film of water . . . stretches over the holes, and the liquid flowing underneath cannot pass through. (OCBP, p. 664)

The result is a marvelously clever piece of fiction which, because of the effective use of scientific theory, is startlingly believable.

As *Faustroll* has rebounded from the verisimilitude of literature toward fictionalizing science, so Jarry now (Chapter 7) bounds back by fictionalizing the realism of literature. This is accomplished by being microscopically analytical. For instance, Jarry forces the reader to select a single fact from the "Equal Books," such as Lautréamont's famous image of "the beetle, beautiful like the trembling hands of an alcoholic." The result is, of course, ridiculous. Another example is taking "the fifth letter from the first word of the first act of *King Ubu,*" which is the last letter in "shitr" (OCBP, pp. 665-67). In both cases, the intention of the work and its value are lost because of this inordinate concern for minutiae. As in the "Lintel" to *The Records of the Black Crest,* Jarry invites the reader to decide for himself whether the microscopic investigation of a work is rewarding.

The first seven chapters of *Faustroll* place the reader's mind at a "crossroads" between fact and fantasy, reason and imagination. The principal method is to becloud the line of demarcation between the two elements and then to show that when the fanciful becomes too imaginative it loses it verisimilitude and value. However, the picture is incomplete because Jarry has not applied the same principle to science; he finishes the cycle with his statement of Pataphysics.

The theory of Pataphysics has received so much unwarranted attention that it is essential to recall not only the position of Pataphysics in *Faustroll* but its history in Jarry's work. The expression "pataphysics" is by no means unique to *Faustroll,* and the previous appearances of the word have proven to be seedbeds of considerable misunderstanding. The term appears in the Preface to *Being and Living* (April 23, 1893), in which Jarry excerpts parts of the dialogue between Ubu and Achras in *The Uninvited Guest,* which was published in *L'Echo de Paris* on the same date (OCBP, p. 341). Specifically, Achras reads Ubu's calling card and learns that Ubu is "ex-King of Poland and Aragon, Doctor of Pataphysics" (OCBP, p. 496). The term is not defined until scene iii, when Ubu announces that Pataphysics is "a science which we have invented and for which the need is becoming generally felt" (OCBP, p. 497). There is no elaboration, nor can the intent of the expression be justifiably inferred from the Ubu episode. Moreover, it would be erroneous to conclude that Jarry had precisely defined the expression. The situation is quite the opposite; these quotations within the context of *Ubu Cuckolded* show that Jarry was using the term as a schoolboy's ridicule of a professor's vocabulary.

On the reverse side of the title page of *The Records of the Black Crest* Jarry noted that *Elements of Pataphysics* was "in preparation," although there is no reason to suppose that he had clearly defined the term. It then appears in a fragment of "About the Physik-stik" in *Real and Future Visions* (May-June 1894), and Arnaud concludes that it was about this time that Jarry was "in full possession of his doctrine" of Pataphysics (Arnaud, p. 127). It is true that Jarry offers a definition: Pataphysics is "the science of . . . beings and machines, real or future, with the Power of their Usage" (OCBP, p. 341). This definition is hardly workable, and the chaotic context of *Real and Future Visions* does not provide any assistance in understanding the expression. However, this definition demonstrates that Jarry was experimenting with varied usages of the expression, and the extant ones were not intended to complement each other. The word *Pataphysique* next appears in the title of a prose work, *The Pataphysics of Sophrotatos the Armenian*, which was written about 1894, but the expression is once again left undefined. The term disappears from Jarry's vocabulary for almost four years, a surprising omission if he felt the term was significant. Morever, Jarry makes no use of it in *King Ubu*, which is markedly indebted to *The Uninvited Guest*. The expression suddenly appears in the title of Book IV, Chapter 2 of *Days and Nights*, but it is once again undefined, although the episode focuses on some of Sengle's experiences with understanding the world and cosmos. Jarry then uses the expression in Chapter 39 of *Faustroll*, "According to Ibicrates the Geometer." This section is an integral part of the central theme of *Faustroll* but not to the discussion of Pataphysics in Chapter 8. For instance, Ibicrates refers to the Pataphysics of Sophrotatos the Armenian, but the chapter focuses on a subject unrelated to Pataphysics. The term is used solely to give a tone of authority to Ibicrates' statement. Then Pataphysics appears significantly in *Faustroll*'s Chapter 8 where it brilliantly satisfies the demands of the work's organization. The context of the expression is most important: immediately prior to the chapter on Pataphysics, Jarry shows how the verisimilitude of fiction is lost when fantasy becomes so extreme that the mind cannot accept it; now the organization necessarily rebounds to science in order to show that when the logic of science is overextended, the result is what Shattuck rightly calls "brilliant anti-reason" (Shattuck, p. 211).

Jarry wisely begins his presentation of Pataphysics by discussing the etymology of the word in order to show that it represents an extreme position. He rightly states the ancient Greek dichotomy between nature *(∅ysis)* and those ideas not related to or which are beyond nature *(meta∅ysis)*. Jarry defines "Pataphysics" as "the science of that which is superinduced on metaphysics, whether within or beyond it, extending as far beyond metaphysics as the latter extends beyond physics . . . pataphysics will be, above all, the science of the particular. . . . It will study the laws which govern exceptions and will explain the universe supplementary to this one" (OCBP, p. 668).

Jarry then proceeds in strict accordance with the "scientific method" of definition and elaboration:

> Definition: *Pataphysics is the science of imaginary solutions, which brings into harmony symbolically to the lineaments the properties of objects depicted by their potentiality.*
> The actual science is based on the principle of induction: the majority of men have seen most often a particular phenomenon preceded or followed by another, and conclude that it will always be like that. But this is only the most frequent case because of one's viewpoint, and it is codified according to convenience. (OCBP, p. 669)

The ensuing discussion wanders in a stream-of-consciousness manner, although the tone and formal vocabulary retain the atmosphere of erudition.

The chapter on Pataphysics ends with a colon, which signals a formal explanation to follow, but the subsequent chapter, "Faustroll Smaller than Faustroll," seems tenuously related to Pataphysics. However, the two chapters are integrated by the organizing principle of *Faustroll*: the work rebounds from the overextension of science to the advanced study by Sir William Crookes, an English physicist and chemist (1832-1919). He was known in France for his work on the relativity of human knowledge and the problems of the infinitely small, which was published in French in May 1897. In order to clarify his thesis, Crookes tells a story of a minuscule man placed on a cabbage leaf; Jarry uses the story by grafting Faustroll onto it. Thus, the chapter effectively functions to demonstrate the Pataphysical principle of the relativity of knowledge.

With the chapter on "Faustroll Smaller than Faustroll," the examination of science and its relation to fantasy comes to an end and Jarry returns to the theme of extreme imagination, which he had previously treated by extending the "Equal Books." That chapter ends with the promise that the third character in the book will be introduced. However, the subsequent section deals with Pataphysics, but Jarry resolves the suspension immediately after discussing "Faustroll Smaller than Faustroll." As the "Elements of Pataphysics" and "Faustroll Smaller than Faustroll" are related by the movement from the theory to the particular, so "Equal Books" moves from the sublime to the ridiculous: "The Large Cynocephalus Monkey Hump-o-Rump Which Only Knew the Human Word 'Ha Ha,' " which is a chapter about Christian Beck.

The work then moves on to Faustroll's voyage, and most of the next twenty-five chapters are dedicated to writers, artists, and musicians. These sections are also organized according to the fundamental duality of idealism and realism, such as those people who were admirable creators and those who were artistic cretins. The elite corps is composed of such people as Thadée Natanson; Vallette; Aubrey Beardsley; Léon Bloy; Franc-Nohain, who helped establish *Le Canard Sauvage* in 1903, a periodical to which Jarry frequently contributed; Paul Gauguin; Gustave Kahn, who was one of the first critics to befriend Jarry; Mallarmé; Henri de Régnier; Marcel Schwob; Laurent Tailhade; Claude Terrasse; Rachilde; Valéry; Pierre Quillard, who lived with Jarry at Corbeil and founded *La Pléiade,* a magazine which preceded the *Mercure de France;* A. F. Hérold, who was a fine poet and translator from Greek, Latin, and Sanskrit; Pierre Bonnard, a painter and decorator; Paul Fort, founder of the Théâtre d'Art in 1891 which was a forerunner of the Théâtre de l'Oeuvre; the anarchist Félix Fénéon, who contributed to *La Revue Blanche* and gave significant encouragement to Jarry; and Louis Dumur, also one of the founders of the *Mercure de France.*

Such were the elevated and sophisticated, the creators and achievers; Jarry then rebounds into the realm of the mundane, and this theme is devoted to those who were incapable of superior work and who remain negative force fields in the realm of art. One such is Christian Beck (1879-1916). He had become a friend of Jarry's through the auspices of the *Mercure de France*, to which he contributed from 1896 to 1897, sometimes using the pseudonym "Joseph Bossi." The animosity between Beck and Jarry began at a dinner party, and while the precise cause remains a mystery, the conflict became physical. Beck's name would be forgotten except that one of Jarry's most memorable characters, "Hump-o-Rump," [17] is named after him. Jarry describes the character as "a large cynocephalic monkey, less cyno- than hydrocephalic, and because of this defect he was less intelligent than his fellow cynocephalic monkeys" (OCBP, p. 672). His knowledge of language is limited to pronouncing a few words with a Belgian accent and calling the lifebelt at the stern of Faustroll's skiff "swimming bladder with writing over it" (OCBP, p. 672). His most frequent utterance is "a tautological monosyllable: Ha ha" (OCBP, p. 672). This oaf is fit only to draw Faustroll's skiff onto the bank each time Faustroll decides to stop (OCBP, p. 675). Jarry also uses Hump-o-Rump to remind the reader of gross reality by frequently having him utter "ha ha" after an episode dealing with the creators and cognoscente.

Jarry also castigates and berates "Louis L. . . . ," a faintly disguised reference to "Louis Lormel," the pen name of Louis Libaude (1896-1922). He founded a small literary journal in 1892, *L'Art Littéraire*, which became the first periodical to publish Jarry's work. Later, he and Jarry quarreled; this led Libaude to publish *Entre Soi* (1897) in which he implied that Jarry and Fargue were homosexuals. Jarry took his revenge in the twelfth chapter of *Faustroll*, which he had finished by the spring of 1898. In this chapter Libaude is described as "sterile and dreary" (OCBP, p. 676), and his associates are called by the Pataphysicians "Shit Diggers" (OCBP, p. 677).

The second section of *Faustroll* terminates with the end of Faustroll's voyage and his death (Book XXXV); the third part of *Faustroll* expands the fact-fantasy dualism into an examination of religion and cosmology. Faustroll dies, but death, he says, "is only for the mediocre" (OCBP, p. 724). From "the kingdom of the unknown dimension" (OCBP, p. 723) he sends two "telepathic letters" to his "dear confrère," Lord Kelvin,[18] whose investigations into solar energy, electricity, and magnetism are justly famed. The first letter provides a fine example of Jarry's humor as he mocks the concept of "ethernity" and afterlife. Faustroll uses his "post-humous leisure" to examine the ether of this region, and his erudite study enables him to report to Kelvin that his "astral body" ad-heres "exactly to the ideal mathematical conditions postulated by Navier, Poisson, and Cauchy." [19] Moreover, Dr. Faustroll also ver-ifies that Faraday [20] was correct in his work on the polarization of light (OCBP, p. 727). The second letter to Kelvin exemplifies sci-ence gone insane. Faustroll states as truth a rhetorical hypothesis of Kelvin: "The sun is a cold, solid, and homogeneous globe. Its sur-face is divided into squares of one meter, which are the bases of long inverted pyramids . . . [which] point to one kilometer at the center" (OCBP, p, 727). The veracious tone of this statement is intensified by Faustroll's name-dropping, but this technique is only a varnish of verismilitude to his error.

As Jarry treated science as it deals with cosmological problems, so he treats religion and its focus on theology. As his work has shown, Jarry found this subject to be one of the most fertile for his erudition and wit, and *Faustroll* is no exception. Chapter 41 is a delightful mockery of the pitiful attempts by theists to prove math-ematically various elements of their beliefs. Jarry addresses the problem of "The Surface of God," and his mathematical calcula-tions are authoritative, clearly formulated, and logically presented. From these calculations, he initially concludes that *"God is the short-est distance between zero and infinity"* but quickly notes that "God, being without extension, is not a line, but a point." "Therefore, *definitively: God is the tangential point from zero to infinity"* (OCBP, pp. 733-34).

Jarry ends *Faustroll* by returning to Pataphysics, which is the logical extension beyond God; but now science and fiction, fact and fantasy, literature and science, imagination and reality result in no definitive conclusions; thus, the examination of that which is beyond metaphysics must end without answer. Jarry terminates *Faustroll* with the incomplete sentence that "Pataphysics is the sci-ence . . . " (OCBP, p. 734). The reader, then, is left at the ultimate and final "crossroads."

So ends Jarry's masterpiece, *The Gests and Opinions of Dr. Faustroll,*

Pataphysician, It is unquestionably his most complex achievement, both philosophically and artistically. It is Jarry at the height of his powers and prowess: confident of his erudition, experiences in his craft, mature in perspective, wonderfully youthful in his zest and playfulness. Some of the most delightful moments are found in his descriptions of his friends; and his delight in, appreciation of, and respect for them overpowers his pessimism. Well might he salute them, but they pose a major problem: How did they become illustrious? Are they biological mutants or self-made? How did they succeed where Sengle failed? Can their presence and work significantly influence others? Such questions failed to attract Jarry; he was content to note that many of his friends were memorable stops on Dr. Faustroll's aimless voyage. Unfortunately, Jarry's satisfaction does not sate the reader's justified curiosity.

Jarry's compressed style serves him well when depicting friends because the cameos are superbly drawn. At times, however, the brushstrokes are so fine that only an intimate of Jarry's circle would understand let alone appreciate the pictures, but the dedications to individual people provide a useful guide. The variety of cameos is also impressive. Each picture is drawn with such remarkable attention to detail and with such a superb eye for the most salient personal qualities that the montage brilliantly depicts the end-of-the-century attitudes and concerns of the avant-garde.

Faustroll, then, is a strange work: a brilliant depiction of people and ideas, an intimate view of intellectual and artistic attitudes, an intriguing critique of Christian theism; a labyrinth of problems from which the reader can escape only with the infrequent signposts and dim signal lights. *Faustroll* also shows Jarry's intellectual profundity and his dedication to free thought and expression. *Faustroll,* in this regard, restates Jarry's attitude in *King Ubu:* art must never become "preserved." He salutes those creators who have dared criticism and failure in order to look anew, experiment with novel relationships of fact and fantasy, and thus achieve the unique and meaningful. Of course mistakes will be made—and Jarry made many—but *Faustroll* exemplifies how an experiment, replete with error, can still be justifiably judged brilliant and masterful. *Faustroll* is a tribute to himself and a trailmarker to those yet to follow.

While *Faustroll* represents the continuing evolution of some facets of Jarry's artistry and philosophy, its optimism is unexpected and unique. Those happy days Jarry spent at "The Phalanstery" and Coudray proved to be few; ahead were years of terrible poverty and illness which forced him to surrender his optimism and return to misanthropy. As in the past, this attitude spawned some of his finest work, especially *Messalina* and *The Supermale*. Although his last years were strikingly productive with most of his work being hastily written for a commercial market, *Messalina* and *The Supermale* remain remarkable achievements and valuable gifts of Alfred Jarry.

Notes

1. A quotation from Rutebeau, a thirteenth-century French troubador, poet, and writer. The reference is to the relations between Sengle and his friend.
2. Jarry changed *médecins* into *merdecins,* that is "doctors" into "dungsters."
3. "Une Introduction à Mes Poèmes avec Quelque Considérations sur L'Affaire Wilde."
4. Hervey de Saint-Denys, *Ethnographie des Peuples Etrangers à La Chine* (Genève: H. Georg-Th. Mueller, 1877-1882). "Leao of the Flying Heads" is one of the chapters. See OCBP, p. 1241.
5. The autobiographical facets of *Days and Nights* are reflected in the portraits of other charcters. Lieutenant Vensuet is Jean Tixier, a lieutenant in the regiment in which Jarry served. Nosocome was Maurice Dide, a medical student and close friend of Jarry's. See OCBP, p. 1242, n. 756; p. 1244, n. 776.
6. The varying styles of this work suggest that it is yet another example of Jarry stitching together various vignettes he had written earlier, perhaps, as "Madame Ubu" shows, as early as his Rennes years.
7. Initially Jarry included *The Other Alceste* in this collection, but it was deleted because the editor thought the manuscript too long. See OCBP, p. 1249. Jarry's original organization for his work is outlined; see OCBP, pp. 1248-49.
8. André Lebois, *Jarry L'Irremplaçable* (Paris: Le Cercle du Livre, 1950), p. 105. Hereafter cited in the text as "Lebois."
9. André Rousseau, *Le Monde Classique* (Paris: Editions Albin Michel, 1956), vol. 4, pp. 250-51. He cites Maurice Saillet; "Relativement à

L'Amour Absolu," *Cahiers du Collège de 'Pataphysique,* nos. 8-9 (1952), p. 69.

10. For other anecdotes, see André Gide's *The Counterfeiters;* Roger Shattuck, *The Origins of the Avant-Garde in France: 1885 to World War I* (New York: Vintage, 1968); and Guillaume Apollinaire, *Il Y A . . .* (Paris: Editions Messein, 1925).

11. Sacha Guitry, *Souvenirs* (Paris: Plon, 1934), vol. 1, p. 177.

12. The apostrophe is used in French to avoid a pun ("pattes à physique"); the apostrophe is frequently omitted in English.

13. Roger Shattuck, "What Is 'Pataphysics'?" *Evergreen Review,* no. 13 (May-June 1960), p. 30.

14. Shattuck, *The Banquet Years,* p. 243. Hereafter cited in the text as "Shattuck."

15. A troll is a nature spirit sometimes conceived of as a giant, sometimes as a dwarf. It was thought to live underground or in caves. A troll was also thought to have prophetic powers. Jarry learned about trolls from his acting the part of the Old Courtier Troll in Ibsen's *Peer Gynt,* which was produced by Lugné-Poe.

16. This essay was translated into French in 1892. See OCBP, p. 1222.

17. His name is "Bosse-de-Nage." "Bosse" is a play on Beck's pseudonym, although the word means "hump" of a camel; *nage* or *nache* in Old French means buttocks or rump.

18. Lord William Thomson, 1824-1907.

19. Denis Poisson, 1781-1840; celebrated French mathematician. Baron Augustin Cauchy, 1789-1857; French mathematician.

20. Michael Faraday, 1791-1867; English physicist and chemist.

5.

Thus Spoke Alfred Jarry:
The Prophetic Vision

Jarry rebounded from the hermeticism of *Faustroll* and exploded
with two brilliant works, but, tragically, they never gained the
audience he so ardently desired. The first of these achievements is
Messalina (Messaline), a novel which he published in fragments
from July 1 to September 15, 1900; the book appeared in 1901.
The novel focuses on the historical figure of Messalina, the profli-
gate empress of Rome who was executed in 48 A.D. Massat, editor
of the Monte Carlo edition of Jarry's "complete works," suggests
that Jarry retells her story,[1] but this interpretation is suspect because Jarry recognized that he most certainly was not a historian.
He consistently used the past to expose points pertinent to modern
man. Jarry's attitude toward history is fully reflected in *Days and
Nights* where he utilizes contemporary events, such as the Panama,
Wilde, and Dreyfus scandals, to exemplify problems, themes, and
conditions. *Messalina* is no exception; it is a tool by which Jarry
presents some of his conclusions about the human animal's ability
to gain happiness.

The philosophic underpining of *Messalina* is found in *Haldernablou.* While the degree of artistry and philosophy between the

two works demonstrates Jarry's remarkable creative and intellectual development, their similarities show that the former was indeed the progenitor of the latter. For instance, in *Haldernablou* Jarry concludes that man is a sexualized protoplasmic creature striving toward absolutes, a theme which reappears in *Messalina* where man is depicted as a beast trapped between Venus and brute (OCMC, III, p. 27). Messalina, like Haldern and Ablou, combines both the abstract and concrete, but Jarry had so matured artistically that she becomes a more sophisticated and significant representative of his views than Haldern. He is a pallid person vacillating among "Pure Thoughts," homosexuality, and Christianity, but she is a tellurian goddess, "Earth begetting life . . . the bride of Pan" (OCMC, III, p. 20), the sycophant of the male gods of love: Priapus, Bacchus, Mercury, and Phallus (OCMC, III, p. 33). But she is also "a very expert and irresistible prostitute" (OCMC, III, p. 96) who wants to experience the ecstasy of sexual intercourse, and as a prostitute she hopes to enjoy "unbroken moments of love" (OCMC, III, p. 22). Jarry delights in describing her seeking her goal "in one of [the] basest brothels. . . . Buckets of excrement are on the doorstep, and on each side of the brothel the storefronts of the butcher and hangman are cracked . . . in the executioner's window a bloodstained whip is drying; on the closed shutters a dragon has been painted in order to scare off the children who might piss against the shopfront and the tramps who might steal sausages" (OCMC, III, p. 20). Messalina enters the brothel, goes to her cell, and soon her first customer appears. He is a soldier, and their sexual activity serves to inflame her desire, which leads her to copulate with an athlete, a gladiator, a chariot driver; and "other men came, and others, and others" (OCMC, III, p. 24).

Messalina's sexual encounters leave her unsated because the line of men ends. Confronting the ephermeral nature of her sexual pleasure, she decides that she must seek a supermale, "the beast-god who never sleeps. . . . Man always erect" (OCMC, III, p. 22). She accelerates her search for Happiness, a trip which, like Fear's visit to Love in *The Visits of Love,* proves labyrinthine. Ultimately, her search returns to sexual gratification, but this cyclical quest has driven her insane, and it is ironical that only in madness can she find her god and happiness. Her expedition has led her to have extramarital affairs, and when her husband learns about one of them he orders Messalina killed; the emperor's soldiers mindlessly carry out his dictum. The insane Messalina sees the approaching soldier and, thinking that the drawn sword is a phallic symbol of Phallus, she ecstatically plunges the knife-penis into her body. "Oh, Happiness, how you hurt me! Kill me, Happiness! . . . I knew very well that one could only die of love" (OCMC, III, pp. 109-10). Early in the work Jarry prophesied that "the crimson stem of love [is] the twin of the bloody sword of steel: the god which fecundates also sows death" (OCMC, III, p. 49). *Messalina* demonstrates the fateful veracity of *Haldernablou:* love is homicidal.

Jarry's examination of love easily permits him to investigate marriage and to ridicule it, especially the marriage vows. He exposes the fantasy of people thinking their mutual love is so binding that it can be broken only by death or God. Jarry overwhelms this ideal by showing that Messalina continues to have amorous affairs, each as sincere as the last. One of the most blatant and torrid was the affair with a young patrician, Caius Silius Silanus, the handsomest of the Romans. He had recently married Junia, but he yields to the seductive nature of the empress, divorces his wife, and marries Messalina in the ceremony called *confarreation.* Jarry notes that this "was an indissoluble union, without the possibility of divorce." But Silanus was married in this same ceremony to Junia (OCMC, III, p. 93). Ceremonies, then, prove to be fragile bonds. Well might the representative of priestcraft smile when the couple naively promises to love, honor, and obey forever. Messalina states the truth: "the lover of that very minute was her legitimate husband" (OCMC, III, p. 94).

Jarry interrupts the plot's development in order to present his last major aesthetic statement. This occurs in the scene when the mime Mnestor dances for the emperor and empress. Jarry informs the reader that Mnestor's name was *"Nester* or *Nestor* or *Vester"* (OCMC, III, p. 50), a reference to Nestor, the Greek hero whom Homer describes as "the lucid speaker . . . from whose lips the streams of words ran sweeter than honey." [2] Moreover, Nestor has become wise because of his active participation in life and, in old age, gaining proper perspective on it. Because of his abilities, consequently, he is the one who teaches the other warriors by engendering in them the capability to inspect their own thoughts and actions. Jarry recasts Nestor into Mnestor, a poet-seer who, through his artistic wizardry, mesmerizes the spectators with his knowledge and brilliance. The climactic moment of his performance occurs during a dance when each part of his body is followed by a fragment of the sun. Portraying the artist's inability to accept traditional cosmology, he uses his art to juggle "with the sun's wreckage" (OCMC, III, p. 71). Because the masses cannot understand the artist, they consider him to be an "evil omen" (OCMC, III, p. 73). Jarry's point is inadequately developed. What are these truths the poet-seer knows, and how does he know them? Jarry does not provide answers; he is content to assert and believe rather than substantiate.

Mnestor taught that traditional cosmology is no longer tenable because its "sun" is "wrecked." But where Mnestor lacks the courage to demolish the "sun"—he admits that he "would no longer know how to restore it" (OCMC, III, 71)—Jarry-Macaber, unlike Mnestor-Faust, carry out their desires to the fullest extent, and the result is a restatement of *Emperor Antichrist*'s cosmology. Jarry returned to the good-evil cycle, which is translated in *Messalina* as the sun-moon relationship: the sun is eclipsed by the moon, "the sower of death," a phrase from *Days and Nights* which describes much of the action of *Messalina*. Shortly after the eclipse, Claudius quickly dismisses Messalina from his thoughts, and as he begins to contemplate taking a fourth wife, his centurions blindly follow his order, heap vituperation on Messalina, mouth the usual borgeois hypocritical moral strictures (OCMC, III, pp. 107-10), and kill her (OCMC, III, p. 110). For Messalina, then, the sun-moon cycle is completed with her death.

A second facet of Jarry's cosmology appears when Caligula is killed. Claudius falls on his knees begging for his life from a Pretorian, but, as chance will have it, instead of killlng him, the soldier proclaims him emperor (OCMC, III, p. 30). Jarry underscores the point about the absurdity of life when Mnestor declares that *"under my feet, up There, / Someone is playing a game with your bones"* (OCMC, III, p. 71). The fate-chance dichotomy is poorly integrated into Jarry's pessimistic cosmology. He attempts a synthesis by having Claudius note that destiny is chance (OCMC, III, p.

30), but this conclusion is fragile. The fundamental principle is an old one to Jarry—pessimism. It is the malignancy of the cosmos which allows Claudius to ignore flagrantly the demands of justice in the case of Valarius the Asiatic, who dressed in blue silk from China, which was considered "promiscuous" and feminine and therefore was forbidden by the government (OCMC, III, p. 45). His strange attire gave rise to myths about him. A soldier says that Valarius "tried to corrupt us by the strange profusion of his riches" (OCMC, III, p. 43); others spread rumors that he mounted a horse from the off side, fed his father soup made of human flesh, made love in his bath, and built his library and picture gallery by beginning with the roof (OCMC, III, p. 46). Considered bizarre, he is an enemy of the state (OCMC, III, p. 46); consequently, Claudius, fully cognizant that Valarius is innocent of these ridiculous accusations, facilely orders his subject to commit suicide (OCMC, III, p. 47). Well might the emperor and his wife weep in Valarius's defense, but tears and innocence cannot deter or mollify the unjust and deathbound direction of life. Such is also the fate of the artist as well as of the nymphomaniac. The field is left to others: the "herd," the ignorant soldiers, and Claudius dreaming of his next wife.

The relationshp between Mnestor and the herd provides a fine opportunity for Jarry to manifest his antidemocratic sentiment. During Mnestor's performance, an eclipse occurs. The people panic, blame Claudius for the phenomenon, scorn his reasonable explanation of it, and call for his death as well as bay for Messalina's. Then they become superstitious and believe that Caligula, Claudius's predecessor, "Has left the underworld" (OCMC, III, p. 73). Their frenzy subsides only when the sun reappears. The herd also misunderstands the role and power of the artist-seer; similarly, they reject all who do not agree with the societal norm. Jarry's work shows that his sympathies lay with those who were detested by society, and, as in the case of Messalina, he was at times willing to compromise his misogyny in order to support them.

Many of the concepts of *Messalina* are striking and intriguing, but too frequently they are marred by inadequate development. For instance, Messalina tries to find the god of love, but Jarry's examination of her experiences is too abbreviated. For example, why is the love between woman and child so fleeting (OCMC, III, p. 83)? The brief episode does not provide an answer. An analysis of religious feeling could have become a telling assault on his hated enemy, Christianity. Moreover, an investigation of the nebulous connections between the maternal, religious, and sexual forms of love might well have proven fruitful, but Jarry overlooked the opportunities and concentrated on describing Messalina's emotionalism. The result is a fine scene called "The Priapus of the Royal Garden" (OCMC, III, pp. 58-64), but the episode should have been expanded. Jarry should have addressed himself to defending his thesis that sexual gratification can bring happiness whereas the other forms of love cannot. It is also unfortunate that the statement of aesthetics is not more elaborate. He comes enticingly close to integrating his aesthetics with this cosmology, but his synthesis is inadequate because he leaves unanswered the significant questions of how the artist-seer comes to know the nature of the cosmos and how that knowledge is to be communicated.

Although *Messalina* is flawed because of Jarry's failure to develop his ideas fully, the work remaims interesting and sound. The most enthusiastic assessment of its artistic value is that of Rachilde, who sees it as a work "which marks a new evolution, perhaps a definitive revolution, in the original stylistic obscurities." [3] It is true that the work is less obscure than some of Jarry's other works, but the episodic style remains vintage Jarry. Fortunately, Jarry has fully developed some of these scenes and tantalizing questions, such as the essential qualities of love, its psychological ramifications, and the nature of the artist-seer. That Jarry failed to provide adequate answers is a shortcoming; that he posed the questions in an interesting manner is to be applauded.

The complementary work to Messalina is *The Supermale (Le Surmâle;* January 1, 1902), which is Jarry's last significant work. *Messalina* focuses on the past to demonstrate the homicidal and illusionary nature of love and happiness; *The Supermale* extends this view into a prophetic vision of man's mental and sexual evolution, his ability to find contentment, and his fateful confrontation with the Age of the Machine. This novel is a superb finale, but the encores are pale and mostly insipid.

The protagonist of *The Supermale* is André Marceuil, who asserts that "The act of love is of no importance because it can be performed indefinitely" (OCMC, III, p. 117). The statement is so extraordinary that Jarry faces the "Faustrollian dilemma" of making the imaginative appear reasonable. He is equal to the challenge: *The Supermale* is a pyrotechnical display of artistry.

The first "proof" Jarry offers for the truth of Marceuil's statement is physiological. Marceuil states the supposedly scientific principle that "Complex muscular and nervous systems enjoy absolute rest . . . while their opposed muscle works . . . [for instance,] each leg of a cyclist rests and even benefits from an automatic massage . . . while the other functions" (OCMC, III, p. 121). Jarry's contention has some anatomical foundation, although it is exaggerated because the relaxation of an opposed muscle can hardly be "absolute" since the muscle becomes fatigued. Moreover, comparing the relationship of opposed muscle groups to the reproductive organs is erroneous, but the logical fallacy is deliberately obfuscated by the strength of Jarry's methodology. He also refers to the heart in order to support his statement that some muscles are capable of enormous activity. He notes that "The number of diastoles and systoles [of the heart] surpasses all imaginable numbers" (OCMC, III, pp. 120-21). The statement is correct, but the contractile tissue of the heart is anatomically quite different from the erectile tissue of the genitalia.

Jarry reinforces his use of science by turning to history, a discipline sometimes considered to be scientific. Now Jarry presents some historical examples of sexual prowess and stamina. The most graphic is from Theophrastus,[4] who tells of an Indian who was known to copulate, "with the aid of a certain herb, seventy times and more" (OCMC, III, p. 127), which defies the medical opinion that "man can [copulate] nine or twelve times at the most in twenty-four hours, and then only in exceptional cases" (OCMC, III, p. 126). Assuming that the reader accepts the supposed truth of history, Marceuil concludes that *"what one man has done, so can another"* (OCMC, III, p. 128). Thus begins the search for the man and woman who can copulate indefinitely, that is, beyond significant number; by observing their actions and reactions, Jarry analyzes the nature of love.

Jarry's depiction of the Supermale, André Marceuil, poses major artistic problems. In order to show that his sexual exploits are within the realm of human capability, Jarry portrays him as being common and ordinary: "thirty . . . medium height, although he seemed to enjoy appearing shorter because he stooped. [He] gave the impression that [he was] remarkably weak" (OCMC, III, p. 118). But Marceuil is the Supermale, and consequently he must be depicted so that the reader will accept Marceuil's feats. For instance, he must have a superb physique in order to be believable in the pivotal episode, "The Ten Thousand Mile Race," which in turn is intended to give credence to his sexual expertise. Consequently, Jarry describes him as having "incomparable proportions. . . . His armpits and the muscles in the back of his knees bulged out . . . a physique that hadn't been seen since the celebrated weightlifter Thomas Topham" (OCMC, III, p. 182). "The Ten Thousand Mile Race" pits a locomotive against a five-man bicycle team are so numerous and knowledgeable that Lebois thinks that *The Supermale* is, above all, an exaltation of a rather new invention, the bicycle (Lebois, p. 149). It is true that Jarry had long been infatuated with the bicycle, but the details serve to give verisimilitude to the race. The episode reaches a climax when the team's efforts are overshadowed by a mysterious cyclist—Marceuil. Ted Oxborrow, one of the members of the bicycle team, observes that "The [calf] muscles of [Marceuil] were palpitating like two alabaster hearts" and that "His racing shorts were ripped over his thighs because of the flexing of the extensor muscles" (OCMC, III, p. 174). In retrospect it is hard for the reader to believe that such a specimen, bedecked with muscles and ripped shorts, is the bestooped and enfeebled Marceuil.

The same problem of packaging the extraordinary in the ribbons and bows of normalcy occurs in the description of Ellen. Jarry asks the reader to believe that she is "just a rather small girl" (OCMC, III, p. 145); but Marceuil, after looking deeply into her eyes, concludes that if there is really metempsychosis, this innocuous female was really "a veteran courtesan" (OCMC, III, p. 154), one who has the stamina to have sexual intercourse with Marceuil eight-two times in order to set a new world sexual intercourse record, and then, after a short rest, copulate with him many times more for personal pleasure.

Initially, the couple is devoted to surpassing the sexual inter-course record, and their interest demonstrates the veracity of Jarry's view that "Assiduous lovemaking detracts from experienc-ing love" (OCMC, III, p. 217). Marceuil exemplifies the point: during his eighty-two copulations with Ellen "he had never asked himself whether he had loved her or whether she was beautiful" (OCMC, III, p. 215). Then Marceuil "perceived that at this stage of the expenditure of his energy he was becoming sentimental. This was his way of manifesting the *post coitum animal triste*" syndrome (OCMC, III, p. 218), a reaction which proves to be quintessential to Jarry's analysis of love. Overpowered by sentimentality, Mar-ceuil experiences love, represented by his comparision of Ellen with Helen of Troy (OCMC, III, pp. 218-20). But Marceuil makes a "Faustrollian bound and rebound" between conflicting emotions. Initially he experiences the joys of rapture, then realizes that the moment of delight in sex was also "the best time to roar with laughter" (OCMC, III, p. 217). Marceuil, rebounding, then over-comes his disgust, kisses her genitalia, and appreciates them as "rare gems" (OCMC, III, p. 217).

To Jarry, love is simply a psychological reaction to the *post coitum animal triste* syndrome, and at best this reaction is ephermeral be-cause societal and parental pressures, fueled by traditional moral-ity, interfere. Ellen's father becomes a moral zealot when he learns of the sexual contest, and he insists that Marceuil marry Ellen (OCMC, III, p. 223). The father's attitude and actions not only allow Jarry to expose the dangers of this morality, but they also permit him to show how science can be made subservient to anach-ronistic religion. Seized with moral rectitude, the father calls upon Arthur Gough, an engineer, "to make the most unusual machine in modern times, the machine which was not designed to produce physical effects, but to influence forces considered until this time to be elusive: the Love-Generating Machine" (OCMC, III, p. 224). Marceuil is quickly attached to it, and in the ensuing titanic clash the machine falls in love with the man (OCMC, III, p. 227). His victory is his undoing because the flow of electricity causes "the platinum crown [which has been placed around his head to be-come] white-hot":

> In a painful paroxysm of effort, Marceuil ripped the
> straps which held his forearms . . . his crown curved in-
> wards. . . .
>
> Drops of molten glass ran down the face of the Super-
> male like tears.
> Marceuil, breaking his last bonds . . . bounded down
> the stairs . . . [and ran down the driveway]. . . .
> And the body of André Marceuil, naked . . . stopped—
> twisted around the bars, or the bars around the body. . . .
> The Supermale was dead. (OCMC, III, pp. 228-29)

Morality has once again triumphed! Likewise over Ellen, who is
forced to return within the bounds of the sacred norms: "Ellen
Elson was cured and married. She insisted on one condition when
she accepted her husband: that he was capable of keeping his love
within wise limits of human forces" (OCMC, III, p. 229). Gone are
the people who extended human capabilities; all that remains is
morality, normalcy, remembrance—and "one of the solid tears of
the Supermale, which Ellen wears" (OCMC, III, p. 229).

While Jarry disparages science for allying itself with traditional
morality and being guided by it, "The Ten Thousand Mile Race"
brilliantly demonstrates that beneath science's assistance to mankind lurks grave spiritual danger. The men are fed "Perpetual Motion Food," which the father of Ellen, the American chemist
William Elson, invented. Although he refuses to give the formula,
he admits that the miraculous nutrient "has a strychnine and alcohol base" (OCMC, III, p. 123). From such poisons he makes a
substance which allows the bicycle team to defeat the locomotive.
While the Perpetual Motion Food permits man to extend his physical limits, it has a deleterious effect upon his artistic and spiritual
development because the scientific discovery intensifies man's focus
on the mundane and pragmatic. Ultimately, man becomes a machine. Jarry brilliantly makes the point in a delightful scene in
which one member of the team, Jewey Jacobs, dies during the race.
The deadweight is a hindrance, and in order for the team to be
successful every member must perform his duties; therefore, Jewey

Jacobs must function properly—alive or dead. Thus begins his education, and soon his body becomes once more a usable part of the team (OCMC, III, pp. 163-64). The individual, then, is of concern only in relation to the degree he helps or hinders the team effort, and it is the group which is of commanding importance. Man infused with the *principium individuationis* cannot survive "the tyrannical preeminence of the machine" (Perche, p. 114). The dilemma confronting modern man is frighteningly clear: become an automaton.

Jarry's misogyny surfaces once again in *The Supermale,* but the artistic demands of the work force some awkward statements of this theme. He argues that "the organs of the two sexes are composed . . . of the same elements, although somewhat differentiated . . . ; [therefore,] there is no reason why a man cannot experience the same physiological phenomena as a Messalina, except for a certain difference in number" (OCMC, III, p. 141). This marks the first time that Jarry acknowledged the equality of the sexes—if not the superiority of women; however, Jarry was not retreating from his misogyny; he was using the equality of the sexes solely to give veracity to the biological aspects of the sexual marathon. The same problem occurs when Marceuil reconsiders his view that "The only real women are Messalinas" (OCMC, III, p. 141); later he falls in love with the Super-Messalina, Ellen, thereby proving that not all women are strumpets. But it is noteworthy that this reassessment occurs while he is overpowered by sentimentality caused by the *post coitum animal triste* syndrome, and thus it is part of the disparagement of love.

Chauveau rightly assesses *The Supermale* as the best of Jarry's novels (Chauveau, p. 157). It is well constructed, and the episodes are generally well integrated, although "The Ten Thousand Mile Race" tends to dominate much of the work. The care with which Jarry establishes a tone of veracity is remarkable, and this control helps the reader enjoy the novel. Jarry superbly tempers his imagination in *The Supermale,* and as a result it becomes an intriguing fictional analysis of several facets of reality.

The Supermale is marred, however, by the needless inclusion of a diatribe about God. The incident occurs when Balthybius, a scientist who is to testify to the record-setting copulatory marathon, dozes while waiting for the bout to begin. When he awakens, he finds that he has written a "strange, scientifico-lyrico-philosophical elucubration" (OCMC, III, p. 192), which is a wearisome discussion of God being "INFINITELY SMALL" (OCMC, III, p. 192). The discussion is a logical quagmire, which Jarry was uniquely gifted to construct, but it does not belong in *The Supermale*. Once again Jarry stitched material into a fabric which was artistically weakened by its inclusion. But this flaw can be easily overlooked in view of the success of the novel, which remains a testament to his extraordinary artistic development and achievement.

Jarry's last years were filled with activity increasingly punctuated by illness and poverty. On January 15, 1901, he became a regular contributor to *La Revue Blanche,* but in October 1902 he received a letter from Binet-Valmer, a member of the editorial staff of *La Renaissance Latine,* a periodical directed by Prince Bibescu. Jarry was given a tantalizing offer: he could write for *La Renaissance Latine* and dictate his fee, but he would have to stop writing for *La Revue Blanche.* Because the future of *La Revue Blanche* was in doubt, Jarry rightly looked to other sources of income, and subsequently he accepted the offer from Bibescu. On November 15, 1902, Jarry's first essay appeared in that periodical, and the next month his second article was published concomitantly with his last essay in *La Revue Blanche.* Bibescu, misunderstanding the terms of Jarry's departure from *La Revue Blanche* and thinking that Jarry was repudiating the agreement with him, refused to publish Jarry's third essay. Severed from *La Renaissance Latine,* Jarry returned to *La Revue Blanche* and contributed a chapter, "The Battle of Morgore," from *The Persecuted (La Dragonne)* to its April 1903 issue. Two weeks later he wrote two articles for the final issue of this periodical. Now Jarry sought another magazine to which he could contribute, and he settled on *Le Canard Sauvage,* with which he collaborated the month before the demise of *La Revue Blanche.* He wrote for *Le Canard Sauvage* until it stopped publication in October 1903. He also contributed essays to several other magazines, and by September 1905 he had written 162 pieces. These articles would have gone almost unnoticed if they had not been brilliantly edited by Maurice Saillet. He successfully argues that Jarry intended collecting his essays into a book tentatively entitled *The Green Candle, Light on Things of This Time (La Chandelle Verte, Lumière sur les Choses de Ce Temps.*[5]

The great majority of these articles are hardly more than brief comments on a variety of subjects ranging from postage stamps, languages, women, policemen, and the military, to reviews of books and plays written by his friends. His critiques show that he continued to be interested in the theater, but unfortunately the comments are too superficial to attract much interest, although the best review, "Inverse Mimeticism in the Characters of Henri de Régnier," sheds considerable light on several facets of Jarry's dramaturgy. These works in *The Green Candle* are also sprinkled with antireligious comments, the best of which is typified by "The Passion Considered as a Bicycle Race" ("La Passion Considérée comme Course de Côte"), which he published in *Le Canard Sauvage* (April 11-17, 1903). "Barabbas," Jarry begins, "showed up, but was scratched." Pilate then "gave the signal to start [and] . . . Jesus, in great shape, took off, but at once he had a flat tire. A bed of thorns riddled the circumference of his front tire" (GC, p. 356). "Then Jesus, after the flat, climbed the slope on foot, carrying on his shoulders his bike—or, if you wish, his cross" (GC, p. 357). "On the twelfth turn the well-known terrible accident occurred. Jesus was at this time in a 'dead heat'[6] with two thieves. It is known that he continued the race as an aviator, but that's another story" (GC, p. 359). "The Passion Considered as a Bicycle Race" reflects the disappearance of the swashbuckling tactics of his youth, which culminated in *King Ubu*. Now the tone has changed from the buffoonery and belligerence of his earlier works, but the essential quality of black humor remains because, as in *King Ubu*, Jarry employs the weapon of wit to expose, ridicule, and denigrate.

While Jarry was writing these articles he was preoccupied with his fixation of writing an opera libretto. He began work in this genre with *Pantagruel*, which he sought to have accepted for the Paris Exposition of 1900, and while he failed in that goal the idea nevertheless remained subterranean for several years. On July 22, 1903, he was busy putting what proved to be the first sketch of *The Big Head (Moutardier du Pape)* to music. In November he accepted an invitation from Terrasse to come to Grand-Lemps, where Terrasse had a mansion, ostensibly to continue work on the opera, although the invitation was probably an amicable plot to entice Jarry away from his haunts in order to break him of his alcohol habit. The project was not finished, and Jarry determinedly worked on *Pantagruel* in the spring of 1905, but the project came to an end when Terrasse finally left it.

In 1904 and 1905 Jarry bought some land at Plesis Coudary and had a shack built over the water. The house rested on four stilts, and it is for this reason that Jarry named his home "The Tripod." But in late 1905 Jarry's life took a significant turn which kept him from living in The Tripod. In September he had to have some extensive and painful dental work done, and in November he was very ill with influenza. He recovered the following month, but the winter was unusually severe and Jarry suffered terribly. His fortunes grew worse, and he borrowed money from Terrasse, ate at the Vallettes', and frantically tried to publish in order to earn money. His haste and commercial concerns determined the direction of most of his post-*Supermale* period, and they doomed his work: Jarry was an artist, not a craftsman of the marketplace.

He made friends with Dr. Saltas, who convinced him to translate *Pope Joan* by Emmanuel Rhoïdes, which he did in the winter of 1905. Actually, the project was a scheme to get Jarry to come to Saltas's home where he could be given decent food because there were times when he was so poor that his only food was the fish he caught. But it was not difficult to get Jarry to work on this manuscript, which was written in his beloved Greek and was anti-Christian. *The Cut of Love* was published in 1906, but this paltry work gave little hope of financial success. In the spring he welcomed Terrasse's invitation to come to Grand-Lemps, and in early April 1906 he accepted an offer from Tailhade to produce *King Ubu*, but the project did not develop. During his illness in the spring of 1906 Jarry went back to Laval so that his sister and an old family doctor could care for him; it was while ill that he revised *The Persecuted* with the help of his sister Charlotte, who took dictation and wrote significant parts of it. On regaining his health, he returned to Paris and his articles, and, desperately seeking money, published *Ubu on the Mound*, but it too was a failure. Vallette and Fénéon attempted to raise an advance on the publication of *The Big Head*, but before they did Jarry again became ill, and on

May 11, 1906, he left Paris to return to Laval. Terribly sick, Jarry asked for and received the Last Rites, a request brought on by fever. Expecting to die, he wrote to Rachilde on May 28, 1906 telling her that he was "full of insatiable curiosity" about death (Rachilde, pp. 220-23). When he regained his composure, he quickly ridiculed his action and the sacraments. Recognizing that "The Tripod" was hardly a suitable habitat for his recovery, he sold it to Charlotte.[7] With this money as well as the 120 francs Vallette received as the advance on *The Big Head,* Jarry returned once again to his beloved Paris in late July 1906 and to his old haunt at 7, rue Cassette. *The Big Head* was delivered to the subscribers in June 1907, but it proved to be "mediocre" (Chauveau, p. 171). Artistically, the play is worthy only of scant notice because the choral odes are clumsy and the rhymes are stilted. Jarry delights in presenting some English dialogue and toying with its pronunciation, and he enjoys the subject matter, which focuses on the story of a girl who left her English husband and, concealing her femininity, becomes pope. Once again Jarry returns to the attack on church and women, but the assault is lackluster and effete. Again he paints women as being dishonest and disloyal, exemplified by Pope Joan when she sees her husband and falls in love with him again, which raises the question as to why she left him previously. Her actions also show that she is an expert prevaricator as well as contriver of plots, but her machinations are of little interest; when compared with Messalina, she is the paler and less dynamic of the two. *The Big Head,* then, is far removed from the zenith of Jarry's creative powers and revolutionary intensity.

Upon his return to Paris, Jarry anticipated contributing to *Chanteclair,* a medical and pharmaceutical advertising magazine, because it would be a source of desperately needed money, but the project did not materialize. Jarry tried to borrow 750 francs from Terrasse, which was surely a painful request aggravated by the refusal. On April 16 Jarry became very ill and again returned to Laval. Barely recovered, he traveled back to Paris and 7, rue Cassette on July 6; two days later he was very tired and asked Vallette to stop by; shortly afterward he went back to Laval. Toward the end of August, Alexandre Natanson, brother of Thadée, paid

Jarry's rent and in early October loaned him enough money so he could return to Paris, which he did on October 17. His health declined very rapidly, and at one point he and a friend stopped in a café so Jarry could write a letter to his sister. He gave it to the friend to correct, but the friend found the letter unintelligible because of its truncated phrases and missing or partly written words (Chauveau, p. 196).

Dr. Saltas and Vallette became alarmed about Jarry when he failed to appear for a meeting he had promised to attend. Saltas and Vallette went to Jarry's apartment, and after vigorous knocking Jarry responded, but he was too ill to open the door. They forced it open: "We found him at the back of the room, on the floor, unable to get up. Around him were two empty bottles and a third which was a candleholder. A guitar was hooked to the wall like a mobile; there was a stuffed owl, a vase of flowers, which gave off an aroma different from roses." [8] Saltas and Vallette carried Jarry in their arms down the steps and into a carriage, and during the trip to the hospital Jarry wanted to know how the hospital bill was going to be paid because he had no money and did not want to impose on anyone or be a burden (Saltas, p. 87). He was assured that there was no problem.

Dr. Stéphen Chauvet was the attending physician, and he noted that when he first saw Jarry in the hospital Jarry "was in terrible condition, and had not eaten for at least two days." [9] He noted that Jarry had "an unhealthy waxy pallor which highlighted a strange physiognomic expression; despondency; lack of attention . . . . It was difficult for him to answer questions . . . ; he had a moderate and irregular fever . . . ; the poor man was in an appalling condition: his sphincter was paralyzed or else he was no longer continent" (Chauvet, pp. 78-79). The next day Jarry was still in "a rather marked state of prostration; his breathing was more constricted than before; his lips were pale, his pulse was light and diminishing" (Chauvet, p. 82). "I asked him if he wanted anything. His eyes began to sparkle. There was something which would be very nice . . . a toothpick. . . . He took one between two fingers of his right hand. Pleasure was visible on his face. I had hardly taken several steps to speak to the orderly when the orderly signaled for me to turn around: Jarry was dead" (Saltas, p. 88). It was 4:15 P.M., November 1, 1907—All Saints' Day. He was thirty-four years old.

On November 3 Alfred Jarry was buried in the Bagneux cemetery after a brief service at Saint-Sulpice. In the cortège were Vallette, Rachilde, Saltas, Paul Léautaud, Thadée Natanson, Appollinaire, Octave Mirbeau, and Valéry. After the burial the group adjourned to eat and drink in honor of their friend.

Because of Jarry's legendary drinking, it was thought that he had died of alcoholism. Jarry began his drinking at the age of three when he found some wine and was later found terribly inebriated (Lebois, p. 27). Rachilde later recalled one of his ordinary days—he

> began by taking down two liters of white wine, three drinks of absinthe between 10:00 A.M. and noon; for lunch he washed down his fish or beef with some red or white wine alternating with more absinthe. In the afternoon, some cups of coffee augmented with marc brandy or alcohol the names of which I have forgotten. During and after dinner some aperitifs, of course. He could still hold at least two more bottles of wine. (Rachilde, pp. 180-81)

His favorite drink was absinthe, which he called "a sacred herb" (Rachilde, p. 90), but he would drink the cheapest wine when he could not afford absinthe, and when he could not afford wine he would drink ether (Rachilde, p. 182). He was even known to have had a glass of absinthe, vinegar, and ink (Bellerie, p. 79). However, it was yet another of the ironies of his life that the autopsy showed that Jarry was indeed correct: he did not die of an alcohol-induced illness, he died of meningitis tuberculosis (Chauvet, p. 85).

In 1935 Frederick Pottecher tried to find Jarry's grave and could not. Its disappearance befits much of Jarry's life: except for a few friends and for *King Ubu,* he was unknown artistically in his own lifetime, and almost all of his works neither gained a significant audience nor earned enough money to lift him out of the ranks of the poor. Even when his literary reputation was resurrected in the 1930s, he was myopically classified as the creator of *King Ubu.* His climb to notoriety was meteoric, and likewise his descent. His celebrity ended when Lugné-Poe shut his doors to him. Thus, from 1896 literary history left Jarry to his own paths. France proved to be more concerned with imperialism than with Jarry's prophecies of the machine age, more infatuated with revenge against the Germans for the humiliation of the Franco-Prussian War than with learning about Jarry's views of homicidal happiness, more interested in Symbolism, Neo-Symbolism, and Proust than with the progenitor of the "absurdist" theater. No—this was not the epoch for Alfred Jarry—nor was the period of World War I and its bloodbath and delights of revenge in French gullets, nor the search for optimism in Sartrian existentialism.

But Jarry's name was known to an important few, and fortunately Antonin Artaud, that volcanic genius of modern theater, recognized Jarry's brilliance and legacy and named his seminal experiment in drama after him "The Alfred Jarry Theater." Although the experiment was short-lived, its impact was indeed crucial in the development of modern drama, and with its fame went that of Jarry, now recognized as the standard-bearer of change and progress. The Monte Carlo edition of Jarry's "complete works" in 1948 accelerated his recognition. While this edition quickly proved far from complete, it made Jarry's most important writing widely available. The year 1948 was also significant in the historiography of Jarry because the "Collège de 'Pataphysique" was founded. This nebulous group was dedicated to the study of Jarry, and the work of the "Collège" has proven to be invaluable. The triumph of the "Theater of the Absurd" in the 1950s and 1960s brought increasing awareness of Jarry's role in literary history, a recognition which has been significantly enhanced by the scholarship of Paul Chauveau, Michel Arrivé, and Noël Arnaud.

Jarry's personal life also affected his reception because he was too frequently dismissed as a clown. Even Rachilde, who knew him very well, referred to him as a "monkey" (Rachilde, p. 169), and Gide had reason to misjudge him. There is little question about Jarry's acting: coming from the provinces and social ostracism, he eagerly sought acceptance in Paris. Consequently, he cultivated the role of Ubu, and while he was very successful, the result was disastrous for his literary reputation. If Gide's description of him in

The Counterfeiters is reasonably accurate, it would be understandably difficult to view Jarry as anything other than a boorish buffoon, let alone a serious creator. The problem is highlighted by Chauveau, who, representing a considerable number of Jarry students, thinks that "Ubu invented Jarry" (Chauveau, p. 205), that is, Jarry lost his personality to that of Ubu. The facts, however, are quite different. In public Jarry was indeed Ubu, but only in speech and manner. Personally, Jarry was not bepaunched but was quite muscular; he was witty and charming, not overbearing; he was thoughtful and considerate, not egotistical. At times his buffoonery overlappped his consideration, and consequently there were unfortunate results, such as the episode with Berthe de Courrière. In general his compassion and consideration were long remembered by his friends, and he manifested these qualities even on his deathbed. Therefore, Ubu and Jarry should not be equated.

Jarry was also denied fame because his concepts were too revolutionary for most people of his time. His epoch was not yet ready for the nihilism which he advocated. Only a small coterie recognized the value of Henry Bauer's conclusion that "Society is a lie, social progress is a trap, the social contract is broken." [10] Enter Jarry: "Ubu is not just the appearance of a new character in the cultural universe; it is a conscious effort to find new means of expression" (Morot-Sir, p. 38). *King Ubu*, then, is a stentorian call for the overthrow of accepted assumptions of man, society, and cosmos; new forces were operating which necessitated new definitions and attitudes. Jarry saw that dramatists must break the chains of the past and seek a new dramaturgy to express the transformations of man and of the forces which operate upon him.

Jarry was very much a product of the intellectual and artistic ferment of his epoch. Darwin, Marx, Nietzsche, and Wagner had revolutionized much of Western thought—and Freud was on the foreseeable horizon when Jarry came to Paris. Jarry was specifically influenced by the Symbolists, whose efforts included revising many traditional concepts of the theater and its functions. He was intellectually and emotionally prepared to accept that challenge, and modern drama is consequently indebted to his achievements. His dramaturgy shows that he understood Symbolism very well and that he was more aware of the problems of dramaturgy than were other Symbolists. He saw that if the goals of Symbolist theater were to be realized, then traditional methods would have to be discarded, a new dramaturgical aesthetic established, and revolutionary techniques developed. It was a propitious moment: a major break with tradition had to be made and failure risked in order to gain success.

Jarry's stimulating expansion of Symbolist theater was the first of his many significant contributions to literature. Ironically, one of the most valuable facets of his legacy was the very issue which accelerated his decline: his revolutionary zeal. Before Jarry and *King Ubu,* many of the experiments in the theater were pallid and vapid. A list of the experimental plays produced at the Théâtre de l'Oeuvre exemplifies the point. The most illustrious of these dramatic essays were the plays of Maeterlinck, but, justifiably, literary history has not been kind to them. *The Princess Maleine* is, fundamentally, reworked traditional theater; *The Intruder* is an *étude* for the performers, and *Pelleas and Melisande* is ludicrous at times and generally conservative. Jarry did not compromise his revolutionary convictions. He saw that the traditional concepts and attitudes toward the theater were anachronistic, and his call for the new was made with a clarity, insistence, and precision not seen before. This legacy proved most beneficial to those who followed because, now freed from the past, they could walk in new areas.

Jarry's contributions to the theater were many and affected all facets of drama: director, script, actor, décor, language, and audience. One of the most startling innovations was "black humor." It would be incorrect to presume that Jarry was the first to exploit it.[11] Edgar Allen Poe, for example, used it brilliantly in "The Cask of Amontillado" (1846) in which he wittily tells how Fortunato is walled up alive. For Poe this type of humor was a means of expressing his personal pessimism, misanthropy, and despair; in *King Ubu* "black humor" becomes socially oriented, and by making this transformation Jarry touched a nerve and muscle of twentieth-century Western man. Jarry's comedy remained to be utilized by others, and in the hands of people like Beckett and Ionesco it proved to be a powerful legacy which Jarry bestowed. Francis

Carco correctly assesses Jarry and "black humor" when he concludes that "Jarry is . . . the first who gave humor its complete contemporary expression." [12]

Jarry also contributed to the emergence of atheism. Jarry demonstrates that Christian theology is contradictory and should be awarded the treatment given to a toy. Equally important, Jarry saw the interconnection of Christianity, social mores, and class structures. Thus, to attack bourgeois hypocrisy means an assault on Christian theism because the two are inextricably interlaced. Parallel to his atheism was his pessimism, which is founded on his inability to accept the primacy of reason. *The Records of the Black Crest,* for instance, shows his assumption that man's vaunted reason is easily manipulated at the wish and whim of the artist. Jarry then saw that beneath the veneer of logic lurk forces which dominate man's reason, and this theme emerges fully in *Messalina* and *The Supermale.*

Jarry's critique of the social, economic, and religious foundations of his culture could have been considerably strengthened had he known more about politics and psychology. Certainly he was surrounded by sophisticated students of politics, including many socialists and anarchists, but rather than learn from them he ridiculed them in *Ubu in Chains.* Becuase of his ignorance, his attack is sometimes feeble and easily blunted. Had he been more knowledgeable he might have seen why government is repressive and how it represents Christianity and the bourgeoisie. A fine opportunity to discuss these problems occurred in *Days and Nights* when he could have analyzed the army as an adjunct of government, or in *Messalina* when he could have explored Caesar's rationale for killing Valarius the Asiatic. Similarly, Jarry could have considerably strengthened his work had he known more psychology. The reader would gain if he knew more of Sengle's mentality and why he had such a need for his "adelphic" friend. The problem is acute in *The Visits of Love* where Jarry fails to probe into the subject, and in *The Old Man of the Mountain* he overlooks the fundamental problem of the effects of Christianity upon the mind and how it camouflages cruelty and homicide beneath the façade of love. Jarry was moving toward an understanding of human psychology in *Messalina* and *The Supermale,* but he did not have time to extend his knowledge.

Almost all of Jarry's fame rests upon *King Ubu,* but many of his other works deserve attention. *The Records of the Black Crest* is an important collection, and Gourmont correctly salutes it. At times this collection rivals the youthful work of Rimbaud and Lautréamont, especially the remarkable statement and demonstration of his aesthetics. *Faustroll* is brilliantly organized; the portraits are exquisite; and the manipulation of logic is superb. *Days and Nights, Faustroll, Messalina,* and *The Supermale* show that Jarry's gifts extended far beyond drama.

Jarry is rightly placed in the same group with Baudelaire, Lautréamont, and Rimbaud [13] as one of the illustrious "black angels of literature." [14] The inclusion of Jarry is fitting because he was indeed an "accursed poet," "a literary anarchist," [15] "one of the most original figures in all of French literature." [16] His rebellion was complete: he destroyed, built "handsome buildings," and then welcomed the day when "young people will . . . find us very old-fashioned, and they will write ballads denouncing us, and there is no reason why they shouldn't" (OCBP, p. 418).

Notes

1. OCMC, III, p. 9. It is clear, however, that Jarry had a firm understanding of many details of this period of Roman history.
2. Homer, *The Iliad,* trans. Richmond Lattimore (Chicago: The University of Chicago Press, 1951), Book I, 1. pp. 248–50.
3. Rachilde, *"Messaline," Mercure de France* (February 1901), p. 482.
4. A Greek philosopher and naturalist; died c. 287 B.C.
5. Saillet retained the title. The book was published in 1969.
6. In English.
7. Charlotte sold the property on January 8, 1909.
8. Jean Saltas, "Les Derniers Jours d'Alfred Jarry," *Les Marges,* October 15, 1921, pp. 86–87. Hereafter cited in the text as "Saltas."
9. Stéphan Chauvet, "Les Derniers Jours d'Alfred Jarry," *Mercure de France,* February 15, 1933, p. 77. Hereafter cited in the text as "Chauvet."

10. Cited in Chauveau, pp. 56–57.
11. André Breton's *Anthologie de l'Humour Noir* (Paris: Editions du Saggittaire, 1940) are particularly illuminating.
12. Francis Carco, "Réflexions sur l'Humour," *Mercure de France,* July 1, 1914, p. 56.
13. Renaud Matignon, "Comme Caligula," *Le Nouvel Observateur,* no. 6 (December 24, 1964), p. 25. See also Jean Amrouche, "Jarry en Enfer," *L'Arche,* no. 21 (November 1946), p. 103.
14. Georges Pillement, *Anthologie du Théâtre Français Contemporain* (Paris: Editions du Bélier, 1945), vol. 1, p. 23.
15. Paul Chauveau, "Alfred Jarry à Laval," *Revue de France,* November 15, 1932, p. 378.
16. Patrick Loriot, "Ubu Plus Jarry," *Le Nouvel Observateur,* no. 311 (October 26–November 1, 1970), p. 47.

Bibliography

Alexander, Ian Welsh. *Bergson; Philosopher of Reflection*. London: Bowes and Bowest, 1957.

Amrouch, Jean. "Jarry en Enfer," *L'Arche* (November, 1946), 103-107.

Apollinaire, Guillaume. "Contemporain Pittoresque: Feu Alfred Jarry," *Les Marges* (November 15, 1909), 161-170.

———. *Il Y A. . . .* Paris: Editions Messein, 1949.

Arnaud, Noël. *Alfred Jarry, D'Ubu Roi au Docteur Faustroll*. Paris: La Table Ronde, 1974.

———. "La Vie Nouvelle d'Alfred Jarry," *Critique* (December, 1959), 1011-1025.

Arrivé, Michel. *Les Langages de Jarry, Essai de Sémiotique Littéraire*. Paris: Publications de l'Université de Paris, 1972.

Barrault, Jean-Louis. *Jarry Sur la Butte. Spectacle d'Après les Oeuvres Complètes d'Alfred Jarry*. Paris: Gallimard, 1970.

Barthes, Roland. "Alfred Jarry: *Ubu* (TNP, 1958)"; *Théâtre Populaire*, no. 3 (May, 1958), 80-83.

Bastide, Francois-Régis. *"Jarry Sur la Butte.* Spectacle de Jean-Louis Barrault," *Les Nouvelles Littéraires*, no. 2250 (November 5, 1970), 13.

Beaubourg, Maurice. *"Ubu-Roi* aux Quat-z-Arts," *La Plume*, XIII, no. 2 (July-December, 1901), 1029-1030.

Beausire, Pierre. *Mallarmé, Poésie et Poétique.* Lausanne: Mermod, 1949.

Béhar, Henri. *Etude sur le Théâtre Dada et Surrealiste.* Paris: Gallimard, 1967.

———. *Jarry, Le Monstre et la Marionnette.* Paris: Librairie Larousse, 1973.

Belaval, Yvon. *Poèmes d'Aujourd'hui.* Paris: Gallimard, 1964.

Bensky, Roger-Daniel. *Structures Textuelles de la Marionnette de Langue Française.* Paris: Nizet, 1969.

Bentley, Eric. *The Playwright as Thinker.* New York: Meridian Books, 1957.

Bergson, Henri. "Le Rire, Essai sur la Signification du Comique," in *Oeuvres.* Paris: Presses Universitaires de France, 1959.

Bernard, Marc, "Soirée Ionesco. Le Petit-Fils de Jarry," *Les Nouvelles Littéraires* (March 13, 1966), 13.

Billy, André. *L'Epoque 1900, 1885-1905.* Paris: Editions Jules Tallandier, 1951.

———. "Le Père Ubu Réhabilité," *Le Figaro Littéraire* (August 30, 1958), 2.

———. "Un Repas de Jarry," *Le Figaro Littéraire* (March 12, 1960), 4.

Bizot, Jean-François. "Ubu dans la Rue," *L'Express* (June 29-July 5, 1970), 50-51.

Blackwell, Vera. "The Avant-Garde in Prague," *The Nation,* no. 24 (June 14, 1965), 650-652.

Blanchart, Paul. "Gémier Precurseur et Vivant," *Europe* (April-May, 1962), 23-37.

Blanchot, Maurice. *Lautréamont et Sade.* Paris: Editions de Minuit, 1949.

Bonnefoy, Claude. "Les Visages de *La Dragonne,*" *Arts,* no. 1007 (May 26-June 1, 1965), 8.

Boulenger, Marcel. *"Le Surmâle,"* *La Renaissance Latine* (July 15, 1902), 447-448.

Bowen, Barbara C. *The Age of Bluff; Paradox and Ambiguity in Rabelais and Montaigne.* Urbana: University of Illinois Press, 1972.

Breton, André. "Alfred Jarry Initiateur et Eclaireur: Son Role dans les Arts Plastiques," *Arts* (November 2, 1951), 1, 10.

———. *Anthologie de l'Humour Noir.* Paris: Editions du Saggittaire, 1940.

———. "Alfred Jarry," *Ecrits Nouveaux* (January, 1919), 17-27.

———. *Les Pas Perdus.* Paris: Gallimard, 1970.

Brice, Jacques. "La Dernière Incarnation d'Alfred Jarry: Chroniqueur Pataphysique. Ubu Journaliste," *Le Figaro Littéraire,* no. 1206 (June 30-July 6, 1969), 27.

Brisson, Adolphe. *Le Théâtre et les Moeurs.* Paris: E. Flammarion, 1906.

Brun, Jean. *"Ubu-Roi* à Londres," *Cahiers du Collège de 'Pataphysique,* nos. 5-6, 105-106.

Brunet, Gabriel. *"Alfred Jarry* par Paul Chauveau," *Mercure de France* (February 1, 1933), 642-647.

Brunet, Gabriel. "Alfred Jarry, Son Oeuvre," *Mercure de France* (March 1, 1935), 341-343.

————. "Littèrature: Rachilde; *Alfred Jarry, Ou Le Surmâle des Lettres,*" *Mercure de France* (July, 1928), 148-151.

Cahiers du Collège de 'Pataphysique; also *Dossiers, Subsidia,* and *Viridis Candela* of the "Collège."

Carco, Francis. "Réflexions sur l'Humour," *Mercure de France* (July 1, 1914), 42-63.

Chassé, Charles. *Dans les Coulisses de la Gloire, D'Ubu-Roi au Douanier Rousseau.* Paris: Nouvelle Revue Critique, 1947.

Chauveau, Paul. "Alfred Jarry à Laval," *Revue de France* (November 15, 1932), 377-382.

————. *Alfred Jarry, Ou La Naissance, La Vie, et La Mort du Père Ubu.* Paris: Mercure de France, 1951.

Chauvet, Stéphen. "Les Derniers Jours d'Alfred Jarry," *Mercure de France* (February 15, 1933), 77-86.

Clancier, G.E. *De Rimbaud au Surrealisme, Panorama Critique.* Paris: Seghers, 1953.

Clouard, Henri. *Histoire de la Littérature Française, Du Symbolisme à Nos Jours* [I: *De 1885 à 1914*]. Paris: Albin Michel, 1947.

Coe, Richard N. *Ionesco.* London: Oliver and Boyd, 1961.

Cohn, Ruby. "The Comedy of Samuel Beckett: Something Old, Something New . . . ," *Yale French Studies,* no. 22 (summer, 1959), 11-17.

————. *Samuel Beckett: The Comic Gamut.* New Brunswick: Rutgers University Press, 1962.

Coolus, Romain. "Ubu Roi," *La Revue Blanche* (January 1, 1897), 38-40.

Cooper, Lane. *An Aristotelian Theory of Comedy, With An Adaptation of the Poetics and a Translation of 'Tractatus Coislinianus.'* New York: Harcourt, Brace and Company, 1922.

Corrigan, Robert (ed.). *Comedy: Meaning and Form.* San Francisco: Chandler Publishing Co., 1965.

Crubbs, Henry-Alexander. "L'Influence d'Isidore Ducasse sur les Débuts Littéraires d'Alfred Jarry," *Revue d'Histoire Littéraire de la France* (July-September, 1935), 437-446.

Décaudin, Michel. *La Crise des Valeurs Symbolistes, Vingt Ans de Poésie Française (1895-1914).* Toulouse: Editions Privat, 1960.

Ducasse, Isidore ("le Comte de Lautréamont"). *Oeuvres Complètes.* Paris: Librairie Générale Française, 1963.

Esslin, Martin. *The Theatre of the Absurd.* Garden City: Doubleday, 1961.

Fargue, Léon-Paul. *Portraits de Famille.* Paris: J.B. Janin, 1947.

Fergusson, Francis. *Aristotle's Poetics.* New York: Hill and Wang, 1961.

Fort, Paul. *Mes Mémoires, Toute La Vie d'Un Poète.* Paris: Flammarion, 1944.

Gandilhon, Gens-d'Armes C. "Alfred Jarry au Lycée Henri IV," *Les Marges* (January 15, 1922), 41-46.

Géroy. "Mon Ami Alfred Jarry," *Courrier d'Epidaure* (March-April, 1949), 3-15.

————. "Mon Ami Alfred Jarry," *Mercure de France* (July, 1947), 493-509.

Gide, André. "Le Groupement Littéraire Qu'Abritait le *Mercure de France,*" *Mercure de France* (December, 1946), 168-170.

Giordanengo, Jean-Pierre. *Petit Traité Théorique et Pratique Sur La Dramaturgie d'Alfred Jarry.* Marseille: Université de Marseille, 1965.

Gourmont, Remy de. *"Minutes de Sable Mémorial,"* *Mercure de France* (October, 1894), 177-178.

Greene, Thomas. *Rabelais, A Study in Comic Courage.* Englewood Cliffs, New Jersey: Prentice-Hall, Inc., 1970.

Grossman, Manuel. "Alfred Jarry and the Theater of His Time," *Modern Drama,* XIII (May, 1970), 10-21.

Grossman, Manuel L. "Alfred Jarry and the Theatre of the Absurd," *Educational Theatre Journal.* (December, 1967), 473-477.

Grossvogel, David I. "The Depths of Laughter: The Subsoil of a Culture," *Yale French Studies,* XXIII (summer, 1959), 63-70.

————. *The Self-Conscious State in Modern French Drama.* New York: Columbia University Press, 1958.

Hanna, Thomas (ed.). *The Bergsonian Heritage.* New York: Columbia University Press, 1962.

Hertz, Henri. "Alfred Jarry, *Ubu Roi* et Les Professeurs," *Nouvelle Revue Française* (September 1, 1924), 263-273.

————. "Jarry, Collégian et la Naissance d'Ubu Roi," *Ecrits Nouveaux* (November, 1921), 73-75.

Highet, Gilbert. *The Anatomy of Satire.* Princeton: Princeton University Press, 1962.

Hirsch, Charles Henri. "Les Revues . . . à Propos d'Alfred Jarry . . . ," *Mercure de France* (March 1, 1922), 479-481.

Jarry, Alfred. *Albert Samain.* Paris: Lemasle, 1907.

————. *La Chandelle Verte, Lumières Sur Les Choses de Ce Temps.* Dessins de Pierre Bonnard. Edition établie et présentée par Maurice Saillet. Paris: Le Livre de Poche, 1969.

————. *La Dragonne.* Paris: Gallimard, 1943.

————. *King Turd* (B. Keith and G. Legman, trans.). New York: Boar's Head Books, 1953.

————. *L'Objet Aimé.* Paris: Arcanes, 1953.

————. *Oeuvres Complètes* (Michel Arrivé, ed.). Paris: Gallimard, 1972.

————. *Oeuvres Complètes* (René Massat, ed.). Monte Carlo: Edit. du Livre, 1948.

————. *Selected Works* (Roger Shattuck and Simon Watson Taylor, eds.). New York: Grove Press, 1965.

————. *A Supermale, A Modern Novel* (Barbara Wright, trans.). London: Jonathan Cape, 1968.

————. *Tout Ubu: Ubu Roi; Ubu Cocu; Almanachs du Père Ubu; Ubu Sur La Butte; Avec Leurs Prolégomènes et Paralipomènes* (Maurice Saillet, ed.).

Paris: Librairie Générale Française, 1962.

———. *The Ubu Plays* (Simon Watson Taylor, ed.). London: Methuen and Co., Ltd., 1968.

———. *Ubu Roi, Drama in 5 Acts* (Barbara Wright, trans.). London: Gaberbocchus Press, 1951.

Jasper, Gertrude. *Adventure in the Theatre: Lugné-Poe and the Théâtre de l'Oeuvre to 1899*. New Brunswick: Rutgers University Press, 1947.

Jean, Marcel, and Arpad Mezei. *Genèse de la Pensée Moderne*. Paris: Corrêa, 1950.

———. "Jarry et le Tourbillon Contemporain," in *Almanach Surrealiste du Demi-Siècle*, special edition of *La Nef,* nos. 63-64 (March-April, 1950), 189-196.

Jouffroy, Alain. "Jarry Nu," *L'Express* (February 1-7, 1965), 44-45.

Jourdain, Francis. *Né en 76*. Paris: Edition du Pavillon, 1951.

Juin, Hubert. "Le Père Ubu n'a pas Mangé Jarry," *Les Nouvelles Littéraires,* no. 1948 (December 31, 1964), 7.

Knowles, Dorothy. *La Réaction Idealiste au Théâtre Depuis 1890*. Paris: Librairie E. Droz, 1934.

Koch, Stephen. "Père Jarry," *Partisan Review,* XXXIII, no. 1 (winter 1966), 143-144.

Konigsberg, Isidore. "A French Complement for Coleridge," *ADAM International Review,* nos. 316-318 (1967), 93-96.

———. "New Light on Alfred Jarry's Juvenilia," *Modern Language Quarterly,* XXVII, no. 3 (September, 1966), 299-305.

Konigsberg, Isidore. "Some Unpublished Letters by Alfred Jarry," *Modern Language Review* (June, 1958), 38-43.

Kostrowitzky [Guillaume Apollinaire]. "Feu Alfred Jarry," *Les Marges* (January 15, 1922), 21-27.

Lalou, René. *Histoire de la Littérature Française Contemporaine*. Paris: Crès, 1922.

Laulan, Robert. "Le Vocabulaire d'Alfred Jarry et Ses Surprises," *Mercure de France* (November, 1959), 521-524.

Léautaud, Paul. *Entretiens avec Robert Mallet*. Paris: Gallimard, 1951.

———. *Journal Littéraire,* I. Paris: Mercure de France, 1954.

Lebois, André. "Alfred Jarry Anecdotique," *Quo Vadis* (June-July-August, 1950), 1-19; (September-October-November, 1950), 44-51.

———. "Christian Beck et Jarry," *Mercure de France* (October, 1949, 383-384.

———. *Jarry L'Irremplaçable*. Paris: Le Cercle du Livre, 1950.

Legrand-Chabrier. "De Gargantua à Ubu," *Gaulois* (November 5, 1921), 1-2.

Lehman, A.G. *The Symbolist Aesthetic in France, 1885-1895*. Oxford: Blackwell, 1950.

Leiris, Michel. *Brisées*. Paris: Mercure de France, 1966.

Lévesque, Jacques-Henry. *Alfred Jarry*. Paris: Seghers, 1951.

Levron, Jacques. "Saint Jarry, Pape et Martyr," *Les Nouvelles Littéraires* (November 5, 1970), 11.

Loriot, Patrick. "Ubu Plus Jarry," *Le Nouvel Observateur* (October 26-November 1, 1970), 46-47.

Lormel, Louis. "Entre Soi," *La Plume* (October 1, 1897), 605-606.

———. "Remy de Gourmont, Alfred Jarry et *L'Art Littéraire,*" *Gaulois* (December 3, 1921), 4.

Lot, Fernand. *Alfred Jarry, Son Oeuvre*. Paris: Nouvelle Revue Critique, 1934.

Lugné-Poe, Aurélien. *Acrobaties, 1894-1903*. Paris: Gallimard, 1931.

Mallarmé, Stephane. *Oeuvres Complètes*. Paris: Gallimard, 1945.

Mauclair, Camille. *Servitudes . . . Littéraires*. Paris: Ollendorff, 1922.

Mauvoisin, J. "L'Equivoque de Jarry." *Carrefour* (October 30, 1957), 7.

Mendès, Catulle. "Premières Représentations," *Le Journal* (December 11, 1896), 2.

Michaud, Guy. *Message Poétique du Symbolisme*. Paris: Nizet, 1966.

Mille, Pierre. *Anthologie des Humoristes Français Contemporains*. Paris: Delagrave, 1925.

Mollet, le Baron. *Mémoires*. Paris: Gallimard, 1963.

Montfort, Eugène. "Les Livres: *Les Sources d'Ubu-Roi*, par Charles Chassé," *Les Marges* (January 15, 1922), 63.

Moore, Will G., "The French Notion of the Comic," *Yale French Studies*, XXIII (summer, 1959), 47-53.

Moréno, Marguerite. *Souvenirs de Ma Vie*. Paris: Flammarion, 1926.

Morienval, Jean. *De Pathelin à Ubu: Bilan des Types Littéraires*. Paris: Bloud et Gay, 1929.

Mornet, D. *Histoire de la Littérature et de La Pensée Française, 1870-1925*. Paris: Larousse, 1927.

Morot-Sir, Edouard. "Apparition de l'Humour dans la Littérature Française au XXe Siècle," *Bulletin de la Société des Professeurs Français en Amerique* (1970), 35-52.

Murphy, Patricia. "Rabelais and Jarry," *The French Review* (October, 1977), 29-36.

Onimus, Jean. *Face au Monde Actuel*. Bruges: Desclée De Brouwer, 1962.

Parisot, Henri (ed.). *Les Poètes Hallucinés*. Paris: Flammarion, 1966.

Perche, Louis. *Alfred Jarry*. Paris: Edit. Universitaires, 1965.

Pia, Pascal. "Jarry en Lumière," *Carrefour* (December 16, 1964), 18.

Pierron, Sander. "Alfred Jarry à Bruxelles," *Mercure de France* (November, 1931), 718-727.

Pieyre de Mandiargues, André. *Le Cadran Lunaire*. Paris: Robert Laffont, 1958.

Pieyre de Mandiargues, André. "Narcisse Déserteur," *Le Nouvel Observateur* (December 10, 1964), 24-25.

Pillement, Georges. *Anthologie du Théâtre Français Contemporain*, I. Paris: Editions du Bétier, 1945.

Pronko, Leonard C. *Avant-Garde: The Experimental Theater in France*. Los Angeles: University of California Press, 1966.

Quillard, Pierre. "De L'Imagination et de L'Expression Chez Alfred Jarry," *La Revue Blanche* (May 15, 1902), 198-200.

Quillard, Pierre. "L'Infaillibilité du Sabre," *Mercure de France*, (February 1898), 353-365.

Rachilde. *Alfred Jarry, Ou Le Surmâle des lettres*. Paris: Grasset, 1928.

———. "*L'Amour en Visites*," *Mercure de France* (June, 1898), 834-835.

———. "*Les Jours et Les Nuits*," *Mercure de France* (July, 1897), 143-145.

———. "*Messaline*," *Mercure de France* (February, 1901), 482-486.

———. "*Le Surmâle*," *Mercure de France* (June, 1902), 753-755.

Raymond, Marcel. *De Baudelaire au Surrealisme*. Paris: Corrêa, 1933.

Régnier, Henri de. *De Mon Temps*. . . . Paris: Mercure de France, 1933.

Rémond, Georges. "Souvenirs sur Jarry et Autres," *Mercure de France* (March, 1955), 427-446; (April 1, 1955), 656-677.

Renard, Jules. *Le Journal de Jules Renard, 1887-1910*. Paris: Gallimard, 1927.

Robichez, Jacques. *Le Symbolisme au Théâtre: Lugné-Poe et Les Débuts de l'Oeuvre*. Paris: L'Arche, 1957.

Rolland de Renéville, André. "*Les Minutes de Sable Mémorial*," *Nouvelle Revue Française* (April 1, 1933), 682-686.

———. *L'Univers de La Parole*. Paris: Corrêa, 1953.

Rousseaux, André. *Le Monde Classique*. Paris: Albin Michel, 1941.

Russell, John. *Edouard Vuillard, 1868-1940*. Norwich, Great Britain: Jarrold and Sons, 1971.

Saillet, Maurice. "L'Oeuvre de Jarry," *La Critique* (February, 1949), 99-112.

———. *Sur La Route de Narcisse*. Paris: Mercure de France, 1958.

Salmon, André. *L'Ami du Lettré*. Paris: Crès, 1924.

Saltas, Jean. "Les Derniers Jours d'Alfred Jarry," *Les Marges* (October 15, 1921), 83-88.

Schneider, Marcel. *La Littérature Fantastique en France*. Paris: Fayard, 1964.

Screech, Michael. *The Rabelaisian Marriage: Aspects of Rabelais' Religion, Ethics, and Comic Philosophy*. London: Edward Arnold, 1958.

Shattuck, Roger. *The Banquet Years, The Origins of the Avant-Garde in France: 1885 to World War I*. New York: Vintage, 1968.

———. "What is 'Pataphysics?" *Evergreen Review* (May-June, 1960).

Smith, Homer W. *Man and His Gods*. New York: Grosset and Dunlap, 1957.

Soupault, Philippe. "Confrontations: Alfred Jarry," *Cahiers de la Compagnie Madeleine Renaud-Jean-Louis Barrault* (May, 1958), 174-181.

Styan, J.L. *The Dark Comedy; The Development of Modern Comic Tragedy*. Cambridge: Cambridge University Press, 1962.

Symons, Arthur. *Studies in Seven Arts.* New York: E.P. Dutton, 1907.

Sypher, Wylie. *Comedy: Meaning and Form.* San Francisco: Chandler Publishing Co., 1965.

Szathmary, Arthur. *The Aesthetic Theory of Bergson.* Cambridge: Harvard University Press, 1937.

Tailhade, Laurent. *Quelques Fantômes de Jadis.* Paris: Editions Française, 1920.

Taylor, A. Carey. "Le Vocabulaire d'Alfred Jarry," *Cahiers de L'Association Internationale des Etudes Française* (May, 1959), 307-322.

Trohel, Jules. "Alfred Jarry et Les Huissiers," *Mercure de France* (May 1, 1934), 627-636.

Updike, John, "Death's Heads," *The New Yorker* (October 2, 1965), 216-228.

Van Roosbroeck, G.. "Alfred Jarry: The Genesis of *Ubu Roi,*" *Romanic Review* (1934), 415-417.

Index